christopher dresser

a pioneer of modern design

WIDAR HALÉN

To Barbara

Phaidon Press Limited
140 Kensington Church Street
London W8 4BN

First published 1990

First paperback edition 1993

© 1993 Phaidon Press Limited

ISBN 0 7148 2952 8

A CIP catalogue record for this book is available from
the British Library

Printed in Singapore

Photographic Acknowledgements:
The author and publisher wish to thank all who have graciously
contributed photographs, and in particular: the Trustees of
British Museum, London, 208; Christie's, London, 171, 199,
201; Chubb & Son Archive, London, 58-64, 213; Cooper-
Hewitt Museum, The Smithsonian Institution, New York, 78;
Courtaulds Plc., London, 92; Fine Art Society, 166, 178, 179,
181, 182, 190, 191, 205, 206, 210, 211; Getty Center for the
History of Art and the Humanities, California, 137, 163, 173;
Haslam & Whiteway, London, 56, 57, 165, 167, 169, 216;
National Trust, 72; Oadby & Wigston Borough, Bushloe
House, Wigston, Leicester, 34, 196, 197; Phillips Fine Art
Auctioneers, London, 180, 209, 219, 222; Public Record
Office, Kew, London, 2, 11, 17, 32-3, 35-6, 40, 43, 45, 47, 55,
65-7, 73, 85-6, 139, 161, 164; Royal Doulton-Minton, Stoke-
on-Trent, 8, 42, 97-8, 100, 102, 104, 119-22, 126-36, 140,
142-4, 146-58 (Northern Counties Photographers); Sotheby's,
London, 3, 170, 174, 175, 177, 200, 202, 204, 221, 226, 228,
229; Silver Studio Collection, Middlesex Polytechnic, 71, 82,
83; United States Patent and Trademark Office, Washington
D.C., 21; the Trustees of Victoria & Albert Museum, imprint
page, 1, 13, 31, 37, 41, 44, 81, 90, 94-5, 115, 160, 214, 223,
227; Wedgwood Museum Trustees, Barlaston, 138.

Half-title
James Dixon & Son, electroplated teapot with ebony handles,
shape no.2277. 25 November 1880. 9 in. high. Fine Art
Society, London.

Frontispiece
Benham & Froud, brass and lead flower pot. 1885. 22 in. high.
Private collection.

Right
Jeffrey & Co., wallpaper. Paris International Exhibition, 1878.
Prints and Drawings, Victoria & Albert Museum, London

.Contents

1
James W. & C. Ward silk
damask. c. 1875. Victoria &
Albert Museum, London.

.PREFACE

Since Nikolaus Pevsner's rediscovery of Dresser in 1936, most writers on nineteenth-century design have placed him among the 'pioneers of modern design', and a thorough monograph on Dresser has long been due.

A few of his designs were featured in the Victorian and Edwardian Decorative Arts exhibition at the Victoria & Albert Museum in 1952, when Elisabeth Aslin, Shirley Bury and Barbara Morris undertook their initial studies on Dresser. These eminent museum officers inspired the Norwegian scholars Stephan Tschudi-Madsen and Alf Bøe, whose respective publications, *Sources of Art Nouveau* (1955) and *From Gothic Revival to Functional Form* (1957), assessed the importance of Dresser's work. I am deeply indebted to all these scholars for their supervision and encouragement, and particularly to Barbara Morris who first introduced me to Dresser's designs and from whom I have learnt more than I can say. This book is dedicated to her.

In 1972 the exhibition of Charles Hanley-Read's Victorian and Edwardian Art at the Royal Academy gave another boost to a revived interest in Dresser, and in the same year the Fine Art Society in London under Andrew McIntosh Patrick's direction arranged the first retrospective show of Dresser's works in collaboration with Stuart Durant, Richard Dennis and John Jesse. This was followed by another Dresser exhibition arranged by Michael Collins in 1979 at the Camden Arts Centre and the Dorman Museum. In 1981 Rüdiger Joppien and Michael Collins organized a comprehensive Dresser show at the Kunstgewerbemuseum in Cologne, and Dan Klein and Adrian J. Tilbrook staged a sales exhibition of his work in London, which sparked off a keen interest in Dresser among dealers and collectors of nineteenth-century decorative art. I would particularly like to thank Michael Collins, Richard Dennis, Stuart Durant, Dan Klein and Adrian J. Tilbrook for much encouragement and the pleasure of argument, as well as my friends

Elisabet Hidemark, Joan Jones, Linda Parry, Takako Shimizu, Jeremy Cooper, Gilbert & George, John Fleming, Hugh Honour, Hasobe Mitsuhiko, Andrew McIntosh Patrick, John Scott, Albert Steen, Thoshio Watanabe, Paul Reeves, Peter Rose and Albert Gallichan, and Michael and Mariko Whiteway for instructive discussions and fine photographs.

This book is based on my D.Phil thesis on 'Christopher Dresser and the Cult of Japan' which was submitted to Oxford University in 1988. I would like to thank my supervisor Stan Smith, then of the Ruskin School of Art, Dr Jaynie Anderson, Dr Oliver Impey, Professor Francis Haskell, and Sir Stuart Hampshire, then Warden of Wadham College, as well as Professor Michael Podro of the University of Essex, Professor Magne Malmanger of the University of Oslo, Professor Per Jonas Nordhagen of Bergen University, Professor Yokoyama Toshio of Kyoto University, and Professors Haga Toru and Suzuki Hiroyuki of Tokyo University, who supervised my studies at these institutions. Many thanks also to the staff of the libraries at these universities, and to the officers in the archives, libraries and museums mentioned in my list of manuscript sources and in the photographic acknowledgements. I am particularly grateful for the grant towards the cost of photographs which I received from NAVF – the Norwegian Academy of Science and Research.

I am much indebted to my publishers – particularly to Penelope Marcus; to Diana Davies for her meticulous editorial care, to Andrew Nash and Julian Bingley for their skill in designing the book, and to Lark Gilmer, Andrew Kolesnikow and Jon Bjørnsen for their excellent photographs. My last thanks go to my dear friends Fiona Fleming-Brown, Lill Scherdin and Ronald Craig who have commented on various chapters of this book, and to my parents whose confidence and care have been a constant source of inspiration.

.|NTRODUCTION

Christopher Dresser was one of the most radical and prolific designers of the nineteenth century, as well as an influential writer on the decorative arts. His works were well known in Europe, America and Japan, and his doctrines were regarded as among the most advanced of his day. Dresser stressed the importance of function, simplicity and mechanical skill, believing that industrial and scientific progress would lead to an entirely new style in art. Above all, he promoted a rational and scientific attitude to design, based on appropriate and inexpensive materials combined with suitable and restrained ornamentation. He was one of the first professionally trained designers for machine production and may arguably be the first industrial designer in Europe.

His production was far ahead of his time and covered a wide range of materials, styles and techniques in the media of ceramics, glass, metalwork, furniture, carpets, textiles, wallpapers and in all interior decorations. A quick worker, Dresser produced designs for at least fifty of the most prestigious and forward-looking Victorian manufacturers (see Appendix), and his clean-cut art furniture, colourful ceramics, and surprisingly simple metalwork and glass still make a powerful impression. Although essentially a Victorian, he fully accepted the implications of industrialized production, and worked in a field barely touched by most contemporary designers. In this respect, he was undoubtedly an outsider, and triumphing over the orthodox dullards of his time, he asserted the designer's rights in this new system of manufacturing. Advocating the equality of status between the designer and the manufacturer, he was one of the first European designers to imprint his signature next to the maker's mark.

Dresser pioneered the elevation of design and interior decoration to the status of art, which in turn gave rise to the terms art furniture, art pottery and art glass, thus helping to bridge the gap which had emerged between art and industry in Victorian Britain. He saw this gap as a fictitious division, and emphasized that the artistic capacity of modern manufacture was equal to that of the craftsman in former times. Clearly, with the advent of the Arts and Crafts Movement, Dresser felt the need to develop the discoveries of his own time. His enthusiasm for the machine was in contrast to the pessimism expressed by William Morris and John Ruskin, and by stressing the importance of design and modernism rather than antiquarian craftsmanship, Dresser emerged as a greater design-innovator than any of the artists in the Arts and Crafts Movement. He published his ideas fifteen years ahead of Morris, and was certainly the most influential theorist of his time. Although both Morris and Dresser preached the gospel of art for the masses, Morris could never match Dresser's tremendous output of design for mass production. Their practical efforts for improvement in British design were fundamentally different, but their principles frequently coincided, and it was largely due to their teachings that greater care was given to design and to the interiors of ordinary houses in Britain. Dresser, however, must be credited as the first to launch these new ideas. Many of his doctrines probably also influenced the Aesthetic Movement, which had emerged in the early 1860s with the work of a few artists and designers,

2
Opposite. William Woollams & Co. wallpaper. March 1863. Public Record Office, London.

notably Edward W. Godwin and James M. Whistler. They joined in rebelling against academic art, but where Dresser adapted the cultural language of the time to new purposes more in tune with the urban and industrial society of which it was a part, the aesthetes offered 'art for art's sake' as a counterbalance to industrialism. Dresser in strict terms was certainly one of the most ardent aesthetes, but he would have rejected this appellation with scorn, and always referred to himself as an 'art workman'. He believed that all men, regardless of class, should enjoy the freedom to be creative and artistic in the true sense. It was his desire to relate design to its social and functional context that was to have the most lasting influence on his contemporaries and on twentieth-century artistic thinking.

The idea of a liaison between art and industry had been topical at the Government School of Design where Dresser spent his first formative years as a student from 1847 to 1854, and as a lecturer between 1855 and 1868. Here he came under the influence of such formidable theorists and designers as William Dyce, Henry Cole, Owen Jones, Richard Redgrave, Gottfried Semper and Matthew Digby Wyatt. Like these vociferous arbiters of design reform, Dresser sought to codify the principles of design and ornamentation, but whereas his teachers embraced the use of historical sources, Dresser called for an imaginative sifting of the ideas of the past and their recasting into a wholly new style.

Dresser and his mentors expressed great dissatisfaction with the output of British design in this period, and following the School's policy of 'wedding science with art' Dresser decided to specialize in botanical studies. As a botanist, and as a designer, he was sympathetic to John Ruskin's and Augustus W.N. Pugin's belief in nature as a basis of ornament, but he objected strongly to Ruskin's false naturalism and to Pugin's Neo-Gothic style, which he claimed was unsuitable for a modern Protestant society. Condemning the meretricious décor which dominated contemporary design, Dresser pushed the concept of ornamentation towards greater stylization and abstraction. Although basically an ornamentist, he went as far as devaluing the importance of decoration altogether, asserting that it was entirely subservient to form and could be readily omitted in design. In Dresser's view form should be allowed to speak for itself, a purist stance which is intriguingly close to that of modern contemporary designers.

3
Hukin & Heath decanter with electroplated fittings and amphora-shaped glass container, shape no. 2045. Marked 'Designed by Dr. C. Dresser'. 9 October 1878. 9 in. high. Private collection.

Dresser was born in Glasgow in 1834, the third child of Christopher Dresser senior (1807–69) and his wife Mary, née Nettleton, both of Yorkshire families. He proudly referred to himself as a Yorkshire man, although he was born in Glasgow and lived most of his life in the London area. Tradition has it that the Dresser family descended from Danish Vikings who settled in Whenly and Shackleton near Hovingham, but the genealogy can be traced only to Robert Dresser (1518–88) and his son Christopher (died 1626). Several members of the family were Excise Officers, as was Dresser's father, who worked in Glasgow, Sussex and Hereford, subsequently rising to the rank of collector. There is no record of artistic proficiency in the family, and as the bearer of an old family name Christopher junior was probably originally destined to become an Officer like his father and grandfather before him. His natural talents were not immediately accepted by his father, according to his childhood memories:

As a child I spent a large portion of my time in drawing and painting and I was never happy without a paint box. I once got into trouble for exchanging a box which my father had given me to lock my little treasures in, for one of the old-fashioned two-penny boxes [of paints]. .... That I was intended by nature as an artist, I doubt not, but let it be remembered, that with the view of causing me to become one, my parents placed me in a 'school of design'.[1]

When the Dressers moved to Sussex in about 1847 Christopher was enrolled at the Government School of Design in London, where he remained for seven years. He graduated in 1854, and married Thirza Perry (1830–1906) of Maidley, Shropshire, in the same year. She was his lifelong companion and they subsequently had thirteen children, five of whom died in childhood. The surviving children were Christopher, Frank, Louis Leo, Mary, Thirza, Rosa Ada, Nellie and Anne. Christopher went to Japan in 1878, married a Japanese and settled in Kobe. Louis Leo was the only son who followed in his father's profession and went to work at Liberty's in 1882, but without recorded success.[2] The five daughters never married; they remained close to their father and helped to carry out his designs in the studio.

The family first lived at 4 Swiss Cottages, Black Lion Lane in Hammersmith, before moving to St Peter's Square, Hammersmith, in about 1860, when the studio was established. Dresser remem-

bered having spent five years in continuous struggle after finishing his education before he succeeded in earning any income from his profession; he kept the family alive by teaching and writing on Art Botany and Botany proper. In 1854 he began lecturing at the School of Design 'on the best mode of investigating the form and structure of plants with a view to the treatment in ornament', and executed a number of botanical illustrations and diagrams, which have been preserved in the Victoria & Albert Museum. The year after, he was formally engaged as a lecturer on this topic at the School, a position he held until 1868. It was largely thanks to his efforts that Art Botany in the form of stylized plant ornamentation eventually ousted the false naturalism and ostentatious ornament which characterized mid-Victorian design.

In 1856 Dresser supplied a plate of 'Plants and Elevations of Flowers' to Owen Jones's famous *Grammar of Ornament* (plate 4). This shows his art botany at its best and contributed considerably to the young Dresser's fame, but he appears to have been more drawn to science than to art during the later 1850s. He published a series of articles on 'Art Botany as Adapted to the Arts and Art Manufacturers' in the *Art Journal* between 1857 and 1858, and in 1857 registered a method of 'nature printing' with the Patent Office. He also lectured for various scientific societies on botanical subjects.

His books on *The Rudiments of Botany* (1859), *Unity in Variety as Deduced from the Vegetable Kingdom* (1859) and *Popular Manual of Botany* (1860) earned him a notable reputation among botanists and a doctorate from the University of Jena in 1859 for his work on Goethe's doctrines on metamorphosis in relation to plant morphology.[3] Pleased and flattered by this honour, Dresser adopted the title of Doctor; his books listed him as Professor of Botany at six different institutions in London. Despite these appointments, it was perhaps too presumptuous of him to apply for the Chair of Botany at the University of London in 1860. Having been rejected, however, Dresser finally dedicated himself wholeheartedly to work in the area of design and the theory of art.

In 1862 he published two major works, *The Art of Decorative Design* and *Development of Ornamental Art in the International Exhibition*. He also supplied a number of designs for the International Exhibition, notably to Minton's stand. He was particularly struck by the beauty of Japanese art,

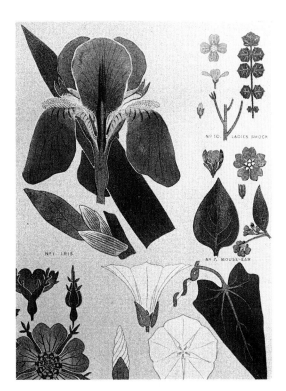

4
Detail of Dresser's Leaves and Flowers from Nature in Owen Jones's *Grammar of Ornament*, 1856, pl. XCVII.

which for the first time was shown on a grand scale in Britain. A sketchbook and two pattern books from the 1860s show several designs for ceramics, metalwork, and surface patterns, which display Dresser's originality and sophisticated artistic vernacular. By 1868 Dresser was not only more prosperous but also famous, and the family moved to the impressive Tower Cressy in Aubrey Road, Campden Hill, which had been built in 1854 by Thomas Page (plate 9).

During the 1860s Dresser was engaged as a designer by at least thirty of the most prestigious British manufacturers of all kinds of art industry, and he wrote extensively on Japanese ornamentation in 1863 and on the Paris International Exhibition in 1867. In 1870 he began his series of articles on 'Principles of Decorative Design' in the *Technical Educator*, which treated all the media of design in which he worked and were published in book form in 1873. He lectured on 'Ornamentation Considered as High Art' and 'Hindrances to the Progress of Applied Art' in 1871 and 1872, defending the status of design and ornamentation and suggesting the establishing of a Royal Academy of Design. Dresser was at the peak of his career during the 1870s and extraordinarily prolific as a designer, lecturer and writer. Most of his lectures and articles were published in the *Furniture*

5
Old Hall Earthenware Co.
vases and jug. 1880s.
Private collection.

6
Page 14. Linthorpe Art
Pottery vase no. 449. 1880.
18¾ in. high. Private
collection.

8
Minton & Co. seau
no. 1919. 1876. 8¼ in. high.
Minton Museum, Royal
Doulton Minton Co.,
Stoke-on-Trent.

7
Page 15. Coalbrookdale Co.
cast iron chair. Maker's
mark and date cipher for 8
March 1870. With James W.
& C. Ward textile. 1871.
Private collection.

9
Dresser's house, Tower
Cressy, Aubrey Road,
Campden Hill, London.
Drawing by Frank L.
Emanuel. Kensington
Public Library, London.

Gazette, of which he became a freelance writer in 1874 and editor in 1880, a position he held for a year. He debated hotly the topics of 'Good Taste in House Furnishing', 'Eastern Art and its Influence on European Manufacture', 'The Grotesque in Decorative Art' and 'The Expression of Egyptian Ornament', and in 1875–6 published his sumptuously illustrated book, *Studies in Design*, as well as a volume on *Carpets* in G.P. Bevan's *British Manufacturing Industries*.

Dresser participated in the International Exhibitions held in London in 1871, 1872 and 1873, in Vienna in 1873, in Philadelphia in 1876 and in Paris in 1878. He wrote perceptively on these exhibitions, served as a juror on wallpapers in Paris, and lectured on 'Art Industries, Art Museums and Art Schools' in Philadelphia. He was responsible for arranging the Japanese stand at the International Exhibition in London in 1873 and for bringing the Japanese village from Vienna to Alexandra Palace Park in 1873. That same year he founded the Alexandra Palace Company and became art adviser to the newly founded Londos & Company, both of which traded extensively with Japanese goods supplied by the Japanese company for Industry and Commerce, Kiritsu Kosho Kaisha.

Dresser thus became one of the main promoters of Japonism in Britain, both commercially and artistically, and in 1876 he was invited to visit Japan as a private guest of the Japanese Government. He set out in December that year, bringing with him a substantial collection of contemporary British art-manufactures, mostly of his own design, as a present from the South Kensington Museum to Tokyo National Museum. The Japanese Government asked him to report on the development of modern industry in Japan, and this was published as a sort of blue guide under the title *Dresser Hokoku* ('Dresser's Report') in 1877 and widely distributed among designers and manufacturers.

Dresser spent some four months in Japan, visiting national monuments and centres of traditional manufacture. He was the first European designer to visit the country after the opening of its borders in 1853, and his extensive book on Japan, *Japan, its Architecture, Art and Art-Manufactures*, published in 1882, was acclaimed as the most scholarly treatment on the topic to appear in the West.

Dresser had been commissioned by Tiffany's to bring back a large number of Japanese goods, and he stopped off in New York to deliver them en route back to London in 1877. The collection was reported to be the hit of the exhibition season in New York that year. Dresser took the opportunity to make contact with American manufacturers, for whom he supplied some designs. His influence on the American art milieu was generously acknowledged in 1986 in the exhibition on 'Americans and the Aesthetic Movement' at the Metropolitan Museum in New York.

Back in London, Dresser organized a Japanese exhibition for the firm of Jackson & Graham. His efforts to promote Japanese art and the Anglo-Japanese style were supported by the Prince and Princess of Wales and by the art critic George Augustus Sala. He exhibited a Japanese room, which had been given to him by the Governor of Kyoto, Makimura Masano, and lectured for the Architectural Association on 'Japanese Woodwork' and 'Japanese Architecture and Ornament', in 1878 and 1884 respectively. It was largely due to his activities that Japanese architecture and design became influential on Western architects and designers during the latter part of the nineteenth century.

In 1878 Dresser lectured on 'The Art Manufactures of Japan' and entered into partnership with Charles Holme, later the founder of *The*

Studio magazine. Trading under the name of Dresser & Holme from 1879 onwards, the company established a branch in Kobe in Japan and imported Japanese and other Oriental wares. In 1879 Dresser was instrumental in founding the Linthorpe Art Pottery at Middlesbrough, for which he acted as 'art superintendent' until 1882. He was particularly active in enlarging his commercial interests during the 1880s and in 1880 founded the Art Furnishers' Alliance, 'manufacturing, buying and selling high-class goods of artistic design'. The company was one of the first interior decorating firms in the modern sense and covered virtually all fields of design, from ordinary household goods to textiles and wallpapers. Contemporary critics referred to it as being unlike anything that existed at the time. It was perhaps too avant-garde for it failed in 1883. Nevertheless Dresser managed to make his mark on British interiors, and in this period was responsible for decorating Bushloe House near Leicester.

Following a bout of serious illness and a temporary decline in fortune, Dresser withdrew from the Art Furnishers' Alliance and moved to Wellesley Lodge, Brunswick Road, in Sutton. In 1886 he published his *Modern Ornamentation*, which also included some plates by his assistants, but concentrated mainly on surface ornamentation and showed 'no examples of architectural work, of designs for furniture, glass earthenware, metalwork or the numerous things that emanate from this office'. Probably as a result of improving finances, the Dressers moved to Elm Barnes, near Barnes Bridge in London, in 1889, where the studio continued to flourish. The Dresser daughters and some ten assistants were employed at the studio, which operated very much like a twentieth-century design studio.

During the last ten years of his life Dresser was principally engaged in designing textiles and wallpapers. When the Wallpaper Combine Company was established in 1899 he went to Alsace, then in Germany, and was engaged by the famous wallpaper manufacturer, Jean Züber & Company. While on a business trip to the firm, accompanied by his son Louis, Dresser died in his sleep at the Hotel Centrale in Mulhouse on 24 November 1904. A fitting tribute had appeared in *The Studio* in 1899 which described Dresser as 'perhaps the greatest of commercial designers, imposing his

10
Christopher Dresser in his conservatory at Elm Barnes, c. 1900.

fantasy and invention upon the ordinary output of British Industry'.[4] An obituary in *The Builder* in 1904 said that in his last years Dresser spent most of his time 'in preparing designs for manufacturers and in the enjoyment of his garden and flowers' (plate 10).[5]

Dresser's most talented daughters, Ada and Nellie, attempted to continue the studio after their father's death, and delivered a few designs to Arthur Sanderson & Sons in 1904–5, but they soon had to abandon the venture. Unlike his contemporaries, such as Morris for example, Dresser never established a proper company or workshop to provide financial security for his studio. He appears to have been entirely dependent on the changing fashions in the manufacturing industries, but unfortunately he did not foresee the increasing demand for novelty and the numerous competitive design companies which were to emerge toward the end of his life. This in part explains why Dresser was virtually forgotten during the first half of this century, since the basis of his activities had itself become extinct.

IN PURSUIT OF TRUTH, BEAUTY AND POWER

The basis for Dresser's motto 'Truth, Beauty and Power' was formed during his time as a student and lecturer at the School of Design. His life and career were closely linked with this institution, and he was a leading figure in its campaign to reform design and industry in Britain. He was one of the first industrial designers to graduate from the School, and the most successful practitioner of its policy of 'wedding science with art'.

During his time at the School from 1847 until 1854, it underwent a number of major changes, which sprang out of the controversy over whether it should be a mere drawing school or a practical training place for industrial designers. Important questions were posed by this divergence of critical opinion, and the issue was fiercely debated in early Victorian art circles: John Ruskin's concept of the imitation of divine nature in art was opposed to Augustus N.W. Pugin's and William Dyce's belief in the flatness of form and in greater stylization in design. Pugin's great love of the Neo-Gothic style and his numerous publications on architecture and design of the 1830s and 1840s helped to raise the status of design in Britain. His books were a constant source of inspiration to the people connected with the School of Design, particularly to William Dyce, the first director of the School from 1838 to 1843.

Dyce, a painter who had trained with the Nazarenes in Rome, was less slavish in his choice of style, but his *Drawing Book of the Government School of Design* (1842) owed much to Pugin. He promoted one of the first programmes for stylization and abstraction in Western art, maintaining that 'ornamental art is rather abstractive than reproductive'. His plans for the School included practical training classes. We know, for example, that he set up a loom, a kiln and a potter's wheel, which immediately aroused the criticism of Ruskin, who believed that 'the greatest decorative art is wholly conventional – downright pure, good painting and sculpture'.[1] These divergent attitudes formed the background to the debates and upheavals which dominated the School during the first decades of its existence and marked the early artistic training of the young Christopher Dresser.

Dresser's first book on design, *The Art of Decorative Design*, published in 1862, drew on Dyce's *Drawing Book* as well as on Pugin's *Floriated Ornament* (1849). However, he rejected the Neo-Gothic as being unsuitable for a modern Protestant society, and he was pleased to note a waning interest in the ideas of Ruskin.[2]

Dyce had left the School in 1843 after disagreements with the management, but subsequently returned as a Master of the Class of Design in 1847, a position he was to hold until his retirement in 1849. Three of his former students, Richard Redgrave, John Rogers Herbert and Richard Burchett, were appointed joint headmasters of the School in 1847,[3] and exerted a great influence on Dresser. Later in life he frequently referred to their teachings. Dresser, however, was the only one to realize their vision of the professional industrial designer.

Richard Redgrave's lectures on 'The Importance of the Study of Botany to the Ornamentist' in 1848 and Pugin's *Floriated Ornament* sparked off a keen interest in what Dresser later was to term 'artistic botany'. Redgrave and Pugin, who were probably the most persuasive writers on design around the middle of the nineteenth century, argued that the general laws of vegetation were parallel to essential principles adopted by artists. They propounded the idea of flat and stylized arrangements of plants as opposed to the naturalistic relief decorations which prevailed in Victorian design at the time. Stylization in turn became an important factor in Dresser's designs and publications; he described it as a conventional form of art, thus paying tribute to Redgrave and Pugin.

Two other famous protagonists in the early history of the reform of design in Victorian Britain were George Wallis and Owen Jones, both of whom lectured at the School in the late 1840s and exercised a considerable influence on Dresser's early education. Wallis later became the headmaster of the School in Birmingham, and finally Art Director of the South Kensington Museum.

The architect and designer Owen Jones had become famous for his *Plans, Elevations, Sections and Details of the Alhambra* (1842–6), which had given rise to the fashion for the Islamic or so-called Alhambresque style. These designs caught the spirit of an age at a time when Britain was rapidly expanding its colonial interests in the Orient. This campaign, which took in the Near East and the whole of India and Hong Kong by 1842, was to find its culmination in the opening of the borders of Japan in the 1850s.

Jones established himself as a central figure among British Orientalists and eventually led a revolt against the constraints of Neo-Classicism and Neo-Gothicism, advocating instead an eclectic approach and a 'new style' more akin to the arts of the East.[4] When Jones died in 1874 Dresser was asked to give the memorial lecture. He praised his former tutor as the greatest ornamentalist of all time, saying 'that he owed all that he then was to the manner in which Jones led him to think in a course of five lectures delivered 25 years ago'.[5] He was thinking of a series of lectures given at the School of Design in 1849 under the title 'An Attempt to Define the Principles which should Regulate the Employment of Colour in Architecture'. Jones here had called for an 'intelligent and imaginative eclecticism', combined with the subtlety of Eastern colouring, and when commenting on Dresser's lecture on 'Ornamentation Considered as High Art' in 1871, George Wallis noted: 'A feeling arose in favour of a style of which Dr Dresser was a very profound and learned disciple, about the time of Owen Jones' work on the Alhambra.'[6] Wallis, whose lectures Dresser remembered

having attended 'when quite a boy', was himself to become something of an expert on Oriental art.

Dresser was later to confirm that he had been 'an earnest student of Oriental art' from the time he enrolled at the School in 1847.[7] The ideas of Orientalism together with the concepts of Eclecticism and Artistic Botany formed his young artistic mind and in turn led to the creation of what he called a 'new style'.

Despite the learned theories of these eminent teachers, the School suffered from inefficient management. This resulted in constant debate about its policy during the 1840s. The workshop studios had been closed during Dyce's first period at the School, and the students in fact received little more than elementary theory and drawing classes. Several of the tutors became involved in the Felix Summerly Art-Manufactures, founded by Henry Cole in 1847 with the aim of reviving 'the good old practice of connecting Art with familiar objects in daily use'.[8] Cole, a talented civil servant, had begun publishing his handbooks on historic monuments in 1841 under the nom de plume of Felix Summerly. In 1846–7, he put his efforts into improving the state of industrial products. The Felix Summerly Art-Manufactures represented the most serious attempt at purifying early Victorian design.

This venture, which was to last until about 1851, attracted a number of the School's teachers, including Richard Redgrave, John Calcott Horsley, master of the class of colour from 1847 to 1849, and the sculptors John H. Townsend and John Bell, masters of the class of form in the 1840s. They all provided designs for the factory and probably introduced their students to practical manufacturing methods, thus compensating for the lack of workshops at the School.

Cole and Redgrave also began the monthly *Journal of Design and Manufacture* in 1849, which published many of the designs and lectures from the School (by Bell, Dyce, Horsley, Jones, Redgrave and Wallis). The journal became one of the most important instruments in their mutual strive for a reform of British design, and the coterie gathering around Cole soon became known as the 'Cole group'. In 1847 and 1848 Henry Cole had been asked by the Board of Trade to report on the state of the School of Design, and the parliamentary enquiries which followed his report concluded that the School was a complete failure and that little was done there other than the copying of drawings.[9] The results of this limited curriculum were all too apparent at the Great Exhibition in 1851, which showed the poverty of British exhibits when compared with foreign products. This public failure on an international level finally brought about a total reform of all the Schools of Design under Cole's directorship.

The changes that took place following the exhibition and the effect on the Cole group, who were struck by the superior quality of the Oriental artefacts in particular, were later recalled by Dresser:

> Prior to 1852 there was a very poor class of art applied to industries, but at the time he remembered that Mr. [John] Herbert, whose pupil he was, calling his attention to the Indian objects in the exhibition, and remarking that he could not find amongst them all a single instance of inharmonious combinations of colours. This observation was afterwards repeated publicly by Richard Redgrave and Mr. Owen Jones, and he believed it was to a great extent the cause of the advance which had lately been made in art industries. English manufacturers had made a great deal of money by copying the striped fabrics of Algeria, China, and Japan; again some of Minton's [porcelain] best productions in a decorative point of view, were little more than recasts of fine works from China and some Eastern country.[10]

The Cole reform absorbed the lessons of the Great Exhibition and as a result more practical training was introduced at the School.

Equally central for the impetus to reform was the new attitude to Oriental art. Orientalism by then encompassed Egyptian, Indian, Persian, Chinese and Japanese art, the latter being represented at the Great Exhibition by a few objects on the Chinese stand,[11] which had been organized by the British Consul in Shanghai, Rutherford Alcock.

Dresser later said that Alcock had been responsible for introducing him to Japanese art, and this may well have been as early as in 1851.[12] Dresser certainly studied the Oriental exhibits at the Great Exhibition, and endorsed Owen Jones's enthusiastic report of the event, describing the Eastern collections as 'a boon to all those European artists who had the opportunity of studying them'.[13] The Cole group's *Lectures on the Result of the Great Exhibition* were equally enthusiastic and Henry Cole himself remarked that 'It was from the East that the most impressive lesson was to be learnt.

11
Liddiard & Co. cambric.
April 1853. Public Record
Office, London.

Here was revealed a fresh well of art, the general principles of which were the same as those in the best period of art of all nations.'[14]

Oriental art in general thus became a major source of inspiration to Dresser and the tutors at the School of Design. The School moved to Marlborough House in 1852 and a comprehensive library was added alongside the newly founded Museum of Ornamental Art, later to become the Museum of Manufactures and then in 1857 the South Kensington Museum. The museum housed a large collection of Oriental acquisitions from the Great Exhibition and served to give the students practical training in the recognition of various styles in art.

The first exhibition of students' work in May 1852 included 'Indian ornaments from the Great Exhibition'. Dresser is recorded as having received a medal for his drawings in the class of applied design.[15] These depicted an Indian turban and dagger and have been preserved in the Victoria & Albert Museum.

It is no coincidence that Dresser's first recorded

designs for 'patterns to be printed on fabrics', displayed at the students' exhibition in the following year, appear to be inspired by Indian and other Oriental prototypes. On this occasion he received a special prize for 'the best design to be printed on cambric', which was produced by Liddiard & Company for Hargreaves Brothers of London.[16] Until 1938 this design was preserved in the Victoria & Albert Museum together with another Dresser textile from the time. Fortunately, registry descriptions and the exact dating have led to the identification of these 'Ladies Smock' and 'Blue and Purple Flower' patterns in the Patent Office Design Registry. They reflect the harmonious colouring and simplicity which Dresser admired in Oriental fabrics, but also show his stylized 'art botany', which by then was well developed (plate 11).

Richard Burchett remembered Dresser as 'an extremely clever student, particularly in the matter of floral forms, having distinguished himself in this way, not only at Somerset House, but also at Kew where he made a high reputation'.[17] Burchett was referring here to Dresser's study days at Kew Gardens under the guidance of the keeper Sir William Hooker, who acted as supervisor to Dresser's studies in Botany.[18] Burchett's report on the School for the year 1852 also mentioned some drawings made after a visit to Kew: 'These works were nearly all purchased by the Department for its use, some of them, executed in a special manner, having reference to designing for textile fabrics are being reproduced in coloured lithography for publication.'[19] Since it dates from the same time as Dresser's textile designs, we may conclude that his drawing for 'Plans and Elevations of Flowers' included in Owen Jones's *Grammar of Ornament* (1856) also belongs to this period (plate 4). Ladies Smock flowers were used by Dresser in all these designs, and remained a favourite motif.

Dresser's contribution to the *Grammar of Ornament* certainly established the young designer's fame, and the connection between master and student was evidently close. Jones's *Doctrines of the Department of Practical Art* (1852) were included in the *Grammar*, and were an important influence on Dresser's early ideas. A number of the doctrines were derived from Jones's Orientalism. The first 13 dealt with form, fitness, utility, beauty and ornamentation in relation to design, the basic idea being that the decorative arts are derived from architecture, and should possess 'fitness, proportion, harmony' in a 'geometrical construction'.

The remaining 21 represented Jones's ideas on colour harmonies and contrasts. Particular emphasis was given to 'The means of increasing harmonious effects of juxtaposed colours' and 'Observations derived from considerations of Oriental practice'. Three additional doctrines proclaimed Jones's objection to imitative art and the belief that no improvement could take place until all social classes were better educated in art. Dresser later expressed similar views in his own *Principles of Decorative Design* (1873), where he stressed that art should be accessible to everyone, regardless of their social class.

Dresser's *Art of Decorative Design* (1862) praised the work of Dyce, Jones and Redgrave, but lamented the practical difficulties under which he had worked as a student, and his tutors' lack of co-ordinating theory and practical instruction.[20] In 1871 he described the situation at the School in his day:

Three special classes were organised, one to train young men to design for calico printers, wall-paper, and the decoration of all kinds of surfaces, another for the decoration of porcelain and ceramic art, and another one for metal chasing. These classes were presided over by three gentlemen of great renown in every way, the professor of the first class in which he was placed, being Mr. Hudson. That which was devoted to the decoration of earthenware was entrusted to Mr. Simpson, from Minton's, and the metal chasing under the direction of Professor Semper. With the exception of Simpson's class, he thoroughly understanding the technicalities of applying colour to porcelain, the other two men knew nothing whatever about the practical operation of their duties though they were all men of marvellous skill.[21]

Octavius Hudson and the German architect Gottfried Semper were both influential forces on Dresser's early design theories. They had joined the School as tutors in 1852, and Hudson, who had been head of Spitalfields School of Design, soon embraced Semper's call for a systematic classification of styles in design.

Semper had arrived as an exile in Britain in 1850 and had collaborated with the Cole group in arranging the Great Exhibition in 1851. His review of the exhibition, *Wissenschaft, Industrie und Kunst* (1852), formed the model for Dresser's own *Development of Ornamental Art in the International*

Exhibition in London ten years later. Semper paid tribute to the Indian, Chinese and Persian products exhibited in 1851, and outlined a novel classification of ornamental art based on his study of a primitive West Indian hut at the exhibition. According to Semper's theory objects made of ceramics and metal originated from the fireplace, the shelter or walls gave rise to the art of weaving and plaiting, and finally the art of carpentry and joinery developed from the terrace and roof construction. Semper thus introduced into Western classifications the consideration of so-called primitive cultures. Previously study of the arts had been entirely dominated by the classicists' preference for Greek and Roman art but Semper now expounded his theory that all styles have their origin in craft processes. This new area of study led him to establish a functional coherence between architecture and the decorative arts as well as between Western and other cultures.

His highly influential publication *Der Stil in der Technischen und Techtonischen Kunsten* (1860–3) elaborated upon his revolutionary classification, which analysed the arts in relation to their functional capacity instead of their mere decorative presentation. These ideas were also discussed in Semper's lectures at the School of Design between 1852 and 1855, and Dresser was an attentive listener. He expounded a similar system of classification in his *Art of Decorative Design*, which also drew on Hudson's lectures on 'The Analogy of Ornaments' and 'The Analysis of the Styles', given at the School in 1854; Dresser devoted two chapters to the same topics and considered precisely those styles discussed by Hudson, namely:

(a) Egyptian, (b) Assyrian, Greek, Etruscan, Roman, (c) Mahommedan, Arabian, (d) Indian, (e) Chinese and Japanese, (f) Christian Ornamental art of the 12th Century, (g) Gothic and Early English, (h) Decorated Gothic, (i) Perpendicular Gothic, (j) The Revival of Classic Art.[22]

Semper's and Dresser's publications presented the first overall view of the School's policy in the 1850s, and had an enormous impact on artistic circles in both Continental Europe and Britain.

Semper had been in charge of the School's 'technical courses and practical construction', but even he, according to Dresser, lacked the professional experience required for this kind of teaching. When he left the School in 1855, three of the School's graduates were appointed to replace him:

Mr. Hagreen to be teacher of Architectural Drawing, Mr. Slocombe to be teacher of Practice of Ornamental Design, and Mr. Dresser to be teacher and class lecturer of Botany and to find his own examples and to be engaged two days a week for three hours each day. One day to be devoted to the Students of the Female School.[23]

When Redgrave became superintendent in 1854, he recognized Dresser's talents and asked him as part of his final training to deliver a series of twelve lectures, with diagrams, 'on the best mode of investigating the form and structure of plants with a view to the treatment of ornament'.[24] These lectures on 'Artistic Botany' were described as being 'of the utmost importance in the study of ornamental art'.[25] Dresser had clearly profited from Professor John Lindley's lectures on 'The Symmetry of Vegetation' and 'Form and Colour in the Vegetable Kingdom' given at the School in 1852 and in 1854.[26] Lindley had introduced the new science of morphology in Britain in his *Introduction to Botany* published in 1832, and in his lectures at the School he offered a scientific solution to the problem of classification and evolution of the species as well as of the arts.

In the late 1850s Dresser appears to have been more drawn to science, particularly botany, than to art. Between 1857 and 1858 he patented a new system of nature printing with the help of the professor of chemistry at the School, Sir Lyon Playfair,[27] and published a series of articles on 'Botany as Adapted to the Arts and Art-Manufactures' and on 'The relation of Science to Ornamental Art' in the *Art Journal*. His lectures on morphology for various botanical societies and his books, *The Rudiments of Botany* (1859), *Unity in Variety as deduced from the Vegetable Kingdom* (1859) and *Popular Manual of Botany* (1860), established his reputation as a botanist. In 1859 he was awarded a doctorate in absentia from the University of Jena in Germany for his work on Goethe's doctrines on metamorphosis in relation to plant morphology, and he is listed in his books as Professor of Botany at six different institutions in London. In 1860 he applied for the Chair of Botany at the University of London upon John Lindley's retirement. When his candidature was rejected he decided to dedicate himself entirely to the pursuit of Truth, Beauty and Power in art and design.

Dresser's studies of botany had, however, helped him to develop the idea of 'artistic botany', which was to unite science and art in a way no previous designer had attempted. He analysed plant structures down to their simplest forms, and argued that plants and their vertical sections could provide a significant source of inspiration to the artist. He maintained that plant organisms if scientifically delineated were fundamentally conventional and symmetrical. Starting from the notion that science equals truth, and art epitomizes beauty, he concluded that the artist's task was to acquire the necessary knowledge with which to unite the two: 'The ambition of the true ornamentist will lead him to occupy his true place, which is by his superior knowledge and skill to lead on the minds of the less enlightened towards beauty and truth.'[28]

It was this premiss which lay behind his first motto, 'Knowledge is Power', which for the first time encapsulated his central concept of art: reaching truth and beauty through power. Dresser later epitomized this in *The Art of Decorative Design* with his design of 'frost on windows',[29] a motif which subsequently inspired some of his most inventive ornamentation (plate 12). His source was revealed in his *Studies in Design* (1875–6), which described a moment of genuine artistic inspiration back in 1856: 'I made sketches of the frost which we commonly see on the windows of our rooms in winter, but it was 8 years later that I perceived in these sketches a new style of ornament, hence we have plates XIX & XXXIV.'[30] (See endpapers.)

Dresser's invention of a new style of ornament in about 1864 was also described in an article entitled 'On the Production of Ornament under the influence of Quasi Inspiration', which provides a fascinating picture of his early working methods:

About two years after this I was sitting in my study, which now looked to the west. A glorious pleasant evening and tranquil autumn day was closed by a most glorious sunset, which I watched dreamily till the last streaks of colour had vanished from the sky. I felt an influence coming over me of which now I have learned to know the nature. Pointing a number of pencils, and placing on my table a quantity of smooth paper, I commenced to draw, when, without the least effort of which I was conscious, and without exercising, so far as I know, any control over my pencil, forms and compositions which were new and vigorous, yet often eccentric, were produced with such rapidity, and in such quantities as astonished

12
'Knowledge is Power' from Dresser's *Art of Decorative Design*, 1862, pl. XXIV.

13
'Truth, Beauty, Power' design from Dresser's Pattern books, 2 vols. c. 1862–7. Prints and Drawings, Victoria & Albert Museum, London.

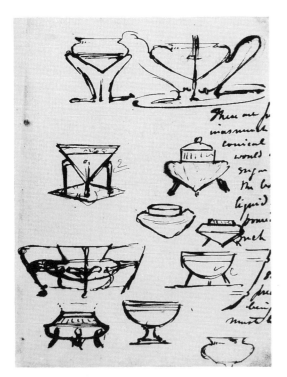

14
Dresser's sketchbook, page 25, showing designs for metalware. Annotated 1864. The book contains 105 similar pages, dated between 1861 and 1865. Ipswich Museum.

me. At two o'clock in the morning I had filled many sheets of papers with drawings, and feeling fatigue, retired to my chamber. I could not, however, shake off this strange influence: so taking a bundle of letters from my pocket, I drew patterns on whatever plain paper they furnished.[31]

In 1972 a sketchbook in the Ipswich Museum containing 104 pages of scrap paper and envelopes dated between 1862 and 1864 was identified as Dresser's. Many of the motifs accord with those described as 'in a new style' in *Studies in Design* (plate 14), and evidently originated from Dresser's great moment of inspiration. Two recently discovered pattern books from Dresser's hand, dating from about 1867, include similar designs (plate 13). These volumes are all that remains of Dresser's private archive and provide a unique source for the identification of his new style.

Such inspired creations also pervade the illustrations of his *Art of Decorative Design*. This important publication was originally presented as a series of lectures to the Royal Society of Arts towards the end of 1861. The abstract was given in a letter to the Society dated 9 October 1861, and listed the following topics:

The Decorative Art, – The true relation of

plants to ornament, – Grades in decorative art, – The affinities of the aesthetic arts, music, ornament &c., – Analysis of Ornamental forms, – Principles common to all ornament, – The Laws in conformity with which plants grow are the laws of ornament, – A parallel between plants and ornament, Curves, – The Union of straight lines with curves, – Proportion, – Repetition or series, – Alternation, – Symmetry, – Adaptation, – The power of Ornament to express feelings and ideas, – Ornament as modified of position, – Horizontal and vertical ornaments, – Varied classes of patterns; Field patterns, Running patterns, Powderings, Diapers & c, – Colour, – Harmonies, – Contrasts, – The Laws which govern application of colour to ornament.[32]

The lectures were intended as a guide to 'the manufacturers and art workmen in view of the coming contest', that is, the International Exhibition in London in 1862, and provided a synthesis of Dresser's artistic and scientific interests. His principles relating to colour appeared in *The Development of Ornamental Art at the International Exhibition*, published later in the same year.

The Art of Decorative Design, which presented Dresser's analysis of 'The Nature and Character of Ornament' and 'The Ministrations of Plants to Ornament' as well as incorporating material from previous lectures, revealed a surprising scepticism to established ornamental values. Most notably Dresser expressed the view that 'the application of ornaments to objects cannot be said to be absolutely necessary'.[33] This advanced idea, which was quite contrary to the accepted practice of the time, served to liberate Dresser from the ornamental and imitative historicism which dominated his teachers' designs.

Dresser's study of the morphology of plants led him to the notion that plants could 'furnish the ornamentist with abstract form'.[34] William Dyce had recognized the importance of the abstract in his *Drawing Book* in 1842, but his generation had failed to realize the perpetual duality between abstract and naturalistic creations. Dresser, however, was less dependent on historical and naturalistic relativity for his designs, and aspired to express in conventional form the morphological laws of organic matter. He considered abstraction and geometric formalism a necessary antithesis to naturalism, and his primary element was not the natural model but the laws he abstracted from it:

The influence of matter in motion upon matter, whether moving or fixed, is at all times worthy of study, for by observing the aspects of matter when acted upon by various influences, and diligently inquiring into the nature of the mental conception of facts and occurrences, it will be found possible to express feelings and ideas by ornaments without the aid of symbolic forms.[35]

Above all, Dresser stressed 'the power of ornament to express feelings and ideas'. He argued that the allegorical symbolism dear to all Victorians could be more successfully embodied in abstract form. This would 'express the sentiments of the age' and act as a 'new scheme of ornamentation'.[36] Dresser was one of the first artists to realize that classicism and historicism had outlived their roles in the wake of industrial progress. He drew attention to other cultures and to contemporary science as more appropriate sources of inspiration for ornamentation and the decorative arts in general.

His search for a principle of order and a basis of classification involved the analysis of patterns down to their simplest units, or 'purely ideal form'. Recent scientific discoveries such as Darwin's theory of natural selection, published as *The Origin of the Species* in 1859, had inspired a general interest in the origins of nature and art. Gottfried Semper had contemplated the 'Urform', and similarly Dresser deduced design principles that are common to all cultures, as outlined in the third chapter of *The Art of Decorative Design*, 'Grades in the Decorative Art'.

The line of argument he adopted represented a severe attack on the imitative naturalist school: 'Natural adaptations are the lowest form of ornament . . . Many brutes can imitate but only few can create.' Following an ascending series he then classified the 'conventional' treatment of natural forms as the next step in the development. The third stage was 'the embodying in form of a mental idea which has been suggested by nature'. Finally he arrived at 'purely ideal ornament', which 'was utterly an embodiment of mind in form, or an offspring of the inner man, and its origin'.

The various grades of ornament in Western and Oriental styles he outlined demonstrated his revolutionary system of classification:

We have as examples of the first, most exalted grade of ornament the Greek, the Moorish, the Early English, much of the Indian, and many features of the Japanese, and some parts of the Egyptian and Renaissance. In the second class, following a descending series, we may instance much of the Egyptian and Chinese, and a few features in the Greek and Japanese. In the third a great portion of the middle-age work, especially the later Gothic, and many features of the Chinese or Indian: and in the forth or last class, much of the Pompeian and our modern floral patterns.[37]

A number of so-called 'anthemion' patterns exemplified this innovative classification, which for the first time in Western terms included Japanese and other Oriental styles. Dresser thus contributed to the basic reinterpretation of art. Departing from conventional concepts, he concentrated on ornamentation and abstract forms. Certain ornaments by virtue of additional features such as colour or composition illustrate different grades in Dresser's system. He explained this at greater length in the fourth and fifth chapters of his book, 'The Affinity of the Aesthetic Arts, Music, Ornament etc' and 'Analysis of Ornamental Forms'.

In 1846 the French poet Charles Baudelaire had introduced the idea of the affinity between colour, music and poetry,[38] and the concept of the mystical properties of colour soon gained credence among artists in Europe. Dresser in fact pioneered the idea that the aesthetic experience was dependent on the perception of a sensuous unity between mind and form: 'Harmonious chords in music when translated into form, furnish examples of beautiful proportion.'[39]

Dresser's analysis of ornamental forms also linked the artist with the scientist by showing that they shared a similar goal: 'To observe the unit out of which all vital forms are wrought, and to discover the "Ultima Thule" of life.'[40] A consideration of basic ornamental forms served to illustrate the infinite variety of construction, founded upon geometric laws of order, namely lines, curves, repetition, proportion, alternation and adaptation, which Dresser treated at length in subsequent chapters of *The Art of Decorative Design*. He believed that curves 'must be of a subtle nature' and that their beauty increased with their complexity and subtlety. In his search for the 'Line of Life', his survey ranged from young plants in spring to tropical vegetation, 'where the leaves are of colossal size and the vitality of the plants at its maximum'.[41] According to Dresser, such tropical plants could inspire powerful designs.

In his discussion of the 'adaptation of ornaments to articles of utility' he emphasized that the purpose or function of the object should be considered first. This should be followed by an analysis of the material to be used, and finally the honesty of the construction should be considered. This last aspect, said Dresser, would 'give force to the intention of every part'. He carefully appraised the nature and substance of the material and its suitability, objecting strongly, for example, to the use of high relief or 'sharp edges that could cause injury to the user'.[42] He preferred flat ornamentation, but permitted low relief in parts of the object which were not in immediate contact with the user.

Dresser's primary concern was with the domestic interior and its contents, and Owen Jones's 'new order of decorative art' was his main source of inspiration. He particularly admired Jones's interiors for St James Palace, which he described as a 'mixture of Greek, Egyptian and other historical elements in a perfect blending'.[43]

It was this kind of sifting of styles, from Orientalism to Eclecticism and Artistic Botany, which in turn dominated Dresser's artistic thinking. In his last chapter, 'Principles Common to Ornament', he concluded that: 'The designer's mind must be like the vital force of the plant, ever developing itself into forms of beauty, yet while thus free to produce, still in all cases governed by unaltered laws.'[44]

Many of the ideas launched by Dresser in *The Art of Decorative Design* related to topics which had been debated at the School of Design. Dresser's great asset, however, was his capacity to unite and synthesize the diverse ideas of his teachers. The International Exhibition provided a valuable outlet for many of his ideas and introduced his readers to the various ornaments and styles treated in his book. His review of the exhibition, published as *Development of Ornamental Art in the International Exhibition* (1862), dealt with specific exhibits, as well as with general principles concerning the design of wallpapers, textiles, carpets, furniture, glass, pottery and ironware. His principles on colour were in part derived from George Field's *Chromatography* (1835) and J.T. Lyon's unpublished 'Ideas on Colouring', but he also included observations on Oriental colour schemes in the exhibition. The Japanese exhibits, whose subtlety and beauty of colour contrasted with the polychrome and harsh colouring dominant in Western styles, made a profound impression on Dresser, and in turn modified his opinions concerning Owen Jones's polychromy. Dresser advocated tints of natural bloom, and hues of secondary and tertiary colours. The colours when viewed from a distance should give the impression of a natural bloom, similar to that of the peach, where all the colours of the rainbow combine to produce a neutral glow of colour.

> Yet, while this is the case, a most desirable effect may in some cases be gained by causing one colour to prevail in one surface, and another in another surface, and so balancing them all, that the hues of colour presented by the different surfaces again harmonize. Thus in the ceiling, while all the primary colours are present, and are so carefully arranged that a soft bloom results from the harmonizing colours, blue may prevail. On the wall the same principle of colouring may be adopted, the distribution of all the colours in small masses, yet yellow shall slightly prevail, and while the flower has a like treatment red shall prevail, and the red hue, the yellow hue and the blue hue shall harmonize.[45]

Dresser recommended this colour scheme as being ideal for drawing rooms, because it inspired 'purity, activity, and enlightenment'. In his next book, *Principles of Decorative Design* (1873), which provided illustrations of this kind of interior (plate 189), he expressed a preference for secondary and tertiary colours such as purple, green, orange, citrine, russet and olive. The idea that colours were capable of inducing certain thoughts or emotions in the viewer was based on J.T. Lyon's unpublished theories, but was expanded by Dresser: 'In the same manner as blue, red, and yellow suggest ideas of strength, beauty, and purity respectively; so purple, green and orange suggest feelings of response, gladness, and excitement, respectively.'[46] This theory provided the basis for Dresser's interior decorating schemes, and he outlined a programme for a blue study, a green breakfast room, a red dining room, a purple nursery, and a yellow drawing room and bedroom. Kitchens, pantries, store-rooms, and other rooms intended for manual work, should be coloured in a way which did not distract their inmates, for example in a dark yellow or buff colour.[47]

Dresser's publications on ornamental art and decorative design in the early 1860s represented the first thorough treatment of the subject by an English writer. They had become popular reading long before other arbiters of design reform such as Charles Locke Eastlake, Bruce J. Talbert and William Morris published their theories in the late 1860s and 1870s.

On the whole, Dresser's books were well received. *The Athenaeum* critic observed that 'One of the most conclusive matters in the scheme of design is set forth by the School represented by Dr Dresser.'[48] The *Art Journal*, although critically appreciative, voiced a more general reaction to his designs, which was to prevail for many years: 'The illustrations his book contains startle us: they are so opposed to everything we have been accustomed to regard as the beautiful in ornament, that we cannot recognise them as such, however true they may be.'[49]

The general reader would indeed have been startled by the sophistication and originality of Dresser's 'Knowledge is Power' design (plate 12) for example, but designers and artists appreciated the new system of intellectualized ornamentation based on abstractions of plant, animal and crystalline forms. However, this did not lead to practical imitation by ordinary Victorians, which probably partly explains why Dresser was virtually forgotten towards the end of the century, although his theories have gained credence today and are highly regarded by contemporary designers.

Dresser's views on art were not dissimilar to those expressed by two other radical British groups in the art milieu: the Arts and Crafts Movement and the Aesthetic Movement. Both groups had emerged from the coterie of design-orientated artists in the Pre-Raphaelite Brotherhood, and, like Dresser, proposed a reformation of British design and industry in the latter half of the nineteenth century.[50]

When Morris set about decorating his house in

1859, he found that all the decorative arts were in a 'state of complete degradation'. Consequently he decided to design suitable items himself. This led to the foundation of Morris, Marshall, Faulkner & Company in 1861, which became Morris & Company in 1875. The firm specialized in the production of alternative furniture, tiles, stained glass, embroideries, textiles and wallpapers, and enjoyed a considerable measure of popular success. In recognizing the heritage of the medieval arts and crafts tradition, Morris expressed ideas which frequently coincided with those of Dresser, particularly with regard to the adaptation of ornaments and objects to their surroundings.

Dresser, however, was fifteen years ahead of Morris in publishing his theories, and it is tempting to surmise that Morris, although he never publicly acknowledged Dresser's influence, may have derived many of his ideas from him. Both men preached the gospel of art for the masses, but Morris was never able to match Dresser's tremendous output of designs for mass production, and his more exclusive arts and crafts products reached a comparatively small circle of admirers. Morris, like his friend Ruskin, was in fact rather sceptical about the role of the machine, whereas Dresser in 1862 boldly asserted that the arts must reflect the knowledge of the age, and 'teach us the perfection of machinery and the greatness of our mechanical skill, and they will also tell in future ages, of the vastness of our power'.[51]

Morris looked to the medieval arts and crafts guilds for inspiration, whereas Dresser delighted in the discoveries of his own time and derived his chief stimulus from the new mechanical processes and from exposure to foreign cultures, notably that of Japan. His professional training led him to exploit the opportunities presented by mass production. He was essentially an innovator in this respect, working alone in a field which received little acclaim from Morris and the artists of the Arts and Crafts Movement, who were rigidly wedded to traditions of craftsmanship. Clearly the practical results of Morris's and Dresser's efforts to improve British design were fundamentally different, but their guiding principles often agreed.

Dresser, in summing up his doctrines on 'adaptation', concluded that 'pretty things when juxtaposed often had an offensive appearance and ought to be adapted to the circumstances in which they are to be placed'.[52] Similarly, Morris, in his lecture on 'The Beauty of Life' in 1880, declared: 'Have nothing in your house which you do not know to be useful or believe to be beautiful.'[53] Indeed, it was largely due to their combined teachings that greater care was taken with the decoration of the interiors in ordinary houses in Britain.

Likewise it was the concern with interiors and the new colour ideas which inspired the Aesthetic Movement – aesthetic being defined as 'the beautiful philosophy of taste', and 'art for art's sake'. Beginning in the 1860s with the work of a few artists and designers, notably Algernon Swinburne, James M. Whistler and Edward W. Godwin, the movement gathered momentum during the 1870s and fostered a highly developed appreciation of beauty. By the 1880s it embraced almost every art form, including architecture and interior decoration.

Dresser published and advocated his ideas long before the 'aesthetes', and many of their doctrines emanated from him. They joined him in admiring Japanese art and rebelling against naturalism and conventional art, but where Dresser adapted the cultural language of the time for new purposes, more in tune with the industrial society of which he was a part, the aesthetes offered art as a counterbalance to industrialism. Their pessimism about the value of industrial design and the implications of mass production set them apart from Dresser. The essentially innovative Dresser saw the immense benefits of the technical processes and advances where his opponents perceived only the disadvantages.

It was Dresser's view of design and interior decoration as a co-operative and harmonious expression, and his ideas concerning colours, which were of especial interest to the aesthetes. This can be seen in the interiors created by Godwin, Jeckyll and Whistler in the 1860s and 1870s.[54] Dresser was certainly one of the most ardent aesthetes, but their creed of 'art for art's sake' had little affinity with his desire to bring art to the ordinary man. Dresser described himself as an 'art-workman', a title which few of the high-minded elitist members of the Aesthetic Movement would have adopted for themselves.

More than any other designer and artist of the time, Dresser worked actively for the right of 'the artisan to take [his] place in the society with the producer', a dictum he first presented when adjudicating the first 'Art Workman's Exhibition' in Manchester in 1865.[55] This remarkably egalitarian consideration of the designer's rights, preceded those expressed by socialist thinkers and the adherents of the Arts and Crafts Movement by at least ten years.

Matthew Digby Wyatt, architect, designer and lecturer at the School of Design, was pleased to note by the time of the Paris International Exhibition in 1867 that ' "Our Artist" is no longer confounded with "Our Traveller" or "Our Warehouseman", but he is put forward as responsible for his own share in the production of the house'.[56] A marked difference in attitude had certainly taken place since the Great Exhibition of 1851. A further decade would pass, however, before designers' names were allowed to appear jointly with the maker's mark. Dresser was one of the first industrial designers to obtain this right and throughout his life he continued to stress the status of the designers as proper artists and art-workmen.

His motto 'Truth, Beauty and Power' was launched with this aim in view and probably originated around the time of the Paris Exhibition. He exhibited a number of his designs and published an extensive review of the exhibition, in which he emphasized that the 'knowledge of truth' would inspire the artist to 'seek out beauty'.[57]

His pattern book from this time includes several of the creations exhibited in Paris as well as a shield-like design with stylized peacock feathers incorporating the words 'Truth, Beauty, Power' (plate 13). In his articles on 'Principles of Decorative Design' of 1870, Dresser recalled the origins of this motto:

> Long since I was so fully impressed with the idea that true art principles are so perfectly manifested by these words, that I embodied them in ornamental device which I painted in my study door, so that all who entered might learn the principles which I sought to manifest in my works.[58]

Dresser's rapid emergence as a designer, writer and educationalist in the 1860s had brought him to the forefront of the artistic milieu in Britain by the 1870s. His position was further enhanced by the publication in book form of his *Principles of Decorative Design* in 1873. Here he especially addressed 'working men', and stressed his solidarity with them: 'Workmen, I am a worker, and a believer in the efficacy of work.'

The first part of Dresser's book covered general principles of design and colouring, which he had written about in 1862. His chapters on 'Truth, Beauty, and Power' and 'Employment of the Grotesque in Ornament', however, presented novel ideas that were probably conceived at the time of the Paris Exhibition in 1867.

Dresser had previously disregarded the grotesque or 'ornamental composition such as tend to suggest the human countenance, or any monster',[59] but in 1870 he suggested that 'the grotesque should frequently be used where we meet with naturalistic imitations'.[60] Implying that it was of a higher order than figurative imitations, he referred to the grotesque as a form of stylization and abstraction. Here again it appears that his experience of Japanese and Chinese art was a main source of inspiration:

> As regards Eastern nations, while nearly all have employed the grotesque as an element of decorative art, the Chinese and Japanese have employed it most largely, and for it they manifest a most decided partiality. The drawings of dragons, celestial lions, mythical birds, beasts, fishes, insects, and other supposed inhabitants of the Elysian plains, which these people produce, are most interesting and extraordinary.[61]

It was this eye-opening experience which had contributed to the final artistic manifestation of his 'Truth, Beauty and Power' motif in 1867.

Dresser's *Principles of Decorative Design* defined truth in relation to imitation – or that which

17
Design for Josiah Wedgwood & Sons vase. 11 March 1867. Public Record Office, London.

militated against the scientific and natural laws of the material – for example faux marble, which he particularly disliked: 'The imitation is always less beautiful than the thing imitated . . . Thus the want of truth brings its own punishment.' Beauty 'must be truthful in expression, and graceful, delicate, and refined in contour, manifesting no coarseness, vulgarity, or obtrusiveness. The beautiful manifests no want, no shortcoming.' Dresser saw art as an expression of power, and the artist as someone who could unite truth and beauty or science and art: 'Power means energy, power implies a conqueror . . . We shall not be believed if we do not utter our truths with power, let truth then be uttered with power, and in the form of beauty.'[62]

His illustrated example displays the most daring and inventive creation from this period of his career. It had been adapted for some vases which he created for Josiah Wedgwood & Sons in 1867:

> I have sought to embody chiefly the idea of power, energy, force, or vigour; and in order to do this, I have employed such lines as we see in the bursting buds of spring, when the energy of growth is at its maximum, and especially such as are to be seen in the spring growth of a luxuriant tropical vegetation: I have also availed myself of those forms to be seen in certain bones of birds which are associated with

the organs of flight, and which give us an impression of great strength, as well as those observable in the propelling fins of certain species of fish (plates 17, 18).[63]

Few if any contemporary Victorian artists possessed a more innovative vernacular of ornamentation. The average man and woman, however, would probably have found Dresser's designs and ideas too avant-garde, and even Dresser himself referred to them as eccentric. In 1871, in his lecture on 'Ornamentation Considered as High Art', he defined this almost organic or abstract ornamentation as a totally new kind of artistic expression – an 'instructive hieroglyph of beauty', which 'symbolized imagination or emotion, such as is calculated to teach some moral lesson or impress some important truth'.[64]

This view contrasted strongly with what was happening at the South Kensington Museum in 1871. The entire lecture in fact was a severe attack on the naturalist school and on the South Kensington Institution which, under the influence of Ruskin and other academicians had, according to Dresser, returned to the methods of the drawing school, even to the extent of decorating the new museum in 'pictorially treated fragments' in Roman and Renaissance styles. This 'misapplied pictorial art' was, said Dresser, 'inferior to the gorgeous ornaments of India, Formosa, China and Japan'.

Dresser raged against 'the authorities of the South Kensington who were not able to find men who had art-knowledge and technical knowledge combined' and he regretted that few students of the School ever developed the liberated and challenging style which had brought him so much success:

As an architect, I have as much work as many of my fellows, and as an ornamentist I have much the largest practice in the kingdom; so far as I know, there is not one branch of art-manufacture that I do not regularly design patterns for, and I hold regular appointments as 'art adviser' and 'chief-designer' to several of our largest art-manufacturing firms.[65]

Vocal and versatile, Dresser was certainly one of the most industrious protagonists of design in

Britain, covering virtually all the media of the art industry, and writing and lecturing extensively on the subject. In 1872 when he lectured on 'Hindrances to the Progress of Applied Art' he was referred to as 'our indefatigable friend', who never tired of advocating new ideas in art and design.

Among the 'hindrances' listed by Dresser were badly educated designers, manufacturers who pirated designs from the inventors, and the antiquarian taste of buyers and art institutions, notably the South Kensington establishment, whose lack of expertise Dresser held responsible for the retrogressive tendencies in the British art industry. He stressed the importance of proper museum labelling and cataloguing,[66] and George Wallis, who was present at the lecture, clearly took note of this, because he soon afterwards encouraged the printing of the *South Kensington Museum Handbooks*, which became very popular during the late 1870s and 1880s.

Dresser's lecture raised the important issue of a Royal Academy for Decorative Artists, which he believed would redress the designers' lack of status. This proposal was taken up by the Chairman, Matthew Digby Wyatt, who suggested that the two schools of art should be united in one Royal Academy, with Owen Jones as Professor of Applied Art. Dresser gave his enthusiastic support to this, praising Jones as the leading spirit of design reform in Britan, an accolade once bestowed on Jones by the South Kensington Institution itself. In the mid-1860s, while still associated with the School of Design, the three friends, Jones, Wyatt and Dresser, had themselves been credited as having 'established a school of decorative art, peculiarly English, pure in its character, and in its colouring perfect'.[67]

Their style was no longer dictated by dogmatic theory, but was based on a general affinity with art of the Early English medieval period and on their admiration for Oriental and Japanese art. A freer play with historical pastiches and with ideas from diverse cultures gave birth to a more personal manner, which reflected the spirit of the times. Dresser's concept of 'borrowing principles rather than forms' and his theories on colour were to inspire a new and original style which in the last third of the century became known as Anglo-Japanese or Modern English.

18
Page 32. Josiah Wedgwood & Sons vase incorporating 'Truth, Beauty, Power' motif. 20 March 1867. Unglazed earthenware. 10 in. high. Private collection.

THE CULT OF JAPAN

Dresser was one of the leading figures in the introduction of Japonism, or the so-called 'Cult of Japan', in the West. This movement covered a period of extraordinary artistic activity and exchange between Japan and the Occident, following the opening of the country to foreign trade in 1853. Japonism soon became a guiding light in Dresser's campaign for artistic reform. His continuous efforts to promote Japanese influences in the mainstream of Western design culminated in his visit to Japan in 1876–7. This was the first tour of the country by a European designer, and his recollections, published under the title *Japan, its Architecture, Art, and Art-Manufactures* (1882), provided one of the most thorough treatments of the subject and became a vital impetus to the Japonism movement.

Broadly speaking, Japonism can be seen as a result of British imperialism in the nineteenth century. As early as 1813 Sir Thomas Stamford Raffles had attempted to break Japan's seclusion, and his collection of 'Japanese Antiquities' were exhibited in London in 1825.[1] Part of this collections was donated by his nephew to the British Museum in 1859.[2]

Studies of museum holdings, exhibitions and public auctions in Europe show indeed that Japanese art could be seen in Britain during the first decades of the century. Joseph Marryat in his *Collections towards a History of Pottery and Porcelain* (1850), which was one of Dresser's textbooks at the School of Design, referred to numerous Arita and Imari pieces acquired from the auction sales of William Beckford's and Horace Walpole's collections in 1823 and 1842 respectively. Large

quantities of lacquer and porcelain in fact were imported to Britain in the early nineteenth century, and gave rise to the Japonaiserie patterns in English porcelain. Japonaiserie, as distinct from Japonism, could be defined as a less fastidious fashion for Japanese motifs in the Chinoiserie style.

During the Indo-China wars, Japanese artefacts filtered through to Europe via diplomats and travellers, and when the conflict came to an end and Hong Kong was annexed to the Empire in 1842, British interests shifted to the closed and mysterious Japan. Rutherford Alcock, the British Consul in Shanghai, collected Japanese objects during his time in China, and some of these were exhibited at the China stand he organized for the Great Exhibition in London in 1851.

The catalogue of this exhibition also mentions Japonaiserie porcelain shown by Mason & Company, which was inspired by the Arita patterns. For the first time such objects were referred to as 'Anglo-Japanese'.[3] Clearly British designers and manufacturers had developed a more sophisticated attitude to Japanese art, and were about to realize the full potential of Japonism.

This trend was greatly accelerated when the Americans forced Japan to open up to foreign exchange. Britain and other Western nations soon secured diplomatic and commercial rights, and Sir Rutherford Alcock was installed as British Minister in Edo, later Tokyo, in 1859. The many travelogues and the great variety of literature on Japan in the Western press provided information about the country and its culture, which presented a new picture of Japanese art products.

The overall body of knowledge, however, was fragmented and the generally enthusiastic descriptions were frequently qualified by such adjectives as 'anomalous', 'bizarre', 'diabolical', 'mysterious' and 'singular'. Condescending attitudes in fact existed alongside a sense of fascination and admiration, but European writers were quick to compare the art of feudalistic Japan with that of medieval Europe, which was popular at the time. This association greatly facilitated the assimilation of Japanese art in artistic circles in the West, and the wide range of objects brought back by the first travellers were shown at major exhibitions of industrial art, and thus helped to spread its influence in Europe.

Large collections of Japanese fine and decorative art were on public display in the Royal Dutch collections in The Hague and at the von Siebold museum in Leiden from 1816 and 1832 respectively,[4] and in Paris there was a Musée Chinois et Japonais as early as 1840.[5] The Museum of Ornamental Art in London acquired several items of Japanese lacquer and porcelain from the dealer William Hewitt in 1852,[6] and in 1854 they enlarged their collection with 37 samples of Japanese artefacts from the first sales exhibition of Japanese art at the Old Water-Colour Society in London.[7] The museum continued to develop its Japanese collection, which by the late 1860s was regarded as one of the best in Europe. Japanese art was also exhibited at the international and industrial exhibitions in Dublin (1853), Edinburgh (1856 and 1857) and Bristol (1861), as well as at the Art Treasures of Great Britain Exhibition in Manchester in 1857.

Dresser's involvement with Japanese art follows three main phases. Although he recalled having been familiar with Japanese Arita patterns from childhood, it was not until later in his career that he began to incorporate Japanese ideas and devices into his writings and designs. At first he was attracted by the sheer novelty of Japanese art, but he soon recognized its distinct aesthetic qualities and the similarities with Western art; finally he reached an awareness and understanding of its artistic criteria. He certainly had access to Japanese art as a student at the School of Design, whose library also housed press reviews and catalogues of the various exhibitions. Indeed, the study of Oriental art in general had been intensified at the School since the Great Exhibition of 1851, and in 1854 Dresser's tutor Octavius Hudson included Japanese study samples in his lectures. Dresser's own lectures on 'The Art of Decorative Design' in 1861 followed the pattern of those of Hudson, but his fascination and enthusiasm for Japanese art led him one step further, and he classified Japanese lotus motifs as belonging to 'the most exalted grade of ornament'.

Dresser was one of the first artists in Europe to respond seriously to Japanese art, and it is significant that this happened before its first comprehensive representation at the International Exhibition in London in 1862. By 1861 certain critics in Britain had already asked for 'true impressions of photographic accuracy' in the plethora of new books about Japan,[8] and Sir Rutherford Alcock provided some 'Views of Japan and Java', which were printed by the London photographers Negretti and Zambra and commercially distributed. These photographs, which were also included in Thomas Westfield's *The Japanese, their Manners and Customs* (1862), were among the first accurate images of the Japanese and their art products. They were certainly known to Dresser, who praised Negretti and Zambra for 'procuring photographs of scenes and lands of the deepest interest'.[9] In fact Dresser's scholarly consideration of Japanese ornamentation helped fulfil the need for more factual information, and was unique in the context of the study of Oriental art at the time. Even at this early stage of his career Dresser had begun to promote Japanese art and challenge the condescension prevalent among most contemporary critics. By showing its authentic connections with other styles, and by removing the false hegemonic barriers between Western and Oriental art in general, he encouraged a more serious study. He also presented a wider spectrum of stylistic prototypes which in turn helped to dethrone historicism and to modernize art in the West. His ideology can be interpreted as an aesthetic result of British imperialism, but his Japonism and his other controversial ideas must be primarily understood as a response to the issue of the reform of design.

The Japanese section of the 1862 International Exhibition prepared by Sir Rutherford Alcock was one of the most influential events in the history of Japanese art in the West. It featured lacquer work, metalwork, basketwork, porcelain, textiles, paintings, prints and other works of art, and a miscellaneous group of objects lent by Captain Vyse, Mr Mcdonald and Remi Schmidt & Company.[10] The latter showed some very fine large bronzes and 33 pieces of enamel work, which were the first to appear in Europe and were subsequently sold by auction at Christie's. The post-exhibition auctions also included a major collection amassed by Edwin Wadham, which had arrived too late to be exhibited. Alcock is not recorded as having offered any of his exhibits for sale.[11]

Among the buyers mentioned in the auction houses were William Hewitt & Company, Murray Marks & Company and Farmer & Rogers. The latter imported goods from the Far East, and Arthur Lasenby Liberty was employed there in 1862, becoming manager two years later and leaving to set up his own rival shop in Regent Street in 1875. Liberty and Murray Marks became the chief London dealers in Japanese art during the 1860s and 1870s and Japan enthusiasts such as Dresser, James M. Whistler, Edward W. Godwin, William Morris, Richard Norman Shaw, and Dante Gabriel and William M. Rossetti are known to have made some of their first purchases from them.[12]

The Japanese exhibits of 1862 were enthusiastically reviewed by the press, and Japanese art began to be compared favourably with the art of other countries. Artists and critics soon recognized a fresh source of art from which they could draw inspiration. Significantly, many of them are recorded as having been positively predisposed from earlier encounters with Japanese art. The architect-designer William Burges for instance observed: 'Since Lord Elgin's visit (1858), numerous articles of Japanese workmanship have come to this country, and been eagerly bought up, but the present Exhibition gives the first opportunity of seeing them collected together in any quantity.'[13] Burges provided one of the most extensive reviews of the Japan stand in 1862, and together with his friend Edward W. Godwin was one of the early collectors of Japanese art in Britain. Their interest may have been aroused at the 1861 Industrial Exhibition in Bristol, where Godwin lived, which featured numerous samples of Japanese and Chinese art. By 1862 Godwin is recorded as having decorated his house with Japanese prints and other artefacts. From that time onward he became one of the main advocates of Japonism, and the Anglo-Japanese style.

Burges was one of the most brilliant architects of the Medieval Revival and soon combined this style with elements of Japanese design, advocating closer study of Japanese art:

I hope I have said enough to shew the student

of our reviving arts of the thirteenth century, that an hour, or even a day or two, spent in the Japanese department will by no means be lost time, for these hitherto unknown barbarians appear not only to know all that the Middle Ages knew, but in some respects are beyond them and us as well.[14]

Writers like John B. Waring also underlined the didactic value of Japanese prototypes. In his *Masterpieces of the International Exhibition* (1863) he illustrated Japanese lacquer, porcelain and enamels, observing that 'Our manufacturers would have derived great advantage from a close study of them'.

Dresser, in his book about the exhibition, described some ebonized furniture 'of a quaint and unique Japanese character' exhibited by Bornemann & Company of Bath and by Lemoine of Paris, and some Minton porcelain vases 'enriched with Chinese or Japanese ornament'.[15] The vases appear to have been designed by Dresser himself. The direct impact of Japanese art on Dresser's designs will be dealt with in subsequent chapters but the ideological background upon which he based his theory of Japonism merits further discussion.

Although several artists responded positively to Japanese art in the early 1860s, few, if any, were able to discern its aesthetic criteria, and even Burges's view was rather limited. The affinity between Japanese and medieval art was readily endorsed, but it was left to Dresser and to John Leighton in their reviews of the Japan stand to attempt to describe Japanese art on its own terms. John Leighton had already included some Japanesque ornaments in his *Suggestions in Design*, published in 1853, but these appear more as expressions of Japonaiserie. The book was certainly known to Dresser and the two young designers were probably friends, since Leighton is recorded as having supported Dresser's patenting the process of nature printing in 1857.[16] Both were friends of Sir Rutherford Alcock, who presented them with gifts from his Japan collection in 1862.

It was probably Alcock who inspired Dresser and Leighton to publish works on Japanese art. Alcock himself published a number of books, including *The Capital of The Tycoon* (1863) and *Art and Art Industries of Japan* (1878) but his main importance in the history of Japonism was that of an intermediary; it was only Dresser and Leighton at this early stage who were able to relate their enthusiasm for Japanese art to contemporary theories of Western art.

Leighton delivered his lecture 'On Japanese Art' to the Royal Institution on 1 May 1863,[17] and Dresser soon followed with his discourse on 'The Prevailing Ornament of China and Japan', presented to the Architectural Association on 19 May, and published as a précis in the same month. Three anonymous articles appearing under the title 'Japanese Ornamentation' in May–June 1863[18] have been attributed to Dresser since they treat the same topics and art-objects as his lecture. Echoing William Burges, both writers expressed the similarities between Japanese and medieval art, but this view was balanced by a consideration of the more striking differences. The novelty of Japanese art was held to be the main factor in its appeal.

Basically the lectures reflect the authors' specific artistic preoccupations; Leighton, who became famous as a printer and illustrator, devoted most of his attention to Japanese prints, whereas Dresser dealt entirely with Japanese ornamentation, art manufactures and interiors. This must have appealed particularly to Burges, who chaired the meeting on 19 May. Edward Godwin, whose Gothicist drawings of architecture were on show at the Architectural Association, probably also attended the lecture. Indeed the connection between Burges, Godwin and Dresser at this period must have been closer than previously assumed by art historians. One of Godwin's sketchbooks for instance contains a page with Japanese diapers marked 'from drawings of Dr. Dresser', and these appear to be identical with ornaments discussed in Dresser's lecture.[19]

Japanese diapers were also illustrated in Dresser's articles, along with Japanese frets, borders, crests and stylized leaf and floral patterns, similar to those included in *The Art of Decorative Design* and in his Japanese crest album. Dresser observed in Japanese ornaments the same 'rigid flatness' he had introduced in his designs, and he listed a number of much-used themes later incorporated in his own creations, such as the chrysanthemum, lotus, bamboo, blackthorn, cherry, narcissus, hibiscus, pomegranate, reeds, grasses and trees, dragons, deer, storks, small birds, butterflies, beetles, grasshoppers and other insects.[20]

The greatest challenge presented by Japanese ornamentation, however, was the irregularity prevalent in the grouping of certain motifs, which clearly contradicted the geometrical symmetry preached by the School of Design. Dresser expressed a certain scepticism about this lack of symmetry in Japanese design, but he later came to feature it in his own work. Generally he found that Japanese art theories were similar to his own, and he was pleased to discover that 'the principles of preserving the true condition of the surface decorated is maintained rigidly in all Japanese works'.[21]

Even Japanese interiors were assessed in relation to Dresser's principles, and they subsequently dictated his own interior decorating schemes. He was well aware of the Japonism which had developed among the Aesthetes and in artistic milieux in France, but he warned against the dangers of superficial adaptations of Japanese art, believing that:

> In many cases the French artists who have engaged themselves with recasting Japanese designs have failed to discover the purport or significance of the forms they have borrowed. They have taken the form, but have not perceived the sentiment of which the shape is but the shroud; or have copied forms and groupings without seizing the spirit of the work.[22]

Clearly Dresser dismissed the imitative tendency in early French Japonism, which was to prevail in France. However, he was quick to appreciate the merits of Japonism and he encouraged artists to consult the literary sources available on Japanese art in order to arrive at a more thorough interpretation:

> The source of knowledge of the art which the French are now earnestly utilizing in a commercial point of view has been open to us as well as to them, hence our knowledge of this branch of art should not be less than theirs. Indeed we had greater facilities for procuring information upon these works than those who were less familiar with the English language than our selves. So our knowledge should be greater.[23]

Dresser's discourses on Japanese art and early Japonism reveal a remarkable insight which is quite lacking in any other contemporary writer on the subject. Even Burges and Leighton were primarily governed by curiosity and a craving for novelty, rather than by an analytical appreciation. Dresser on the other hand strove to comprehend the true aesthetics of Japanese art, and he concluded his articles with a consideration of symbolic forms and religious significance which had not previously been understood by the Japonists.

In Japanese crests, 'anthemions', grotesques and cloud-patterns, Dresser discerned the 'abstract ornament in conventional form' he had recommended in *The Art of Decorative Design*. He believed that this type of ornament would liberate designers from the allegorical symbolism favoured by most Victorians, and lead to a more sophisticated Japonism than that practised by French artists at the time: 'These considerations of Japanese ornament will aid us in selecting the true art qualities from the Japanese, if we must follow the fashion of the French, and produce designs in the style of worthy character.'[24] He also called for a proper study of the spiritual content of Japanese art, and this attitude played a decisive part in his own career as a designer. In his lecture on 'The Art Manufactures of Japan' in 1878 he stated that Japanese art had been fundamental in forming his 'art character' and that Sir Rutherford Alcock had played a vital part in this:

> In 1862 he kindly permitted me to make sketches of whatever he possessed, and I made about eighty drawings, such as they were, in the Exhibition, from the various articles which he had brought over, and at the close of the Exhibition, I became the possessor of a fair selection of the objects which formed his interesting collection; and to the treasures which I thus became possessed of I have almost constantly been adding, till now my house is rather a museum than a comfortable abode for civilised beings. Feeling the beauty of these objects I have done what I could to encourage their introduction into this country.[25]

Dresser's enthusiasm for Japanese art was soon echoed by other artists, and during the 1860s the coterie around Godwin, Whistler and the Rossetti brothers put forward their plea for aestheticism and Japonism. William M. Rossetti wrote two perceptive articles on 'Japanese Woodcuts' and 'Japanese Fans' in 1863 and 1865,[26] and the paintings of his brother and those of Whistler showed distinct Japonism tendencies. Norman Shaw and William Nesfield incorporated Japanese crest patterns and ornaments into their architectural schemes in the early 1860s, and Burges and Talbert created medieval-inspired furniture with similar decorative details.[27] Owen Jones's designs for the Oriental Courts in the South Kensington Museum

from 1865 showed motifs derived from Japanese and Chinese cloisonné patterns. Since Jones had been rather dismissive about Japanese ornamentation, it is tempting to suggest that he collaborated with Dresser on this early example of Japonism in European architecture; the preliminary drawings in fact came into Dresser's possession when Jones died in 1874.

By the time of the Paris International Exhibition in 1867 Japonism had manifested itself both in Britain and in France. Dresser praised the Japan stand in his review of the exhibition: 'Such an acquaintance with Eastern art could scarcely fail to influence the ornamentation of objects in this country.'[28] His own perception of Japanese aesthetics seems to have been vitally enlarged at this time and he became particularly interested in the aspects of the grotesque and angular, which in turn inspired his personal style. His review stressed the educational value of Japanese cloisonné vessels, bronze teapots, and above all furniture, which he claimed was 'not anywhere surpassed'.[29] The numerous Japanese lacquer étagères, tables and stands made a profound impact on Western critics. The French Japonist Philippe Burty recognized the 'lois des ensembles' in Japanese interiors of the kind that Dresser had advocated in 1863: 'Le mobilier japonais nous est révélé, dans toute son élégante simplicité.'[30]

Even stout Gothicists such as Charles L. Eastlake contrasted the bad taste in contemporary furniture-making with the superior products of 'those nations whose art has long been our custom to despise', his only example of such nations being Japan.[31] Eastlake in fact popularized much of the 'lois des ensembles' recommended by Dresser and Burty.

When the Goncourt brothers proclaimed 'Japonaiserie forever' in 1867, the fashion developed into a veritable cult.[32] In 1869 the painter Fantin-Latour, a close friend of Whistler, coined the word 'Japonisme' for a painting he made using Whistler's kimono, among other Japanese effects. Thus it was that the collaboration of these two leaders of the Japonist painters in France and in England introduced the term which became identified with the whole movement.[33] Japan's triumphs at the international exhibitions, as well as the increasing flow of information and imports of Japanese art, had taken Western artists and critics by storm. The architect and designer Owen W. Davis in a short notice on 'Japanese Ornament' signalled the emergence of a 'little mania':

In the studio of artists and amateurs we find increasing collections of Japanese, Chinese, or other Oriental objects, from inlaid mother-of-pearl cabinets, textile fabrics, faience, trays, fans, and screens, down to the unpretending pot of preserved ginger; in fact it has become a little mania to exercise a show of taste in that quarter.[34]

When he lectured on 'Ornamentation Considered as High Art' in 1871, Dresser held up the 'gorgeous ornaments of India, Formosa, China and Japan' as more appropriate models for the decorations of the South Kensington Museum than the figurative Renaissance motifs applied by Francis Wollaston Moody. Matthew Digby Wyatt had put forward similar views in his articles on 'Orientalism in European Industry' in 1870.[35] Other critics such as the Austrian Jacob Falke also attempted 'to point to a new source from whence might be derived new motifs and a renovation of modern taste and modern Art-Industry'.[36] It was precisely this concept of renovation which had first excited Dresser and other Japan enthusiasts in the 1860s, and the encouragement of well-known art authorities helped consolidate the Japonism movement in Europe during the 1870s. By 1872 The Builder was boldly announcing the arrival of 'The Japanese Craze'[37] and the Art Journal welcomed the 'increasing influence of Japanese art on industry in England'.[38]

Dresser's enthusiasm showed no sign of abating as the decade progressed, but in his Principles of Decorative Design he warned against the deterioration of Japanese art under Western influence. The impact of modernization on Japan attracted considerable attention in the Western press, and members of The Asiatic Society of Japan, founded by Sir Harry Parkes in 1872, were particularly active in highlighting the alarming disappearance of the old Japanese culture.[39]

Strangely enough this strengthened the view of Japan as a mystical and singular country. Despite the increasing amount of information on Japan available in the West, the literature during the 1870s in fact centred on old Japan, but philistine condescension seems to have been replaced by fascination and acceptance.

Japanese art was featured extensively at the International Exhibitions in London in 1871, 1872 and 1873. The 1871 exhibition showed for the first time some 'drab coloured, rough and unglazed earthenware' which made a profound impact on Dresser.[40] In his 'Principles of Decorative Design' articles published that year he referred to 'some specimens of Japanese earthenware, which are formed of coarse dark brown clay' in his own collection. These displayed 'the bold art-effects' he so much admired, and his recommendation in turn inspired the production of art ceramics in the West during the 1870s and 1880s.

Sir Rutherford Alcock, who retired from his post in Japan in 1872, showed samples from his collection at the International Exhibition that year, and several of these were acquired by the South Kensington Museum. Equally important for Japonism in Britain was the visit of the Iwakura mission in 1872, headed by Iwakura Tomomi and Okubo Toschimichi. These distinguished creators of modern Japan were received by Sir Philip Cunliffe Owen, Director of the South Kensington Museum, and plans were made for a comprehensive Japan stand at the International Exhibition in 1873, which Cunliffe Owen and Dresser were asked to organize.[41]

It was probably to a member of the Iwakura mission that the House-Furnisher and Decorator was referring when it announced that 'Dr. Dresser has a resident agent in Japan, a gentleman of artistic judgement and experience, who has already sent home some of the finest specimens of lacquer-ware ever seen in this country, and such as must excite the lively envy of all collectors and curators of the S. Ken. Museum and India Museum.'[42]

Sakata Haruo, a young official of the Japanese Government, personally delivered the Japanese objects required for the exhibition; the catalogue lists silks, leather papers, lacquer and some coarse ceramics, evidently shown on Dresser's recommendation.[43] Sakata remained in London as a student at the Royal School of Mines, returning to Japan in 1876, when he was appointed Dresser's escort during the latter's visit to the country.

It was his personal contacts with Japanese officials which in 1873 inspired Dresser to organize the establishment of a large warehouse for imported goods from Japan and the Far East in conjunction with Charles Reynolds & Company.[44] Within a decade the new company, called Londos, had developed into the 'first and largest importer of Japanese art in Britain'.[45]

Dresser was engaged as art adviser and in 1873 he sent his assistants Caspar Clarke and William Churcher on an expedition to investigate products from Spain, Morocco, Egypt, Italy, Greece, Turkey, Persia, Thailand and China.[46] A letter from Clarke to Dresser, dated Teheran 22 April 1875, proves that Clarke and Churcher arrived in Persia, but whether they reached other Far Eastern countries is not known.[47] Londos & Company subsequently established branches in Paris, China, Persia, Morocco and Japan, and the *House-Furnisher and Decorator* praised Dresser's eagerness in the 'Pursuit of Beauty', a reference to the motto adorning his stationery and Londos's advertising (plate 19).[48] This slogan became virtually synonymous with Japonism and the Aesthetic Movement, and was subsequently adopted by Louis C. Tiffany.[49]

Dresser appears to have been at the peak of his energies in 1873. After organizing the Japan show in London he proceeded to visit the International Exhibition in Vienna, and supplied designs for a number of British manufacturers who participated in the exhibition, notably Minton's, who showed some of his Japan-inspired cloisonné porcelain.[50] Japonism was by then so well established that its influence had spread as far as the United States, and the American critic William P. Blake devoted an entire chapter of his report on the exhibition to 'The Influence of Japanese Art'.[51]

Dresser himself endorsed this trend in an essay on 'Eastern Art and its Influence on European Manufacture', which considered 'especially Japanese influences'. The essay, originally given as a lecture for the Royal Society of Arts, dealt with Japanese porcelain and cloisonné enamel work, which Dresser claimed had led to new industries in Europe. But, he went on, it was also vital for the artist to comprehend 'the feeling, and the poetry of the various forms of Oriental ornament'.[52] He lamented the inadequate capacity of Westerners to assimilate such lessons, and again emphasized the educational value of Japanese functionalism for British manufacturers.[53]

Turning from the consideration of utilitarian truths to those of beauty, he noted that the ornaments of Eastern nations originated from 'the expression of a poetic thought or a beautiful idea'.[54] Dresser had first hinted at the spiritual significance of ornamentation in 1862–3, but it was only after he encountered Japanese scholars that he understood the inherent poetic expression contained in Japanese decorative art.

He concluded his essay with an examination of the religious significance of fire worship, symbolized in the flame and nimbus ornaments. These ornaments, said Dresser, were common to all cultures, including Christianity, Islam, Buddhism

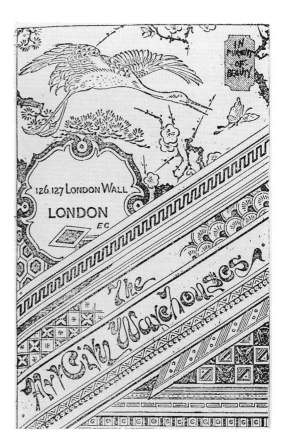

19
Londos & Co. advertisement incorporating Dresser's motto 'In the Pursuit of Beauty'. *The Furniture Gazette*, 8 July 1876.

and Shintoism, and it was this belief in the universality of ornament which provided the main impetus for his journey to Japan in 1876.

Following his visit to Vienna in 1873 Dresser announced the establishment of a new importing company, the Alexandra Palace Company, naming himself as art director and Sir Edward Lee as managing director. The aim was to offer Japanese objects for sale at a Japanese village to be built in Alexandra Park, at Muswell Hill in North London.

This Japanese village presented the British public with their first real view of Japanese architecture. The newly founded Japanese company, Kiritsu Kosho Kaisha, supplied the goods offered for sale, and under Matsuo Gosuké and Wakai Kanezaburo were responsible for promoting some of the most distinguished contemporary Japanese artists in the West. They established branches in New York in 1877 and in Paris in 1878, remaining in business until about 1891.[55]

Clearly Dresser's artistic aims were combined with commercial aspirations, as the guide to the Alexandra Palace Company testifies:

In the bazaar, as well as in a special department

in the Palace, Japanese productions of the highest and rarest, as well as of the most ordinary kinds, are on sale. To ensure their genuineness, the Japanese goods will be stamped. It is the more essential that this point should be dwelt on, because the taste of Japanese work has been somewhat deteriorated by the introduction of goods of inferior workmanship, manufactured expressly for the England market. From the Alexandra Palace such trash will be banished, and the lovers of Japanese art cannot fail to be gratified. Viewed from the Western end of the Palace, the Japanese Village has a very pretty appearance.[56]

Dresser was involved with the venture until at least 1879, when he was responsible for the designs of a Moorish villa, an Egyptian residence and a Chinese teashop, which all contributed to the general allure of the Orient.[57] He was assisted by Henry Tooth, a stage designer from the Isle of Wight whom he had met during his visit to the island in 1870. Tooth subsequently went on to become the manager of the Linthorpe Art Pottery founded by Dresser and John Harrison in 1879.[58]

The Alexandra Palace itself contained departments occupied by such notable companies as Elkington's, Minton's, Jackson & Graham's, Chubb & Sons, Benham & Froud, Edwin Streeter's and Arthur Liberty's, all of which were in contact with Dresser in the 1870s. Arthur Liberty, when starting his own company in 1875, is recorded as having fitted up a Japanese house at Alexandra Park, which must refer to one of the houses in Dresser's village.[59] This is perhaps the first datable connection between the two friends, who were among the foremost promoters of Japanese art in Britain.

The Japanese village provided yet another stimulus to the development of the Japan cult, and the *Art Journal* boldly stated in 1874 that 'Fashion has declared for Japanese art'.[60] By the mid-1870s the cult had influenced the décor and taste of ordinary British households.

Dresser's sumptuously illustrated *Studies in Design*, released in parts between 1875 and 1876, incorporated a number of Japan-influenced designs which could easily be adapted to surface ornamentation in Victorian interiors, and his 'greenery-yallery' and subdued colour schemes made a profound impact on decorators (plate 20).

En route to Japan in the autumn of 1876 Dresser visited the Centennial Exhibition in Philadelphia,

20
Pl. VI in Dresser's *Studies in Design*, 1875–6.

and promoted his ideas in a series of lectures on 'Art Industries', 'Art Museums' and 'Art Schools' at the newly founded Pennsylvania Museum and School of Industrial Art. In his lecture on 'Art Museums' he referred to the South Kensington Museum as a model, but he lamented the fact that the directorship had discontinued the practice of purchasing Oriental and Japanese art, which was of such great importance to British designers and manufacturers.[61]

The hint was taken by the Americans, notably by Charles Louis Tiffany and his son Louis Comfort, whom Dresser befriended during his stay. Tiffany had launched some popular silver designs in the Japanese style in the early 1870s, and now commissioned Dresser to bring back a substantial collection of all kinds of artefacts from Japan, amounting to several thousand items. They were delivered to Tiffany's by Dresser on his way home in 1877.

The *New York Times* of 6 May provides a fascinating glimpse of Dresser at this time:

One of the most perfect specimens of art intellect which England shipped to the U.S. for the exhibition at Philadelphia was, without doubt, Dr. Christopher Dresser. He styles himself 'art adviser' and is well known to American designers and art manufacturers by several publications . . . The Doctor as he is generally termed, is a full grown Cockney – black of beard, bright of eye, and who would talk a man into a state which American ingenuity illustrated some time ago by a skeleton in a deal box; but this is charming.[62]

Louis Comfort Tiffany was greatly influenced by Dresser, and in 1878 he turned his talents to designing, and joined with Candace Wheeler, Samuel Colman and Lockwood de Forest in founding Associated Artists. This sophisticated group became one of the main promoters of Japonism in America, producing designs for entire interiors in the style advocated by Dresser.

Dresser's impact upon American design was recently acknowledged in the exhibition 'Americans and the Aesthetic Movement' at the Metropolitan Museum in New York in 1986. David Hanks in paying tribute to Dresser said that he 'acted as a catalyst for the influence of Japanese art on American manufacturers and designers'.[63] According to a contemporary article, 'Dr. Dresser in America', he also made contacts with American wallpaper manufacturers and supplied thirteen different designs to the Philadelphia firm of Wilson & Fennimore.[64] These were registered with the American Patent Office on 15 May 1877. Japanese diaper and broken patterns prevail in the designs, but some are also marked by his distinctive 'art botany' style (plate 21).

By 1876–7 Dresser's role in the dissemination of Japanese art and the Japonism style was as prominent in the United States as in Britain. Japanese manufacturers were now fully aware of the commercial potential of their products, and actively stimulated the Western market. The Centennial Exhibition in Philadelphia featured the largest Japanese stand ever mounted in the West, and much attention was given to the ancient porcelain, earthenware and stoneware exhibited by Dresser's trading affiliate, the Kirutsu Kosho Kaisha Company.

The increasing interest in Japanese earthenware, as distinct from the earlier fascination with porcelain, marked a change in critical interest. The British reporter Roger Soden-Smith praised precisely those kinds of ceramics which were collected by Dresser, namely Awata, Amaji, Banko, Raku, Tamba and Takatori, emphasizing that 'Where no evil influence of bad European taste has been felt,

21
Two Wilson & Fennimore wallpapers. 15 May 1877. US Patent and Trademark Office, Washington, DC.

the production of these factories afford examples of ornament that in quaintness of fancy, skilful balance of parts and gorgeous effects of colour could not easily be surpassed.'[65]

The Meiji Government had encouraged the production of new ceramics kilns in order to provide work for the large number of artisans left unemployed after the revolution of 1868. This initiative encouraged the national expansion of domestic ceramics, and as these products gradually found their way to the West, there was a growing

need for information on them. Shioda Makato's *Catalogue of Japanese Ceramics at the Centennial Exhibition* provided a model for Western collectors. Dresser himself relied heavily on Shioda, whom he consulted while in Japan.[66]

As a result of Dresser's friendly connections with the Japanese Commissioners in 1876, a representative collection of Japanese pottery from the Philadelphia exhibition was donated to the South Kensington Museum in exchange for a number of British contemporary artefacts collected by Dresser, which were presented to the Tokyo National Museum.

After the interlude in Philadelphia, Dresser travelled to San Francisco and from there left for Japan in the company of the Japanese Commissioners Sekisawa Akiko and General Saigo Yorimichi. They arrived in Yokohama on 26 December 1876. According to Dresser, the aim of his tour was threefold: to instruct the Japanese in modern industrial techniques; to bring the South Kensington Museum exchange donation to the National Museum in Tokyo; and finally to complete his own and Tiffany's Japanese collection.[67]

Dresser was granted semi-official status during his visit, and was asked by the Minister of Home Affairs, Okubo Toschimichi, to act as adviser to the Japanese Government on the modernization of their art industries. The Emperor Meiji honoured him with an audience and offered to reimburse his travel expenses. He also allowed him to examine the Imperial collections in Nara and Kyoto, a rare privilege granted to few foreigners.

During his travels around the country Dresser was accompanied by two young officials of the Home Office, Sakata Haruo and Ishida Tametake. Ishida was asked to report to the Government about the value of the trip, and his account, published in book form as *Dresser Hokoku* (1877), dealt with some seventy different forms of art industry commented on by Dresser. It emphasized Dresser's respect for traditional aesthetics and suggested ways of adapting these to modern methods of manufacturing. Ishida's report, together with Dresser's *Japan, its Architecture, Art and Art-Manufactures*, provided the most substantial coverage of contemporary Japanese art and industry to that date, and had a marked impact on the art milieu in Japan. The *Japan Mail* observed: 'We believe that Mr. Dresser has the further and very weighty object in view of impressing upon the decorative artists of Japan the high importance of preserving intact those distinctive and peculiar

merits in Japanese art of which we have just spoken. That these are now in great danger is certain.'[68]

Another English traveller in Japan at the time was Lady Thomas Brassey, who echoed the sentiments of the Japanese press: 'Dr. Dresser is here, collecting, lecturing, and trying to persuade the Japanese to adhere to their own forms and taste in art and decoration.'[69] The educational value of Dresser's visit was clearly appreciated; it was acknowledged in particular by Okubo Toschimichi in a letter dated 26 March 1877:

> I have notified all through the country your valuable informations, regarding to the important points of industry which you have given to the officer who attended you during your visit to several industrial establishments. It must be for your kindness that I could make all industrial men to understand the points which were obscure heretofore, and I can assure you that in the future time they will make a progress and bring great interest upon the commerce.[70]

The gift from the South Kensington Museum included some sixty wallpaper samples from Jeffrey's, lace from Edward Cope's, textiles from James W. & C. Ward, carpets from Brinton & Lewis, terracotta from Watcombe's, porcelain from Minton's and glass from the retailers Green & Nephews, as well as a miscellaneous collection from Londos.[71] Dresser was engaged as a designer and adviser to all these companies and it seems likely that he had chosen samples of his own designs. The entire collection was exhibited at the first National Exhibition at Ueno Park in Tokyo in 1877. Dresser instructed the organizers in museological methods, which in turn were adapted to museums and exhibitions throughout the country.

As a result of the exhibition the Japanese realized that their own arts were in a state of serious neglect, and Dresser's plea for a return to national standards gained momentum. His friends Kawase Hideharu and Makimura Masano established art schools in Tokyo in 1878 and in Kyoto in 1880, and Kawase and Wakai Kanezaburo founded The Ryuchi Society for the Preservation of Japanese Art in 1879. On a visit to London the next year they brought Dresser several precious gifts as 'a remark of respect to you, whose intelligent suggestions have done so much to promote the arts and manufactures of Japan'.[72] It was probably on their recommendation that Dresser in the same year sent a personal gift of his Linthorpe Art Pottery and three sample books of his textile designs to the Tokyo National Museum. The gift was enthusiastically received by Machida Hisanari, the director of the museum:

This new porcelain and ceramics has provided new ideas for Japanese potters, and your visit to the Orient contributed considerable stimulus for our eyes and minds. Japanese artists should be grateful to your suggestive remarks, and likewise the people of your own country, who thanks to you have been able to become acquainted with traditional products from Japan.[73]

During his stay in Japan, Dresser visited over seventy different potteries, including those in the districts of Awaji, Sanda, Kishiu, Sakai, Awata, Banko, Owari (now called Mino), Seto, Shiba and Makudzu, and various Kyoto kilns, to which he devoted several days of study. He brought back samples of their work, as well as some of the popular Tamba, Takatori and Arita wares. Drawings of his Japanese pottery in the Victoria & Albert Museum and in Tiffany's archive testify to the importance of his collection in Britain and in America.[74] Dresser also paid particular attention to the Japanese lacquer industries, and claimed to have contributed to the revival of the forgotten technique of the purple or vellum lacquer, which he especially admired.[75]

Sano Tsunetami introduced him to some of the leading contemporary pictorial artists, who presented him with drawings (probably those in the albums of drawings preserved from Dresser's collection in the British Museum and in the Victoria & Albert Museum).[76] In Kyoto, the governor of the town, the famous art connoisseur Makimura Masano, acted as Dresser's adviser. He also consulted the Government antiquarian Ninagawa Noritane and the head of the Board of Trade, Kawase Hideji. These three were the principal figures behind the slogan 'Back to Japanese Art'. They also led the revival of interest in Shintoism, whose status as the official national religion was confirmed in 1889.

Dresser was particularly interested in Shintoism, and he frequently stressed that his personal collecting interests were based on the religious symbolism apparent in Japanese art. This attitude was unique in the context of contemporary Western research on Shinto and Buddhist art,

which was not seriously studied until the beginning of the twentieth century.

While visiting Nara, Dresser participated in many discussions about Shintoism. His guide, the director of the National Museum, Machida Hisanari, took him to a Shinto dance ceremony, where he was highly intrigued by a simple bronze wine heater with a long straight handle. This later influenced his own heating vessels.[77] Dresser also visited the ancient Shinto shrines at Isé, and in Kyoto he profited greatly from conversations with Akamatsu Renjo, a priest who played an active role in the separation of Shintoism and Buddhism in the 1880s.[78]

It was on a visit to the temples of Nikko on 28–29 March 1877 that Dresser began to appreciate some of the fundamental differences between Shinto and Buddhist art:

Shinto enjoins the most perfect work, but employs neither colour nor carving in its temples; while Buddhism symbolised by carving and colour the power of the Buddhists' god over all created things, and the loving protection which all that lives enjoys at his hands. The very essence of Shintoism is simplicity, and of Buddhism the tender perception of and care of, all that lives.[79]

The perception of this duality as well as of hybrid forms of Japanese art is rare among Western commentators, and Dresser's studies set the pattern for a more thorough scholarship. The close connection between art and religion in the Far East was not properly understood in the West until much later, and Dresser's ideas anticipate the work of art historians and ethnologists in the twentieth century. His approach, surprisingly, was based upon rules discovered by contemporary linguists, and he pioneered the application of their methods in the arts:

With the simple purpose of showing the probable origin of some of the features which characterise early Japanese art, and of pointing out to the student that research into the affinities and migrations of races may be aided by a consideration of ornament not less than by the study of a language.[80]

Dresser recognized the fire and phallic worship prevalent in Shintoism; he saw the simplicity and conventionality of Shinto art as an expression of an indigenous preference which coincided with Buddhist ideals. Buddhism had made the Japanese receptive to a more sophisticated worship of nature, which was expressed in ornamentation of a naturalistic kind. In Shinto art, however, the ancient ideals of simplicity, utility, perfection of finish and constructional honesty are retained. These aspects were to have a great influence on Dresser's own principles and designs.

His meetings with Japanese artists, connoisseurs and priests had a catalytic effect on Dresser, and enabled him to reach a more profound understanding of Japanese art. They also helped to promote Anglo-Japanese trade. During his trip he established further contacts for Londos and founded his own importing firm in conjuction with the Bradford business man Charles Holme. Holme subsequently wrote perceptively about Japanese art and founded *The Studio* magazine in 1893. The new company became known as Dresser & Holme and was established in Kobe by Dresser's sons Louis and Christopher in 1878. Louis returned to Britain in 1882, but Christopher married a Japanese woman, and his descendants lived in Kobe until 1980, when the last of the line, Stanley Dresser, died.

Dresser travelled back to Europe via New York to deliver the Tiffany collection. This comprised some 8000 objects, and included ceramics, textiles and embroideries, jewellery and objects in mixed metals, as well as translucent enamel screens and plaques. These screens, which Dresser claimed to have introduced to the West,[81] were referred to as 'glass screens' in Tiffany's catalogue, and inspired Louis C. Tiffany and John La Farge's Japanesque stained-glass windows and screens of 1877–8.[82] The Tiffany collection was the highlight of the exhibition season in New York and aroused enormous public interest. About half was retained by Tiffany's but the rest was sold at auction in June 1877; it was described as 'the largest and most important collection of Japanese goods ever offered for sale' and as overshadowing even 'the collection of the Metropolitan, from the fact that its display was more brilliant and varied, and hence more interesting to the modern eyes'.[83]

The *Graphic Journal* critic praised it as:

. . . novel even to those who have long studied Japanese bric-a-brac. This novelty proceeds from the peculiar system of Dr. Dresser, who has made an especial point of collecting the common utensils, the coarser potteries, the conveniences of common life in Japan, well

surmising that articles of this kind would bear as distinctly as any others the cachet of Oriental taste, and would be more fresh for connoisseurs and more suggestive to artisans than the now well-known fabrications of distinctly artistic intention.[84]

Dresser may be counted as one of the first systematic Western collectors of Japanese objects. He was interested in all kinds of Japanese art, and his studies of the historical growth of forms from the primitive to the sophisticated went beyond the taste and interest of most Japonists.

The American collectors Edward Sylvester Morse, Ernest Fenollosa and William Sturgis Bigelow appear to have been the first to adopt Dresser's attitude to collecting. They had certainly heard about the Tiffany collection before they left for Japan in 1877–8, and Morse and Bigelow began amassing Japanese ceramics and tea-ware of the cruder kind admired by Dresser. Like Dresser, these collectors had an eye for all forms of Japanese art, and they undertook similar researches on architecture, fine art, sculpture, ceramics and religion. Their collections were later to enrich the Museum of Fine Arts in Boston. Morse also made a name for himself with his book, *Japanese Homes and Their Surroundings* (Boston 1886), which was the first serious treatment of the subject to appear after Dresser's *Japan* of 1882.

The collecting attitudes among Victorian Japonists remain to be thoroughly analysed, but Joe Earle of the Victoria & Albert Museum recently emphasized that the Americans generally demonstrated a higher level of cultural involvement. Dresser, however, was considered an outstanding exception to the 'pervasive cultural blindness' of the British.[85] In May 1877, *The World* lauded his role in the dissemination of Japonism:

Among the men who are the best known in Europe, since the present 'renaissance' in Decorative Art, none perhaps, has been more thoroughly identified with the new ideas that have grown out of our acquaintance with the Japanese and Chinese methods of decoration, than Doctor Christopher Dresser. The active part he took in forming the invaluable collections of the South Kensington Museum, in London; the exquisite taste he displayed in the decoration of the Alexandra Palace, placed him in position, both as a 'Connoisseur' and an

'Art Decorator', which will identify his name with the most successful efforts made to introduce this new style. His publications of portfolios of colored plates are the basis of many a successful decorator's and upholsterer's reputation, and, when he came to the exhibition in Philadelphia, his influence and erudition were much sought after in the higher artistic circles.[86]

Following his return to Britain in the summer of 1877, Dresser continued his enthusiastic promotion of Japanese art, and offered his expertise to various academic societies, manufacturers and dealers. He gave a number of lectures on the topic throughout the country, and leaders of fashion such as the critic George A. Sala and the Prince and Princess of Wales supported his campaign.[87]

In 1878 he lectured for the Royal Society of Art on 'The Art Manufacture of Japan', and again emphasized the artistic value of Japonism:

I firmly believe that the introduction of the works of Japanese handicraftsmen into England has done as much to improve our national taste as even our schools of art and public museums, great as is the good which they have achieved; for these Japanese objects have got into our homes, and amongst them we live.[88]

Surprisingly, he gave equal credit to Japonism and to the Schools of Art for having contributed to the elevation of public taste in Britain, but he stressed that his own encounter with Japanese art had had a more profound effect on him than the education he had received at the School of Design.

The grand display of Japanese art and culture at the Paris International Exhibition in 1878 provided Dresser and other Japonists with fresh inspiration, and by October that year the *Furniture Gazette* was announcing the Anglo–Japanese as 'the style of the coming season':

Everything is already Japanese. The most progressive tradesman in Regent Street [Liberty] sells Japanese bric-a-brac. All the curiosity shops display Japanese trinkets. Some decorators and art-furniture makers are not content unless their productions are as good imitations of Japanese work as can be found, and in Fleet Street a Japanese cabinet stands at this moment as the triumph of the School of Queen Anne.[89]

Unfortunately, some designers had confused Chinoiserie and Japonaiserie in the Queen Anne style with Japonism, and adapted it to the Anglo–Japanese manner. These hybrid pastiches were chiefly promoted by architects belonging to the Aesthetic Movement such as Richard N. Shaw and to some extent Edward W. Godwin. Dresser objected strongly to this mingling of stylistic effects and publicly condemned it in an article entitled 'Is the Rage for Queen Anne Over?' as 'being alike destitute of both art and constructive merit'.[90] By 1880 the fashion was fading but the Anglo–Japanese style in furniture continued to incorporate elements from the English Medieval, Elizabethan and Queen Anne styles flavoured with Japanese asymmetry. Dresser, however, advocated a more careful sifting and recasting of inspirational sources, which infused a fresh vigour into his designs.

The exhibition of Dresser's genuine Japanese room at the jeweller Edwin W. Streeter's New Bond Street premises in 1878 attracted considerable attention in the press, and it may well have influenced Edward Godwin's Anglo–Japanese designs for Whistler's White House and Frank Miles's Chelsea house executed in the same year. The show of Dresser's lattice panels and other Japanese woodwork at the Architectural Association in 1878 undoubtedly made an impact on British architects, and lattice panels, which Dresser recommended for their versatility, became a popular feature in many interiors and furniture: they were used as 'ventilating panels in room-doors; as enrichments in cabinets; for both dwarf-blinds in our windows – replacing the very modern cane-blinds – and for outside sunshutters, instead of Venetian shutters' (plate 23).[91]

Dresser rebelled against the constraints of Western conformism and continued to search for new ideas. In September in 1878 he canvassed the adaptation of Japanese ceilings to European architecture. His article on 'Works from Japan' described some model ceilings from the Tokugawa Shrine in Tokyo.[92] These coffered ceilings probably served as prototypes for several of the Anglo–Japanese ceilings which subsequently gained popularity in Britain in the 1880s and 1890s. It was not until the turn of the century, however, that the lattice panels, ceilings, beams, brackets, and the simplicity of Japanese interiors recommended by Dresser, began to influence Western architects such as Charles Rennie Mackintosh, Peter Behrens, Ludwig Mies van der Rohe, Louis Sullivan, Bruno Taut and Frank Lloyd Wright.

ton (carpets), Benham & Froud (metalware), Hukin & Heath (silver), and the wallpaper companies Jeffrey's, Lightbown & Aspinall, Scott Cuthbertson, and Arthur Sanderson & Sons.[95] Dresser is known to have been engaged as a designer for these companies and clearly the Art Furnishers' Alliance was intended to promote his work. The company was entirely under his artistic supervision and according to its prospectus undertook to supply 'All kinds of artistic house furnishing material, including furniture, carpets, wall decorations, hangings, pottery, table glass, silversmith's wares, hardware, and whatever is necessary to our household requirements'.[96]

The prospectus was published in leaflet form in 1881 with a preface by Sir Edward Lee, the managing director, and a summary of 114 of Dresser's 'Principles of Art' abstracted from his previous

By 1879 Dresser had become one of the most active and well-known exponents of Japonism in Britain. The opening of his importing company, Dresser & Holme, in London in that year was attended by Sir Rutherford and Lady Alcock, Sir Louis and Lady Pelly, as well as by members of the Japanese Legation and other dignitaries, who all agreed that 'we seemed to have left England and to have been transported to Japan, so completely orientalised was everything around us'.[93]

The showrooms contained the most diverse collection of Japanese artefacts, including Shiba and Hizen porcelain, Makudzu ceramics, ivory work, lacquer objects, silver and bronze work, iron kettles, lattice panels, screens and samples of Dresser's own Linthorpe Art Pottery, which contrasted nicely with their Japanese counterparts (plate 22). Dresser retired from the company in August 1882, but Charles Holme continued the business, and his stand at the Furniture Trades Exhibition in London in 1883 occupied the whole of Berner's Hall and was acclaimed as 'the most novel and striking feature of the exhibition'.[94]

Dresser & Holme were shareholders and suppliers of Japanese goods to the Art Furnishers' Alliance, which Dresser founded in June 1880 with George H. Chubb, Edward Cope, John Harrison and Sir Edward Lee. The firm register lists several other business associates of Dresser as being shareholders, notably his solicitor Hiram B. Owston, Arthur Liberty, Frederick Walton (linoleum and wallpapers), James Dixon (silver), William Cooke (wallpapers) and the Tees Bottle Company of Middlesbrough. These manufacturers are named as suppliers to the company, together with John Brin-

23
Three of Dresser's Japanese
lattice and geometrical
patterns. *The British
Architect*, 1879.

publications. The stationery designed by Dresser was in the Japanese style, and the company clearly hoped to encourage the 'Japanese Mania', as one critic termed it in 1880.[97]

The *Cabinet Maker* also noted with approval the uniform of the female shop assistants of the Art Furnishers' Alliance, who were 'attired in aesthetic colours . . . of "greenery-yallery" dress, ruby sash and mob cap to harmonize' (plate 24).[98] The passion for 'greenery-yallery' by then embraced ladies' fashions, and the vogue for broad sashes with large butterfly knots reflected the current admiration for the Japanese 'kimono'. Similar costumes in Liberty fabrics were designed by Gilbert and Sullivan for their comic opera *Patience or Bunthorne's Bride*, which satirized and popularized the Anglo–Japanese fashion and was the theatrical hit of the season in 1881 in both London and New York.[99]

The opening of the Art Furnishers' Alliance in New Bond Street in May 1881 was hailed as one of the most important retail developments. The *Artist and Journal of Home Culture* was unstinting in its praise for Dresser: 'The critical eye is that of Dr. C. Dresser, and without recognising the possibility, or desirability, of a pope in the matters of taste, we may unreservedly say that there is no one in whose knowledge and taste we would rather trust in regard to such matters.'[100] The Alliance provided the clearest response to the new ideas promoted by Dresser, but the venture seems to have been too avant-garde for commercial taste and the firm went into liquidation in May 1883. *The Studio* suggested that its closure was:

> perhaps partly owing to the fact that it was before its time. For it was alone in its mission in addressing a popular audience. It is true that Morris & Co. were known to a few, and that one or two manufacturers of beautiful things for the house could be found by searching, but no window in a popular thoroughfare was supporting the movement destined to assume such large proportions later. Liberty's at the time was almost entirely a Japanese warehouse, and the ordinary upholsterer, ironmonger, or other furnishing tradesmen kept little, if anything, that was in harmony with the new ideals in domestic appointments.[101]

Arthur Liberty, however, had realized its potential, and he organized his own shop in a similar way in 1883, when he opened his Furniture and

24
Female attendant in 'aesthetic dress', and Dresser's furniture, at the opening of the Art Furnishers' Alliance. *The Cabinet Maker*, 1 July 1881.

Decorating Studio. As Mervyn Levy has recently noted, 'Arthur Liberty's awareness of the need for change derived partly, at least, from his close friendship with Christopher Dresser'.[102]

In 1882 Dresser lectured on 'Japanese Art Workmanship' in Liverpool and Glasgow[103] on the occasion of the opening of a 'Loan Collection of Oriental Art', which included objects from the South Kensington Museum, the Duke of Edinburgh's collection, and 1150 items received as part of an exchange between the Glasgow Art Gallery and the Tokyo National Museum.[104] This last collection has been mistaken for the one sent by Dresser to Glasgow on his return from Japan, but this in fact went to a private collector, Robert Balfour, who lent the objects used to illustrate Dresser's lecture. Dresser's introductory remarks criticized the indiscriminate fashion for everything Japanese, which, he said, had resulted in nonsensical Japanesque products and converted many homes to mere curiosity shops. This timely warning was taken up by Charles Pfoundes, who in the same year published a critical assessment of 'Japanese Art, its Teachings and Meaning, and the Follies and Fallacies of the Japanesque'.[105]

The main part of Dresser's lecture, however, dealt with 'the peculiarities of Japanese art, showing the manner in which it has been moulded and influenced by the two prevailing systems of religion – Shintoism and Buddhism – of the Japanese'. This aspect was treated at greater length in his book, *Japan, its Architecture, Art and Art-Manufactures*, published later that year. The critic of the *Edinburgh Review* wrote:

> There are many passages in *Japan* which have a deeper interest than lies on the surface, from the light that they throw on that very ancient, if not most ancient, form of nature worship, the survival of which in Japan is known by the name of Shinto. And in urging that in architecture and in other arts may be found as distinct memorials of prehistoric man as in language itself, the chapter on analogies and symbols, if not so wholly original as the author supposes, is full of interest.[106]

Dresser's book was described as the first Western attempt to treat the art-manufactures and architecture of Japan as a serious academic subject. The *New York Times* review, entitled 'Wonders seen in Japan, Dr. Dresser's unrivalled and curious experience', particularly praised the section on architecture:

> Accordingly, although every part of his book is valuable, the architectural chapters of it, and especially the illustrations they contain, are inestimable. Japanese architecture is scarcely understood at all in Europe as yet and unfortunately its ancient masterpieces receive at present so little respect from the Japanese Government itself, with its mania for modernisation of national life, that they are rapidly falling into fatal decay.[107]

This positive response was an important directive for British and American architects who fell under the influence of Japanese design during the 1890s. Japanese architecture had in fact been almost entirely neglected by Western scholars. Even Sir Rutherford Alcock had proclaimed that 'the Japanese have no architecture',[108] and this fatal lack of insight permeated Western opinion. As late as 1893 William Morris still believed that 'the Japanese have no architectural, and therefore no decorative instinct'.[109] Dresser attempted to correct this view in his book, which stands apart

from the general literature on the subject, as the *Furniture Gazette* critic noted:

> To the one subject of paramount interest to designers and craftsmen (i.e. the Arts and Manufactures of Japan) there has thus far, however, been but scant justice done by English writers and travellers, who as a rule, have lacked the special training without which their observations on such matters would have been valueless. A volume that supplies this long-felt want is, however, now before us in the form of a handsome octavo of 480 pages, entitled *Japan, its Architecture, Art, and Art-Manufactures*. The author, Dr. Dresser, is well known as a specialist in connection with architecture and decoration, and it is this fact which gives exceptional value to the observations embodied in this work.[110]

Throughout the 1880s Dresser assiduously continued his study and promotion of Japanese architecture and ornamentation. His untiring efforts to enlighten the Architectural Association made a lasting impact on contemporary Victorian architects, and it was largely due to Dresser that Japanese architecture became the object of serious artistic study in Britain and in America. The *Journal of Decorative Art* commented that the influence of Japonism on the arts in Britain

> . . . has been like the infusion of new life into a torpid body, and whilst undoubtedly in those quarters where results could not be discriminated from means, the consequences have been hurtful, it is also true that on the whole our own artistic life has been furthered and developed by the message and story which Japanese art has to tell us.[111]

In a lecture at the Architectural Association on 5 December 1884, Dresser again stressed the importance of understanding Buddhist and Shinto aesthetics. Using Shinto's sacred symbol, the mirror, as an example, he spoke of the purist attitude in Japanese art and architecture, and urged the need for simplicity and purity in the West. He also showed a number of photographs of constructional details, drawing particular attention to the soundness of the bracketing under the curved Japanese roof.[112]

One of the final manifestations of the cult of Japan in Britain was Gilbert and Sullivan's highly popular operetta, *The Mikado*. It prompted the

25
Ebonized doorpanel with
vermilion decoration for a
wardrobe from Bushloe
House, Leicester. 1879–80.

26
Chair and filing box
produced by Chubb & Son
for the Art Furnishers'
Alliance. c. 1880. Private
collection.

27
Chair produced by Chubb
& Son for the Art
Furnishers' Alliance.
c. 1880. Private collection.

28
Opposite. Anglo-Japanese cabinet with Minton cloisonné ware. From bottom to top: pilgrim bottles nos. 13, 48, 1472; bird's head vase no. 1626, beetle vase no. 1644, pair of jugs no. 1607, and seau no. 1630.

29
Coalbrookdale Co. cast iron coat stands. Maker's mark and date ciphers for 11 December 1867 and 22 March 1867. Private collection.

30
Coalbrookdale Co. cast
iron chair. Maker's mark
and date cipher for 22
March 1867. Private
collection.

31
Opposite. William
Woollams & Co. wallpaper.
Dated 1866. Prints and
Drawings, Victoria &
Albert Museum, London.

34
Dado and staircase in
Bushloe House entrance
hall, Leicester. *c.* 1880.

35
Jeffrey & Co. 'Daffodil'
wallpaper. 28 May 1879.
Public Record Office,
London.

32, 33
Opposite. William Cooke &
Co. wallpapers. 18
September 1866. Public
Record Office, London.

36
Jeffrey & Co. 'Indian'
wallpaper. 28 May 1879.
Public Record Office,
London.

37
Jeffrey & Co. 'Pomegranate'
wallpaper. c. 1878. Paris
International Exhibition,
1878. Prints and Drawings,
Victoria & Albert Museum,
London.

38
Jeffrey & Co. wallpaper.
Attributed to Dresser. Late
1880s. Nordiska Museet,
Stockholm.

39
Lightbown, Aspinall & Co.
wallpaper. c. 1886.
Manchester City Art
Gallery.

40
William Cooke & Co.
frieze. August 1878. Public
Record Office, London.

41
Wallpaper frieze, probably
produced by William
Woollams. c. 1877. Prints
and Drawings, Victoria &
Albert Museum, London.

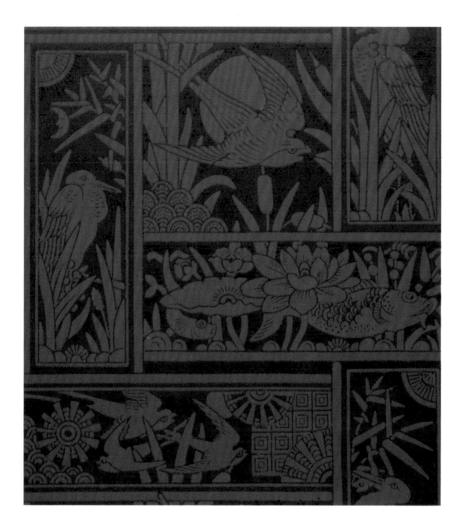

42
Arthur Sanderson & Son
dado paper. c. 1882. Royal
Doulton Minton Archive,
Stoke-on-Trent.

43
William Cooke & Co.
wallpaper frieze. 20 August
1881. Public Record Office,
London.

44
Opposite. Jean Züber & Co.
wallpaper no. 1291. Dated
1903. Musée du Papier
Peint, Rixheim, France.

45
James W. & C. Ward silk
damask. 1 June 1875. Public
Record Office, London.

46
Norris & Co. silk damask.
c. 1867. Private collection.

Opposite. James W. & C.
Ward silk damask. 18 April
1873. Public Record Office,
London.

creation of a Japanese village at South Kensington which was opened by Sir Rutherford Alcock on 10 January 1885. This ambitious enterprise consisted of five streets crowded with stalls and workshops inhabited by more than 200 Japanese people. The *Cabinet Maker* announced it as 'Japan in England' and referred to Dresser as the Japan expert *par excellence*:

> Dr. Dresser – has given clear descriptions of the talent and painstaking methods of Japanese artisans and artists, but, after all is said and done, such things must be seen to be believed, and doubtless a sight of the clever workers of Kensington will be a revelation to the majority of the people.[113]

Dresser's call for a serious study of Japanese art was given further impetus by the interest generated in the village, and was finally answered in the late 1880s and 1890s by such writers as Ernest Hart, William Anderson, Marcus B. Huish and James Bowes.

In 1886 Hart showed his extensive Japan collection at the Library of the Royal Society of Art, and lectured on 'Japanese Art Work'.[114] Following the example of Dresser and other Japan specialists, Hart arranged his collection in 'historic succession'. With the help of the Japanese dealer Hayashi Tadamasa, he focused on various schools and masters, and prepared the way for a kind of taxonomic classification of Japanese art, which is still used in British scholarship. He recommended in particular the collecting of signed and readily classifiable items such as sword-guards, netsukes and lacquer, and these collecting fields have remained the most popular to this day. William Anderson, a physician who lived in Japan between 1873 and 1879, contributed a chronological study of *The Pictorial Art of Japan* in 1886, and his collection later enriched the British Museum.

In the later 1880s information about the masters and schools of Japanese painting and printing also began to filter through to the West. In Paris, Vincent van Gogh and the dealer Samuel Bing organized exhibitions of Japanese fine art in 1886 and 1888 respectively. Bing was aware of the need for a more critical evaluation of Japanese art, and his popular magazine *Le Japon Artistique*, published in French, German and English from 1888 to 1891, featured specialist articles and frequently referred to Dresser and other scholars. Bing subsequently combined his interest in contemporary French art with Japonism. In 1895 he converted

his shop to a gallery showing Japanese art next to the work of young progressive designers, naming it 'L'Art Nouveau'.[115]

The English collectors Marcus B. Huish and James Bowes, however, were less successful in their endeavours, and their respective publications 'Japan and its Art Wares'[116] and *Japanese Pottery* (1890) were criticized as misleading by the American Japonists Ernest Fenollosa and Edward Morse. The latter dismissed Bowes' entire work, concluding with a statement which Dresser would have approved: 'How far may one go astray who undertake to study the products of a country from just the opposite side of the globe.'[117]

Dresser, Morse and Fenollosa all had the advantage of first-hand studies in Japan, and they have been called the first scientific interpreters of Japanese art and culture. Dresser, in particular, stressed the benefits of utilizing methods similar to those practised by botanists, zoologists and linguists, in classifying various branches of Japanese art. He was fully aware, however, that controversies and myths still hampered the development of scholarship. Similar attitudes dominate Western studies of Japanese art to this day, but the writings of Dresser, Fenollosa and Morse have made a valuable contribution. All three acknowledged the importance of Japonism and Morse's view accords with that of Dresser:

> It is an interesting fact that the efforts at harmonious and decorative effects which have been made by famous artists and decorators in this country and in England have been strongly imbued by the Japanese spirit, and every success attained is a confirmation of the correctness of Japanese taste. Wall-papers are now more quiet and unobtrusive; the merit of simplicity and reserve where it belongs, and fitness everywhere, are becoming more widely recognized.[118]

Dresser's *Modern Ornamentation*, published in 1886, added further weight to the movement. As one critic wrote: 'we think that the work will be suggestive and useful, and chiefly in those designs which have their motif in Japanese precedents, for in that direction we much prefer Dr. Dresser's work.'[119] However, Dresser's book was rather too modern for some critics. *The Builder*, for example, described his Japan-inspired 'Evening' pattern with beetles, moths and spiders as 'inherently vicious' (plate 49).[120] It was not until 1904, the year of Dresser's death, that Alphonse Mucha

48
James W. & C. Ward silk damask. 1871. Private collection.

popularized surprisingly similar insect designs in his *Formenwelt aus dem Naturreiche*. It was only then that the influence of Dresser's publication had a tangible effect upon contemporary art, but few if any artists credited his pioneering work as their source of inspiration.

Lewis F. Day for instance wrote about 'Modernity in Decoration' in 1904,[121] but ignored Dresser's work entirely. He had shown a similar neglect in his essays on 'The Victorian Progress in Applied Design', but had at least acknowledged the Japonism style:

> An influence excessive at the time, resulting in a style of art most un-English, but which now that the fever is past, we may believe will effect the design of the near future very favourably, for in workmanlikeness, fitness of treatment, spontaneity, and many other qualities most essential to good ornament, there was everything for us to learn from it.[122]

For more than a third of the century Dresser had been the main spokesman for Japanese art, and

his ideas finally gained full support in Britain towards the end of the century. Several British artists such as Mortimer Menpes, George Henry and Edward A. Hornel travelled to Japan in the late 1880s and became exponents of the Japonism style in painting. Dresser's friends Sir Alfred East, Arthur Liberty and Charles Holme also toured Japan in 1888–9, visiting several of Dresser's associates. Liberty lectured on 'Art Productions of Japan' in Tokyo and praised 'the great wave of Japanese influence over the workshops of Europe'. Like Dresser, he expressed a high regard for the integrity of Japanese art and warned against the indiscriminate adaptation of Western ideas.[123]

Following their visit to the country, Liberty and Holme wrote authoritatively about 'The Industrial Arts and Manufacture of Japan' and 'Japanese Pottery', and in the spirit of Dresser emphasized the need to explore Buddhism and Shintoism.[124] Holme considered Morse and Dresser to be the most influential promoters of Japanese art.[125]

Towards the end of the century Japonism became the focus of more analytical and critical attention. The *Art Journal* in 1889 quoted a German designer as saying that 'we were all bewitched' and that 'English Art had become more strongly influenced by the art of Japan' than that of any other European country.[126]

Another German intrigued by the almost mystical impact of the Cult of Japan in Britain was the critic Peter Jesse. His influential articles 'Der Kunstgewerbliche Geschmack in England' treated Japonism as a serious topic and he called Dresser, whom he described as 'the head of a famous studio outside London', the successor of Owen Jones.[127]

The Anglo–Japanese style also fuelled the increasing interest in English architecture and design on the Continent, which was epitomized in Herman Muthesius' *Die Englische Baukunst der Gegenwart* (1900–4). Unfortunately, Dresser did not participate in the public debate on Japonism around the turn of the century, but his adherence to this style, which led to his detachment from traditional Western attitudes, generated a vernacular which anticipated the Modern Movement. When he died in 1904, the obituary which appeared in *The Builder* recalled among his virtues his lifelong passion for the East: 'He was a most genial companion and interesting talker and never tired of discussion on Art and the habits of the nations of the East, trying to trace their histories by their ornamental forms as a philologist does by their language.'[128]

ART FURNITURE
MEDIEVAL AND
JAPANESE
INFLUENCES

It was Charles Locke Eastlake, in his influential book *Hints on Household Taste* (1868), who first applied the term 'Art Furniture'. Dresser, however, was the first to provide full treatment of the subject, in three articles entitled 'Art Furniture' in 1870. These were subsequently included in his *Principles of Decorative Design* in 1873, and thus reached a wider section of the reading public.

The term art furniture had emerged in the late 1860s as a result of the need to bridge the gap which had developed between art and industry, and between art and craft, in Victorian Britain. The School of Design had encouraged this trend, as did Dresser, Eastlake and William Morris. The firm of Morris, Marshall, Faulkner, Fine Art Workmen, for instance, was founded in 1861 with the aim of mending the split which had developed between art and craft functions. Their pessimism about the value of mass production, however, was equalled only by that of their friends connected with the Aesthetic Movement.

Eastlake's Art Furniture Company, founded in 1868, on the other hand, catered for designs suited to machine production, and Arthur Blomfield and Edward W. Godwin, among others, supplied designs which are surprisingly similar to those of Dresser's.[1] Little is known about this company save that it remained in business until about 1871. It is possible that the art furniture illustrated by Dresser in 1870 was produced by the Art Furniture Company, since no other maker has yet been traced (plate 50).

Dresser had commented favourably on Eastlake's book, which in accordance with his own views advocated the adoption of harmonious interiors and referred to Japanese prototypes and the Early English or Medieval style. In 'Art Furniture', he stressed above all the principles of sound, revealed construction and minimal carving, and he criticized the Neo-Gothic and Reform-Gothic styles favoured by the leading furniture designers A.N.W. Pugin, Bruce J. Talbert and William Burges. Dresser found these styles too elaborate, and unsuited to modern requirements. He was particularly appalled by the architectural appearance of Burges' and Pugin's furniture. Likewise, he condemned the curved frames and legs in some of Eastlake's chairs, which he claimed were falsely constructed and would collapse beneath the weight of their occupants.[2]

Ironically Dresser himself had designed chairs of a similar kind, but these, according to the critics, were designed prior to his articles of 1870,[3] and indeed they are included in his pattern book from about 1867 (plate 51). This also applies to much of the furniture shown by Dresser in the *Furniture Gazette* during his period as editor of the magazine in 1880–1 (plate 52). They bear little resemblance to the art furniture included in his articles of 1870, or to the avant-garde designs he produced for the Art Furnishers' Alliance between 1880 and 1883. However, this furniture can be compared to the designs in Bruce J. Talbert's *Gothic Forms Applied to Furniture* (1867), which were highly influential and praised by Dresser, with some reservations, in his articles.

In *The Art of Decorative Design* Dresser had also recommended the Early English (medieval) style found in much of Talbert's work, because of its 'great breadth and simplicity', in contrast to the

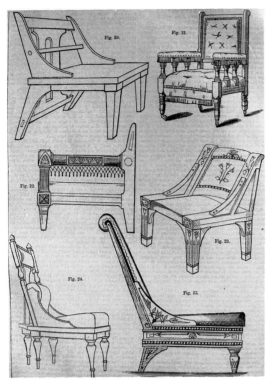

50
Chairs from Dresser's
*Principles of Decorative
Design*, 1873, fig. 30.

later Gothic 'lavish display of ornament . . . quite undesirable for cabinet work'.[4] Both Dresser and Talbert were firm advocates of the Early English style, which inspired their first designs. Both gradually introduced elements derived from Japanese furniture, which they compared to the simple medieval vernacular.

Dresser first made this association between medieval and Japanese styles in 1862 when he saw

51
Chair in Dresser's Pattern
book, c. 1867. Prints and
Drawings, Victoria &
Albert Museum, London.

some of the furniture in medieval style produced by H. Ogden of Manchester; he also praised the first recorded Japan-inspired ebonized furniture made by A.F. Bornemann & Company of Bath:

> They are of a quaint and unique Japanese character, yet manifest one very pleasing feature in the side supports of the back rising from the sides of the chair, and slanting upwards, instead of being an upward continuation of the back legs; but this is not the only merit, for the back of the rail is also supported by a central passage, which rises from the centre of the back of the seat. Altogether there is a quaint elegance about these chairs, and the structural peculiarity might advantageously be applied in a simple form to furniture of a more ordinary character.[5]

52
Sideboard. *The Furniture
Gazette*, 31 January 1880.

These two companies are known to have produced furniture in the distinctive Dresser style, but a definite connection with Dresser has not yet been made. He may have designed the furniture exhibited by them at the International Exhibition in London in 1862, and this hypothesis is supported by the fact that he was the only perceptive commentator who noted the Japanese influence, and that on his own admission he is described as having 'furnished many designs for the manufacturers . . . perhaps as many as any individual'.[6]

Remarkably, the chairs which he described in 1862 also seem to correspond precisely to a chair of his own design illustrated in the 'Art Furniture' articles, where he 'sought to give strength to the back by connecting its upper portion with a strong cross-rail of the frame' (plate 53). Dresser associated this kind of soundness and simplicity of construction with characteristic features of Japanese

furniture design, and the chair represents his first documented piece of furniture in the Anglo–Japanese style.

The chair may well have been designed in 1870 for Allangate Mansion in Halifax. Acording to the anonymous author of *Castles and Country Houses in Yorkshire*, all the furniture of this house 'was manufactured from special designs prepared by Dr. Dresser in ebonised wood with incised gold work'.[7] The bedroom furniture in particular seems to have conveyed the appearance of Japanese lacquer furniture, incorporating patterns 'produced with an enamelled surface of cool grey tint which upon the black of the body has an exceedingly tasteful and charming effect'. Unfortunately, none of this furniture has come to light, but it appears to have been similar to the suite in the Japanese style created by Dresser for Bushloe House, Leicester, in 1879–80 (plate 54). Both houses were decorated in their entirety by Dresser. They featured rooms in the Anglo–Japanese style, as well as a wealth of Japanese objects decorating the furniture and fireplaces. The drawing room at Allangate is described in *Castles and Country Houses*:

> There are two fire-places in the room, each being tiled in an aesthetic shade of electric blue. They are surmounted by elegantly designed overmantels of cabinet form ascending almost to the roof, and whose shelves, as indeed are the tables and wall cabinets in this and other apartments, are filled with a profusion of the choicest old cloisonné, Persian, Chinese and Japanese ware . . . There are also in the room a number of very handsome bronze and other lamps of unusual and artistic designs. The

furniture is of extremely massive and tasteful character.[8]

The typical fireplace mantel of the aesthetic interior advocated by Dresser and other designers was somewhat imposing in character, and often imbued with a mystical, quasi-religious character. One of the Allangate fireplaces, for instance, was flanked by recesses intended for plants, and decorated around the top with a frieze in ebonized wood and gold lettering with the bibilical text: 'Consider the lilies of the field, how they grow, for they toil not, neither do they spin, yet Solomon in all his glory was not arrayed as one of these.'

Dresser's designs, lectures and publications, especially his *Principles of Decorative Design*, testify to his concern with creating a total interior. The favoured aesthetic treatment of ebonized wood and furniture, combined with turquoise tiles, Oriental porcelain and cloisonné, came to dominate the artistic interiors sought after by the leading Victorian arbiters of taste. In his articles on 'Japanese Ornamentation' in 1863 Dresser had alluded to Japanese interiors 'whose wallpapers are as dull and neutral as the lacquered objects are bright and positive', an effect he promoted in his own interior schemes. Unlike Japanese prototypes, however, Dresser's furniture showed features

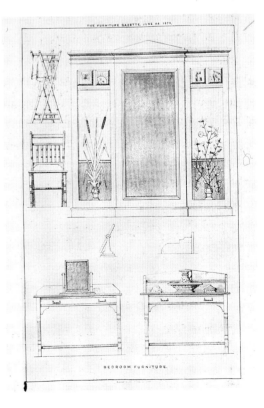

which originated from his studies of Japanese étagères, cabinets, stands and lattice panels, and they can be classed with the Anglo–Japanese furniture produced by Edward W. Godwin in 1867, and distinguished by 'the group of solid and void' and by a more or less broken outline.[9]

At the Paris Exhibition of 1867 Dresser had praised the Japanese furniture: 'The delicate cabinet work of the Japanese is not anywhere surpassed.'[10] But even before this, he had studied the Japanese furniture acquired by the Museum of Manufactures in 1854, and the samples exhibited by Sir Rutherford Alcock at the International Exhibition in 1862, which made such an impact on Dresser, Godwin and other designers.

However, it would be wrong to associate Dresser's furniture designs exclusively with his admiration for Japanese furniture. They clearly reflect his sifting of Early English, Egyptian and Greek sources, as well as Japanese prototypes, but the results are his own independent creations and in their constructional honesty, angularity and above all in their simplicity depart radically from contemporary Victorian furniture.

Dresser was fundamentally opposed to the falsity of structure prevalent in contemporary cabinetwork. He denounced the use of veneer, wood cut across the grain, and excessive carving and upholstery, which he felt concealed the true shape and function of the furniture: ' "Be truthful". An obvious and true structure is always pleasant. Let, then, the "tenon" and the "mortise" pass through the various members, and let the parts be "pinned" together by obvious wooden pins.'[11] The interest in 'constructional honesty' is a prominent feature of all Dresser's work. He even made tenons, mortises and rivets part of his ornamental vernacular, as in eight coalboxes he designed for Benham & Froud in 1870 (plate 55).

Those coalboxes mark Dresser's first connection with this well-known metalwork company; he continued to provide designs for some of their most popular coalboxes, with and without metal fixtures and decorations, during the 1870s and 1880s, pursuing the ideas he expressed in 1874:

With the exception of a few of the wooden coalboxes, all are bad, while many violate every principle of utility and beauty . . . To me the coalbox which I have here sketched meets the case. It is formed of wood, which is an appropriate material, as coals do not make a great noise when placed in or taken from the

vessel formed of this material; the shovel meets with resistance at the lower angle and here the coals are always found, however few they may be; the box stands steadily, and could be carried easily, and the wood is used in the most simple manner, and with the utmost economy.[12]

Dresser was far ahead of his time in advocating functionalist principles. The simplicity of his furniture has frequently been compared to that of Godwin, but Dresser's furniture is usually sturdier and more robust, with deeply incised and gilded decorations, which have little in common with Godwin's light structures. Neither Dresser nor Godwin adhered slavishly to the principles which they laid down, and both remained eclectic in their sources of inspiration. Their most original furniture, however, has the Anglo–Japanese characteristics of ebony and lacquer tints, and contrasting angular shapes. This typifies the furniture which Dresser designed for Hiram B. Owston's residence, Bushloe House, near Leicester, and for the Art Furnishers' Alliance. Some of his furniture for Bushloe House has been located, and reveals the Japonism style, with decorations in ebony, gold, olive and vermilion lacquer colours. Two wardrobes, one decorated with stylized owls and the other with crawling semi-humorous frogs, convey Dresser's love for grotesque imagery (plate 25).

Another bedroom suite was featured in the *Furniture Gazette* in 1879, and was probably also intended for Bushloe House. It incorporates sim-

55
Wooden coalbox for Benham & Froud. September 1870. Public Record Office, London.

56
Corner cabinet in fumed
oak with leather-paper
panels in Japanese style for
Lord George Hayter
Chubb's dining room.
c. 1880.

suite designed for Lord George Hayter Chubb, Chairman of the Art Furnishers' Alliance, in about 1880 (plate 56). The prospectus of the Alliance stated that 'Messrs Chubb & Son, the well-known manufacturers of locks and safes, have fitted up large works for the manufacture of artistic furniture and household metal work, and this firm will constantly keep on consignment in the new warehouse a large quantity of goods.' This explains why the furniture sold at the Alliance had no maker's mark, whereas the metal hinges, locks etc. were stamped Chubb & Son and clearly designed by Dresser. The *Cabinet Maker* enthusiasticly supported the Art Furnishers' Alliance and on its inauguration at New Bond Street in 1881 illustrated four different ebonized chairs.[13] One was 'A sort of a heavy Greek, in black and gold or vermilion enrichment'; two study chairs are more in the simple Anglo–Japanese style (plate 24). Similar study chairs with Dresser's characteristic deep-cut zig-zag borders have recently been located, and were probably also produced by the Art Furnishers' Alliance (plate 57). Notable among the designs illustrated in 1881 is the so-called 'Thebes stool' which was inspired by an Egyptian chair in the British Museum (plate 24). This particular chair had been copied by other artists, including Ford Madox Brown and Edward W. Godwin, but Dresser's version is very similar to the elegant substructures and leather-covered seats he made for the Art Furnishers' Alliance.

ilar Anglo–Japanese ornamentation, showing rectangular panels with bulrushes and Japonica flowers in a broken and angular manner; four smaller panels display typical Japanese motifs such as butterflies, humming birds, the rising sun and an owl (plate 54). A similar owl and sun design occurs in Dresser's Japanesque stained-glass windows in the drawing room (plate 198); it was also used in his silk damasks produced by James W. & C. Ward in the 1880s (plate 92).

The Bushloe House furniture and the striking pieces Dresser made for the Art Furnishers' Alliance may well have been influenced by the comprehensive show of Japanese furniture at the Paris International Exhibition which he visited in 1878, and perhaps by the Japanese samples included in the 'Loan Collection of Furniture' organized by his friend George Wallis at the Bethnal Green Museum in East London the same year. The catalogue describes cabinets decorated with motifs very similar to those adopted by Dresser.

Around this time Dresser also began to use Japanese leather papers as decorative features, particularly in dining-room furniture, such as the

57
Ebonized study chair with
incised ornamentation.
c. 1880. Private collection.

58–63
Chairs produced by Chubb
& Son for the Art
Furnishers' Alliance.
c. 1880. Chubb & Son
Archive, London.

The Thebes stool was registered with the Patent Office Design Registry in 1884 by Liberty & Co. who probably reserved the production rights when Dresser's company went into liquidation in 1883.

The 'Art Furniture Catalogue' issued by the Art Furnishers' Alliance in 1881 contained some 324 entries and stressed that 'Every piece of Furniture has been carefully constructed by experienced workmen under the immediate supervision of Dr. Dresser. The Furniture is priced at a low figure, and can be seen on application to Messrs. Chubb, the Lock and Safe Makers, at their works.' Most pieces were described as ebonized with gold or red incised decoration, the chairs as covered with morocco leather. Contemporary photographs of some of these items have been preserved in the Chubb & Son archive; some were also shown in the *Furniture Gazette* in 1880 (plates 58–63). Early English, and perhaps Greek and Egyptian elements, are recognizable, and several samples reveal the 'quaint and unique Japanese character' Dresser had admired since 1862. This is especially apparent in some of the lattice panel backs and intricate sub-structures which contrast solid and void, and the regular and irregular (plates 26, 27).

Many of the items were in the Anglo–Japanese style. A 'six-foot black and gold drawing-room cabinet with numerous recesses, lined with velvet and enclosed with transparent plate-glass doors' has been located (plate 28). It has the irregular arrangements of shelves and structures which Dresser had praised during his stay in Japan in 1877.[14] A model book of Japanese furniture from his collection has also been traced and provides further evidence of his inspirational sources.[15] When the Art Furnishers' Alliance was liquidated its numerous pieces of furniture were referred to as Anglo–Japanese and 'Japanesque'.[16] Two boudoir safes, described by Chubb & Son in 1882 as being in the Japanese style, again testify to Dresser's preoccupation with lattice panels and Japanese decorations (plate 64).

Dresser's furniture offered one of the boldest alternatives to ordinary Victorian design, and was perhaps regarded as too advanced by most people. The critics, however, were surprisingly unanimous in their commendation. The *Artist and Journal of Home Culture*, for example, wrote that:

A recent visit to the premises of the Art Furnishers' Alliance leads to the observation that here are some of the freshest and boldest things in furniture which are being at present produced. Dr. Dresser, who is the appointed designer, shows an especially varied and robust invention in chairs. In no similar show rooms, perhaps, is there so little of the commonplace and merely imitative. Against the actually false and base there is a guarantee in the censorship which is exercised over the admission of articles.[17]

Dresser's art furniture diverted designers from the elaborate carving and inlay prevalent in much contemporary Victorian furniture. The Dresser style contributed vitally to the formation of the 'Modern English Furniture and Decoration' which the *Furniture Gazette* welcomed in 1882:

What is most noticeable in it is its greater simplicity, a larger variety, and a departure from the rigid symmetry of former days, . . . and a suddenly awakened interest in the products of Japanese art, have resulted in producing an immense multiplicity in the forms of chairs and tables. Wooden chairs are now straight and square.[18]

Although Dresser's production of furniture was relatively small and ceased before the end of the decade, the *Cabinet Maker* critic continued to use Dresser's designs as a measure of novelty. After the Italian Exhibition in London in 1888 he was pleased to note that Carlo Bugatti's first Japanese and Turkish-inspired furniture 'reminds one, in passing of some of the highly original forms which used to come from the pencil of Dr. Christopher Dresser.'[19]

Equally original was Dresser's production of cast iron furniture. As early as 1862 he had heralded works in cast iron as 'the style of the day' because of their low cost. He particularly liked the works of the Coalbrookdale Company of Shropshire, whose designs, he claimed, 'would form excellent studies for the treatment of plants in iron work'.[20] Jones and Pugin had advocated the use of cast iron in the 1830s, but by the time of the Great Exhibition in 1851 Jones was disillusioned and said that 'iron had been forged in vain'.[21] During the later 1850s he and other arbiters of reform attempted to introduce a new style of iron furniture and architecture, which by the mid-1860s was adapted by Dresser, who around this period began producing designs for Coalbrookdale. He seems to have replaced John Bell and Alfred Stevens as the company's chief designer toward the end of the decade.

64
Boudoir safe ebonized with repoussé and lacquer panels in the Japanese style produced by Chubb & Son. 1883. Chubb & Son Archive, London.

7). Dresser was sometimes thought to have a contempt for figure drawing, but this was a misunderstanding, he said in 1871. In fact he enjoyed filling panels with certain stylized and flatly treated figure subjects, such as this table with its Greek-inspired outline of anthropoid beauty.[23]

A ferociously grotesque dragon panel probably inspired by Japanese prototypes adorned a hot-air stove designed by Dresser for Coalbrookdale in 1868, and coincides in time with his Dragon wallpaper for Jeffrey's (plate 66).

According to Dresser's *Principles* 'cast iron should be formed in the easiest manner in which it can be worked and as perfectly to suit its means.'[24] This radical dictum challenged the cluttered historicism prevalent in much of the Victorian cast iron designs, and inspired a new artistic interpretation of this unpretentious material. By the mid-1870s it had an unrivalled importance in

Dresser's first attributed designs for Coalbrookdale include three coat-stands, and a suite of hall furniture registered with the Patent Office on 11 December 1867 (plates 29, 30). These bold creations show Dresser's artistic botany to advantage, and the thistles and banana leaves recall his words from the Paris Exhibition of that year: 'Angularity, when considered from an art point of view, is stimulating; rounded forms are soothing. The crispness of a thistle-leaf is exciting, while the large rounded forms of the banana-leaf present an appearance of tranquility.'[22] His 'Truth, Beauty and Power' design from 1867 was also said to have been inspired by the forms of early spring and luxuriant tropical vegetation (plate 12). Angularity was frequently a feature of Dresser's work, and perhaps originated from his admiration for the Early English and Ecclesiastical style, as well as from Oriental metalwork.

His cast iron hall furniture was supplemented by three matching hall-tables in 1869, 1870 and 1872 (plates 65, 68). They combine spiky foliage and angular scrolls with elliptical mirrors and roundels. The table executed in 1870 was made to match a set of chairs and incorporated roundels depicting the Greek gods Æolius and Boreas (plate

65
Coalbrookdale Co. cast iron hall table. 8 March 1870. Public Record Office, London.

home furnishing. Dresser continued to supply designs for Coalbrookdale's fireplace fittings, grates, furniture etc., and they were much praised at the international exhibitions. In Philadelphia in 1876 he was able to compare his works with the wrought-iron exhibits of Thomas Jeckyll, produced by Barnard, Bishops & Barnards.

Among Jeckyll's exhibits were the Anglo–Japanese sunflower pavilion and andirons, which introduced the taste for Japonism ironwork, and also inspired Dresser's sunflower andirons and flame-patterned stove casing produced by Coalbrookdale's in 1879 (plate 67). He had used similar sunflower and flame motifs in his contemporaneous wallpapers for Potters of Darwen (plate 76). These motifs had by then become identified with Japonism, and with the Aesthetic Movement, whose adherents adopted the sunflower as their symbol. Dresser's cast iron sunflowers constituted a more stylized and less expensive alternative to wrought iron, and are characteristic of his highly individual merging of Japonism and Art Botany.

Dresser's art furnishings embraced not only metal fittings and the iron framing of grates, but

67
Coalbrookdale Co. cast iron stove casing. 19 July 1879. Public Record Office, London.

also window, door and picture frames, as well as curtain poles in wood. In his *Principles of Decorative Design* he recommended simple structures and darker colours for these items, preferably ebonized black, which would fit the furniture and contrast nicely with the walls. Curtains should be hung on a 'simple and obvious pole'.[25] This idea was a major departure from the Victorian preference for ponderous gold frames and elaborate curtain arrangements, and anticipated the practice of modern interior decorators. Above all, Dresser aimed to free his furniture and decorations from the clutches of historicism, and to create a 'new style', which would make 'every homestead artistic in the truest sense of the word',[26] and which can still be seen today in fashionable interiors.

66
Coalbrookdale Co. hot-air stove. 22 January 1868. Public Record Office, London.

68
Top of Coalbrookdale Co.
cast iron hall table. Maker's
mark and date cipher for 25
October 1869. Private
collection.

THE AESTHETIC INTERIOR AND SURFACE ORNAMENTATION

In 1862 Dresser boldly declared that 'the decorative arts arise from and should be properly attendant upon Architecture'.[1] Echoing Jones's words from *The Grammar of Ornament*, he kept alive the Victorian concept of the architect-designer, a term which was widely used around the middle of the nineteenth century. The division between architect and designer was not rigidly defined at the time, and the combination of related disciplines led to a greater interest in decorative media. This in turn fostered a closer association between architecture and design, and helped to direct interest away from the heavier styles of Medieval and Neo-Gothic towards the vernacular-based domestic architecture.

Throughout his life Dresser strove to raise interior decoration and furnishing to the status of fine art. His ideas on the decoration of buildings were first expressed in his *Principles of Decorative Design*:

> It will be said that in my writing I mingle together ornament and architecture, and that my sphere is ornament, and not building. I cannot separate the two. The material at command, the religion of the people, and the climate, have to a great extent determined the character of architecture of all ages and nations, but they have to the same extent determined the nature of ornamentation of the edifices raised. Ornament always has arisen out of architecture.[2]

Dresser's general views on interior decoration accorded with his method of sifting historical models in new forms suited to 'modern require-

ments'.[3] The spirit of his work was more decorative than architectural, however, and he worked on few architectural schemes, restricting himself to the altering of façades and to interior constructions.

'Ceilings'

Among Dresser's favourite themes were the decoration and colouring of ceilings, and again he was influenced by Owen Jones, whose primary-coloured ceiling in St James's Palace he recommended in 1862.[4] His own ideas on the decoration of ceilings were published in leaflet form in 1868 and advocated a similar colour scheme, but 'more colour may be placed upon the ceiling than upon the walls or floor of a room, for it does not serve as a background to the objects in the room'.[5]

In *Principles of Decorative Design*, he went further and stated that 'Any amount of colour may be used on a ceiling, provided the colours are employed in very small masses, and perfectly mingled, so that the effect produced is that of a rich bloom'.[6] And if one part only can be decorated in a room, then it should be the ceiling. He deplored the Victorian habit of whitewashing the ceiling, preferring the flat overall patterns which he had studied in Egyptian, Greek, Moorish and Japanese ornamentation. These were mostly based on repeated motifs, such as the star-formed Japanese patterns on a blue ground, which he particularly liked (plate 189).

Dresser's ceiling decorations always complemented the wall covering, and he was responsible for some of the first British papers which matched dado, frieze, wall, cornice and ceiling

schemes. Similar papers had been produced in France in the early nineteenth century, but they were not popular in Britain until the 1870s. Dresser was one of the main instigators of this fashion and supplied a complete series for Jeffrey's in 1871 (plate 189). The precedent set by these designs was quickly followed by other manufacturers, and mass-produced ceiling papers became one of the most favoured decorations to be used in ordinary British homes.

Some of Dresser's most sophisticated hand-painted ceilings were incorporated in the interiors which he created for Thomas Shaw's Allangate Mansion and John Crossley's Saville Hall, both in Halifax, Yorkshire, between 1870 and 1873. The Saville Hall interiors are no longer intact, but in *Castles and Country Houses in Yorkshire* there is a reference to the Allangate Mansion library ceiling which, according to the anonymous author, Dresser considered a veritable masterpiece. He proudly included the pattern in *Modern Ornamentation* in 1886 and the *Furniture Gazette* compared it to Owen Jones's ceilings at Carlton House Terrace in London.[7] The rich Oriental-inspired pattern does indeed bear a strong resemblance to those popularized by Jones, and the elaborate enamel-like colouring in green, turquoise, blue and gold lent an exotic Moorish atmosphere to the room.

The drawing-room ceiling was equally brightly coloured and was fitted with an open crosswork of joists painted in blue, black and gold, which gave a coffered effect. The square panels visible through the joists were decorated with colourful overlapping floral patterns in the Japanese style (plate 70).

The Saville Hall ceilings were famous in their day and mention is made of them in an obituary of Dresser which appeared in the *Journal of Decorative Art* in 1905:

It was a current report some thirty years ago, that Dr. Dresser spent some £2500 on the ceiling of a dining-room for a Yorkshire carpet manufacturer, and to go one better another brother in the same firm capped it by spending £3500 on his ceiling. There can be no doubt

that the Doctor's income must have run to enormous figures from one source and another.[8]

The Crossley brothers who owned the carpet firm of John Crossley & Sons were among Dresser's best customers; they commissioned him to undertake the redecoration of their factory offices and studios in 1870–1, and he was also asked to supply a number of designs for carpets.[9]

The majority of Dresser's ceiling patterns were in the Oriental style and were often hand painted on the ceiling. Others, however, were mass produced as ceiling papers (plates 71, 189) and as Linoleum Muralis. The latter paper was first produced in 1878 by the wallpaper manufacturer Frederick Walton, and soon became known as Lincrusta Walton, a reference to its embossed and incrusted designs.[10] The similar Anaglypta linoleum papers, launched in 1887 by Walton's manager John T. Palmer, also featured numerous

Dresser designs for ceiling coverings in the Oriental fashion (plate 71). Linoleum papers based on Arabian, Egyptian, Japanese, Moorish and Persian patterns combined with a rich colour effect would, according to Dresser, contribute to the 'sense of snugness' which was considered so desirable during the latter part of the Victorian period: 'Dark ceilings give a cosy effect to a room, which is very appropriate to our changeable climate and to this land of "homes" . . . cosiness, or snugness, is usually associated with our feeling of "home".'[11]

Dresser's ceilings contributed fundamentally to the move away from the more formal decorative schemes of the early Victorians. They were also influential on household taste in America. The picture gallery of John T. Martin's Brooklyn home, for example, is recorded as having been covered with a Dresser paper from the cove of the ceiling to the borders of the skylight.[12] In 1885 *Art*

Amateur published Dresser's article on 'The Decoration of our Homes' and thus ensured that his principles were kept alive among decorators in the United States. As late as 1899 *The Studio* was still citing Dresser's designs as an example: 'In the case of some of the designs for ceiling papers, it is doubtful if any patterns of more recent years are so appropriate and admirable.'[13]

'The Decoration of Walls'

By 1862 Dresser had presented the basic rules which governed his decoration of walls:

> 1st. Ornaments destined to a vertical position may advantageously consist of corresponding halves.
> 2nd. A composition having a radiate character is not offensive on a wall.
> 3rd. A powdering formed by the flower, in full view, being studded over the surface of the wall is legitimate, and is in many cases peculiarly appropriate.
> 4th. Perfect flatness of treatment is most suitable to all wall enrichments.
> 5th. A low-toned neutral effect of colour is desirable in all decorations which are in any way to act as backgrounds.[14]

In 1865 the *Building News* stated that Dresser during the early part of his career had been mainly active as a designer of wallpapers, textiles and carpets, which had earned him the reputation of being 'the most active revolutioniser in decorative art of the day'.[15] Indeed his first recorded wallpaper was produced by William Woollams in 1858 and was exhibited at the Schools of Art exhibition in London in the same year.[16] Two years later the *Art Journal* praised his innovative designs for Scott, Cuthbertson:

> The peculiarity which they present is this, – the ornament is raised, and is of the same colour as the ground . . . The patterns were chiefly Medieval and Alhambra, and were well chosen, reminding one of the rich old decorations which we sometimes wrought in embossed leather. . . The effect is much more pleasing than might be expected; indeed, it altogether surpasses all that we have heretofore seen in the shape of ordinary wall decorations.[17]

71
Anaglypta linoleum
'Moorish' ceiling pattern.
No. 57 in Anaglypta
Catalogue, 1896.

These low-relief patterns set a new precedent in wall coverings, which became increasingly popular during the Victorian period. When they were shown at the Architectural Exhibition in 1861 they were described as 'producing a raised ornamental design not hitherto executed in paper staining'.[18]

Scott, Cuthbertson soon gained a reputation for this kind of decoration and won several prizes at international exhibitions. Although Dresser is known to have continued his connection with the firm until at least 1883,[19] only one of his papers, in citrine and gold, has come to light, at Kingston Lacy in Dorset (plate 72). This corresponds to some Scott, Cuthbertson papers described by Dresser as 'fleur-de-lys and foliage in citrine-green and gold'.[20]

Dresser's lecture on 'The Decoration of Flat Surfaces' in 1864 reiterated his views on wall coverings first put forward in 1862, but he also announced the patenting of a new invention of 'relief wall decoration of the lowest cost', which was to be produced by Catto & Company of London in both England and France.[21] The *Building News* critic recommended seven wallpaper and textile designs exhibited by Dresser at the Architectural Exhibition in London that year.[22] Some of these may well have been manufactured by Catto's, who registered a series of Dresser-like patterns with the Patent Office on 15 July 1864. One of these motifs in fact is identical to figure 54 in *The Art of Decorative Design*, and displays repeated fret or diaper patterns, which stand in sharp contrast to the naturalistic floral patterns produced by other contemporary companies (plate 73). Catto's registered their designs under the name of Wylie & Lochhead of Glasgow, who took over the company some time in the 1860s. In *Principles of Decorative Design* Dresser mentioned having produced three narrow dado papers for Wylie & Lochhead, but he is not known to have maintained any contact with the firm after this time (plate 69).

Dresser's designs for William Woollams, William Cooke's and Jeffrey's are more firmly documented. He had already supplied a design to Woollams in 1858, and in 1863 the company registered some typical Dresser patterns with the Patent Office, which accord with motifs shown in his publications. A sophisticated radiating and interlaced passionflower design in subdued colours shows one of Dresser's most successful adaptations of 'artistic botany' (plate 2).

Similar Cooke, Jeffrey and Woollams designs can be identified in Dresser's pattern books and sketchbooks from the time, and this has led to the discovery of some of their printed wallpapers. One of these is contained in the William Woollams sam-

72
Wallpaper in citrine and gold, probably produced by Scott, Cuthbertson & Co. c. 1860s. The National Trust, Kingston Lacy, Dorset.

ple book of 1866 in the Victoria & Albert Museum (plate 31), and was probably exhibited at the Paris International Exhibition in 1867. Dresser's wallpapers were well received on this occasion. The *Building News*, for instance, observed: 'Many of the designs shown by Woollams & Company are excellent, and those of Dr. Dresser are especially good.'[23] Another critic praised Woollams' production as:

Superb exhibition of manufacture. In all the examples displayed by the firm referred to we miss the atrocious natural imitations of fruit, flowers, and landscapes, once so popular among all classes, and in place of them, a sober, conventional treatment of foliage, exhibiting considerable skill in design and arrangement, the colours used being the warm and cool neutral tints which are well adapted for backgrounds in rooms of every description.[24]

Dresser's theories concerning wallpaper design had obviously reached a receptive public, and his own creations were to contribute fundamentally to the change of taste in Victorian paperhangings. Matthew Digby Wyatt, Dresser's former tutor, reporting on the novel wallpapers in Paris in 1867, recognized Dresser's individuality in his designs for William Cooke's:

> Twenty-four original designs, founded on different flowers and plants, amongst which many are very good and few altogether unpleasing. The treatment of the hop, the hawthorn, and the anemone are particularly agreeable to the eye both in form and colour. The Chinese primrose also make a very pretty delicate diaper.[25]

A series of Cooke designs from 1866 correspond precisely to this description and to motifs in Dresser's pattern books and sketchbooks. They stand out as entirely original compared to contemporary patterns, and have the low-toned and subdued colouring recommended by Dresser in 1862 (plates 32, 33). His 'Japanese Ornamentation' articles of 1863 had also enthused over this kind of colouring, as well as the scroll-work and angularity in the designs of Japanese wallpapers, which continued to exert an influence on Dresser's wallpapers.

Similar characteristics typify Dresser's first designs for Jeffrey's, entitled Dragon, Celtic Knot and Cairo, executed in 1867 (plate 15). His affinity with natural phenomena seems to have been replaced by a certain detachment around the time of the Paris International Exhibition in 1867, when he presented his first overall view on the grotesque in design. His review of the exhibition recommended the stylized Chinese and Japanese dragons and other abstract motifs. He recognized similarities with Celtic ornamentation, which he had studied in J.O. Westwood's edition of *The Book*

of Kells, a source which afforded 'a ready means of comparing these ancient grotesques with those produced by Eastern nations'.[26] Scrolls and entrelac motifs became a popular part of Dresser's artistic vernacular. They occur in many of his later designs and publications, imparting a sense of weirdness and eccentricity.

Owen Jones had included Celtic, Chinese and Egyptian motifs in his *Grammar of Ornament* – but not Japanese – and these styles had been the focus of attention at international exhibitions during the 1850s and 1860s. The exhibit of the Celtic 'Tara Brooch' in 1851 inspired much subsequent jewellery, but Dresser's Celtic Knot wallpaper appears to be one of the first signs of the so-called Celtic revival in architecture and interior design. It was not until the 1890s that this revival became a political, literary and artistic movement under the guidance of the poet William B. Yeats and the architect-designers Charles Rennie Mackintosh and Archibald Knox. These men were undoubtedly influenced by Dresser's predilection for Celtic, Egyptian and Japanese styles, which in turn contributed to the development of the Glasgow and Liberty styles towards the turn of the century.

Above all, Dresser was responsible for promoting the idea of an 'aesthetic interior', which gained momentum during the 1860s and 1870s. In *Principles of Decorative Design* he stressed the necessity of a carefully chosen colour scheme, and outlined a pattern of blue ceilings, citrine or low-toned yellow-orange walls, maroon or purple dados, and bronze green doors surmounted by black architraves for the drawing room. These colours were intended to inspire 'purity, activity, and enlightenment'. Schemes in olive, russet and yellow were suggested for the adjacent rooms.[27] This colouring became the favoured decorative palette of the designers connected with the Aesthetic Movement – Edward Godwin and James M. Whistler, for example, created rooms and furniture based on 'the colours of the pineapple' for the Prince of Wales Pavilion at the Paris Exhibition in 1878[28] – and gained such popularity by the 1880s that Gilbert and Sullivan's satirical operetta *Patience, or Bunthorne's Bride* (1881) spoke scathingly of the 'greenery-yallery' movement. In America, Clarence Cooke's book, *What Shall We Do With Our Walls?* (New York, 1880), also questioned the value of encumbering ordinary homes with the refinements of aestheticism.

Although numerous guides to interior decoration appeared in the 1870s and 1880s, few interiors,

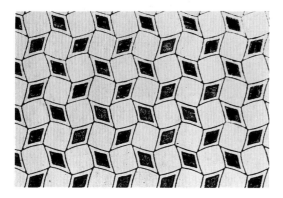

73
J. Catto & Co. wallpaper. 5 July 1864. Public Record Office, London.

except for those created by Dresser, Godwin, Jeckyll and Whistler, could be termed aesthetic in the proper sense. Unfortunately, only a small number of these, such as Jeckyll and Whistler's 'Peacock Room', have survived intact.   All that remain of Dresser's sumptuous interiors at Allangate are the ceilings, stained-glass windows and some of the wooden constructions. However, the anonymous author of *Castles and Country Houses of Yorkshire* provides a telling picture of what must have been one of the first aesthetic interiors in Britain. The writer emphasized that there were no houses in Yorkshire, and few in England, which were decorated in such excellent taste:

> The alterations carried out have been so thorough as to comprise even the renewal of the fireplaces, gas, and other fixtures, and of the whole of the furniture. The fireplaces throughout the building are of polished black marble with incised work in gold, and the whole of the woodwork and the furniture, which was manufactured from special designs prepared by Dr. Dresser, is in ebonised wood with incised gold work. Dados are found in all the rooms, and like the upper portion of the walls are flatted in aesthetic colours with suitable archaic patterns stencilled thereon.[29]

These interiors with their low-toned walls, bright ceilings and ebonized woodwork and furniture were contrasted with bright Japanese porcelain and enamel vases, and were obviously derived from the Japanese interiors admired by Dresser.

The library walls were described as being cool green with a chocolate-coloured dado; the drawing room had cool buff walls with dados in crimson; and the bedrooms were in 'aesthetic green and chocolate tints' – contrasted with ceilings and cornices in blue, black and gold. Evidently 'greenery-yallery' colours were adhered to, but the walls were probably painted rather than papered.

In *Principles of Decorative Design*, which was published around the time of the creation of the Allangate interiors, Dresser stressed that plain coloured or tinted walls, perhaps enriched with a simple powdering pattern, were to be preferred to the popular naturalistic wallpapers which showed huge bunches of flowers combined with animals and the human figure. According to Dresser, the patterns should be very simple, and 'in all cases consist of flat ornament' and of 'small, simple repeated parts, which are low-toned or neutral in colour'.[30]

The interiors Dresser created at Bushloe House for Hiram B. Owston of Leicester also show a preference for the Anglo–Japanese, particularly in the drawing room, where the stained-glass windows display his typical Japonism (plate 198). The house appears to have been decorated on eclectic principles, however, with the library in Persian style (plate 74), and the entrance hall in the Egyptian manner with a 'greenery-yallery' touch (plate 34).

Dresser's publications between 1875 and 1886 featured similar 'aesthetic' patterns, based on motifs derived from Arabian, Chinese, Egyptian, Greek, Indian, Japanese, Early English and Moorish styles, combined with his artistic botany and certain crystalline and grotesque forms (plate 20). In *Studies in Design* (1875–6) Dresser advocated 'newness of design' (see endpapers) and stressed the necessity of seeking inspiration at those moments when one 'became in feeling' 'a Chinaman, or Arabian, or such as the case requires'.[31] He expressed his preference for the Japanese style, and recommended the student 'to study native Japanese drawings of flowers, which now can be got at many fancy warehouses'.[32]

His books were among the first to attempt to solve the problem of combining suitable patterns

74
Dado in Persian style for Bushloe House Library, Leicester. *The Furniture Gazette*, 26 June 1880.

and colours for the whole interior, and to encourage a more aesthetic style of decoration in ordinary houses:

> I look to decorators becoming the great teachers of art in the country. If we, as ornamentists, get knowledge, and explain to our clients why we propose treating their rooms in a peculiar manner, they will readily consent to the production of artistic rooms; and when once they have lived in an artistic house, they will never again like the white ceilings and merely papered wall, for their tastes will have improved.[33]

With this aim in view he designed a series of wallpapers expressly to meet the requirements set out in *Studies in Design*. All the papers had his name printed on the margin[34] and were issued by Jeffrey's. They are recorded in the company's logbook for 1875–6 under the titles Egypt, Ark, Locust, Persian, East Gulf, Cyprus, Crown, Raven, Cedar, Caspian and Moslem,[35] but only the Persian design has been traced. This shows his typical spiky leaves and artistic botany and was inspired by the ancient monuments at Persepolis (plate 75).

In 1873 Dresser had sent his assistants Caspar Clarke and William Churcher on an expedition to establish trading connections abroad,[36] and a letter from Clarke testifies that moulds and drawings of the monuments in Persepolis were sent back to Britain.[37] The entire range of Dresser's designs for Jeffrey's seems to have been inspired by his assistants' travels.

Dresser was particularly active as a designer for Jeffrey wallpapers during the 1870s. His patterns Sultan and Laurel, entered in the company's logbook for 1876, have not been traced, but a range of designs executed in 1878–9 has survived as sample strips, namely Cressy, Gold, Cistus, Lancaster, Oak, Pomegranate, Indian, Daffodil, Flame, Fire and Nemo. Only the Indian, Nemo and Pomegranate printed papers have come to light, and these incorporate respectively stylized cornflowers, daffodils combined with chrysanthemums, and pomegranates and wisteria in the Japanese style and colouring (plates 35, 36, 37). Another favourite motif of the aesthetes, that of the sunflower, was used in his Flame and Fire patterns. Similar themes were also used in one of his contemporaneous designs for Potters of Darwen wallpapers (plate 76), and in a fireplace fitting produced by Coalbrookdale in 1879 (plate 67).

Another hitherto unknown Dresser paper from Jeffrey's log-book has recently been found in the bundle of company wallpapers exhibited at the Paris Exhibition in 1878 and now in the Victoria & Albert Museum (see imprint page). This shows Dresser's Japonism and 'greenery-yallery' style at its best and undoubtedly helped Jeffrey's win a

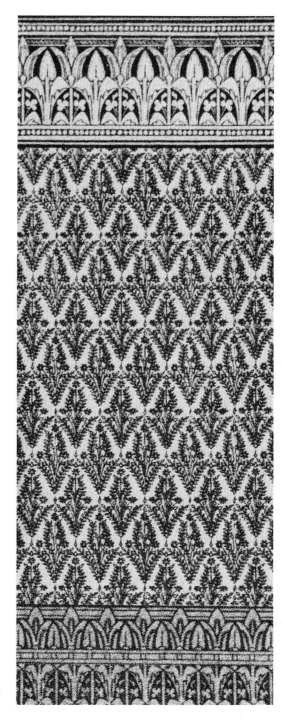

75
Jeffrey & Co. 'Persian' dado, frieze, filling and cornice paper. *The Building News*, 1874, p. 492.

76
Potters of Darwen
(Darwen Wallpaper Co.)
wallpaper. c. 1879–80.
Manchester City Art
Gallery.

By the time of the International Exhibition in Paris in 1878 Dresser was considered one of the most prolific and successful wallpaper designers in Europe, and he was asked to serve as a juror. He later recalled having supplied designs for as many as eleven different manufacturers represented at the exhibition, and among these were certainly the wallpaper companies he worked with at the time, namely Jeffrey's, William Cooke's, William Woollams' and Frederick Walton's.

Woollams' and Cooke's are known to have exhibited a number of Anglo–Japanese designs at the exhibition, and several of their designs executed between 1877–8 show distinct Dresser motifs. A stylized bamboo, flower and crane pattern produced by Cooke's in 1878 is similar to Dresser's 'Quick March' crane design for Minton's (plates 40, 157). Comparable friezes were produced by Woollams' and display Dresser's unobtrusive colour scheme and his typical scrolls, diapers and frets, combined with flower and bird panels in the Japanese style. A frieze attributed to Dresser and incorporating scrolls combined with sweet peas has been preserved in the Victoria & Albert Museum (plate 41).

Dresser is known to have supplied designs for some of the first Lincrusta Walton, which was launched at the 1878 Paris Exhibition. A retrospective article illustrated one of Dresser's early patterns for the dado, fillng and cornice scheme, and shows his overlapping floral pattern in the Anglo–Japanese style (plate 77). Dresser was certainly involved in Frederick Walton's first production of linoleum coverings, for Nikolaus Pevsner recorded him as having executed linoleum designs already in 1874, probably for floors.[38] Lincrusta Walton achieved enormous popularity during the late 1870s and 1880s, and remarkably also in America where samples of the dado and filling mentioned above have been preserved (plate 78).

It is entirely in keeping with Dresser's social convictions that he should have been involved in the first production of linoleum decorations. Linoleum was an inexpensive factory-made product which, according to the *Journal of Decorative Art*, 'placed within the reach of a great bulk of the middle and upper classes, a material peerless as a sanitary agent, and of a beauty that need fear no rival'.[39]

Allan V. Sugden listed Dresser's commissioners of paperhangings in his *History of English Wallpapers* (1925), providing the following names and dates: Potters of Darwen from about 1876, Allan,

gold medal at the Exhibition. He continued to remain a popular supplier of designs to the company until about 1887.

Three Dresser patterns named Coronal, Gotha and Agra were entered in Jeffrey's log-book for 1884, but have not been traced. Some previously unattributed Jeffrey papers from the mid-1880s, however, show distinct Dresser characteristics in their overlapping floral motifs (plate 38). He had introduced these at Lightbown, Aspinall's wallpaper manufactury in 1886, and in his *Modern Ornamentation* published the same year (plate 39).

77
Lincrusta Walton embossed and gilded wallcovering. c. 1878. *Journal of Decorative Art*, March 1884, p. 476.

78
Dado fragment, probably produced by Frederick Walton & Co. c. 1878. Marked 'Dr Dresser Inv.' Cooper-Hewitt Museum, New York.

Cockshut & Company from 1878, Knowles & Essex from about 1882, Lincrusta Walton from 1878, Anaglypta Company from 1887, and John Line & Company, and Lightbown, Aspinall & Company, from about 1880. Later, Nikolaus Pevsner added the name of Arthur Sanderson & Sons to the list.[40] Sanderson's, Jeffrey's, Lightbown, Aspinall's and Lincrusta Walton are all recorded as suppliers of wallpapers to Dresser's Art Furnishers' Alliance between 1880 and 1883.[41] A recently located Sanderson pattern displaying Dresser's favourite Japonism motifs of overlapping panels and diapers combined with birds and flowers compares strikingly with his designs for Lightbown, Aspinall from about 1882 (plates 42, 79, 80). The Sanderson paper may with certainty be attributed to Dresser, but so far remains the only identifiable sample of his designs for the company, although his name appears in their records as late as 1904.[42]

The Anglo–Japanese style, or Modern English as it was also termed, had come into its own at the Paris Exhibition of 1878, and earned Britain the reputation of the leading artistic nation. The Ger-

79, 80
Lightbown, Aspinall & Co.
dado papers. c. 1882.
Manchester City Art
Gallery.

man critic Carl Graff hailed it as 'the style of our time'[43] and another critic observed that 'Things have so far changed that England now stands in the front rank of European countries as regards many branches of her art manufactures, as the last Paris Exhibition showed.'[44] The designer and writer Lewis F. Day, himself an exponent of the Anglo–Japanese style, confirmed Britain's position in his article on 'Victorian Progress in Applied Art' in 1887:

> In the matter of originality that is to say, we
> have made very marked progress during the last
> five-and-twenty years: so much that at the last
> Paris Exhibition in 1878 the 'English style'
> made quite a sensation and was even imitated
> by the Parisian designers.[45]

This remarkable turn of events had been brought about by the efforts of Dresser, Godwin, Jeckyll, Talbert and Whistler, who all showed their work to advantage at the Paris Exhibition. Day's self-congratulatory appraisal was in fact endorsed by several Continental critics, who praised the English style as 'the most genuinely novel' of its time and 'one of the precursors of Art Nouveau'.[46]

The rapid transmission of Dresser's ideas and designs was greatly facilitated by the Art Furnishers' Alliance, founded in 1880. By this time his wallpapers had achieved wide renown and his impact on the American wallpaper industry was considerable, matching even that of Morris. He had supplied thirteen different designs, mostly in the Anglo–Japanese style during his stay in America in 1877 (plate 21), and the American

writer Constance Harrison noted in 1881 that Dresser's and Morris's wallpapers were 'familiar in our homes'.[47] Subsequently, Dresser's article on 'The Decoration of Our Homes' of 1885 presented his main thoughts on the subject to the ordinary American.[48]

In the summer of 1882 Dresser launched the most daring solution yet to the question of what to do with the walls. The Art Furnishers' Alliance exhibited his series of three wallpapers made of plain brown sugarpaper and discreetly ornamented. This eccentric but less costly alternative to the rich paperhangings of the day was generally well received and the *Artist and Journal of Home Culture* commented:

> At the Art Furnishers Alliance, an exhibition
> has been organised with a view to showing that
> really artistic wall decorations may be executed
> in the cheapest possible materials. The
> materials are brown paper, blue paper, and
> yellow paper.[49]

To impress its readers the journal revealed that the plain brown paper scheme had been adopted for a nobleman's dining room, probably that of Lord George Hayter Chubb, for whom Dresser had designed an Anglo–Japanese set of dining-room furniture (plate 56).[50]

Dresser had always preferred unobtrusive wallpapers, and his revolutionary use of sugarpaper seems to have been inspired by the brown papers used in the Japanese sliding-doors or 'Shoji', which were described in his *Japan, its Architecture, Art and Art-Manufactures*.[51] His invention was recalled many years later by the *Journal of Decorative Art*:

> Some 22 years ago Dr. Dresser surprised the
> British public by covering the walls of some
> rooms with what was known as sugar papers
> . . . Dr. Dresser's action was only an intelligent
> anticipation of the taste of the past few years,
> plus a very keen apprehension of what
> intrinsically was a very artistic and suitable
> medium. The experiment or 'fad' of 22 years
> ago is today 'un fait accompli', and the
> charming varied plain surfaces which the
> enterprise of our manufacturers places at the
> disposal of the decorator is a feature well worth
> of commendation.[52]

Most of Dresser's wallpapers from the latter
period of his career expand upon his sugarpaper
colour scheme with discreet patterns in the Anglo–
Japanese style. These were chiefly produced by
William Cooke's, Jeffrey's, Charles Knowles,[1]
Lightbown, Aspinall's, John Line's, Potters of
Darwen, Arthur Sanderson & Sons and Jean
Züber.

John Line's entered the wallpaper trade in 1880
and produced Dresser designs throughout the
1880s and 1890s. Their pattern book includes some
of Dresser's typical layered and grille patterns in
the Japanese style (plate 81). This kind of
ornamentation was perhaps Dresser's most daring
contribution to contemporary wallpaper design.
His stylized net-like juxtapositions of motifs, as
well as the dual balance of superimposed patterns,
were to become recurring devices in John Line's
wallpapers even into the new century. In 1905, a
year after Dresser's death, the *Journal of Decorative Art* applauded the 'brown papers with a
singularly rich and silky mottled surface' produced
by Line's, and described two patterns in particular

81
John Line & Co. dado
paper. Prints and
Drawings, Victoria &
Albert Museum, London.

as having 'that touch of weirdness which was often
associated with the work of the deceased gentleman',[53] whom they considered one of the creators
of the modern style of wall covering.

In 1882 William Cooke's produced one of Dresser's most attractive friezes in sugarpaper colours,
displaying stylized flowers, butterflies and palmtrees, similar to those illustrated in his *Art of Decorative Design* (plate 43). A comparable design
entitled Palm and annotated 'Dresser's design' was
produced by the Charles Knowles company in
1894. The wallpaper designs from this late period
of his career are remarkably close to motifs in
Modern Ornamentation and to Anaglypta patterns
from the 1880s and 1890s.

The Anaglypta company was founded in 1887
by J.T. Palmer, a former employee of Frederick
Walton, who had patented a new version of
linoleum paper which he called Anaglypta. It was
similar to Lincrusta Walton, but perhaps with a
slightly higher relief, and was welcomed as a good
alternative in bathroom sanitary decoration. The
Journal of Decorative Art contributed much to its
popularization and in 1891 stated that:

> Although this decorative material has not yet
> reached its fourth year of existence, yet to-day
> it is one of the most popular of wall decorations.
> No. 117, decoration 5593, is a design by Dr.
> Dresser, in the popular Moresque manner. For
> a dado in a room where such a style of
> decoration would be admissible we can
> conceive nothing better.[54]

Dresser supplied some of Anaglypta's first patterns, including Persian, Japanese XV Century,
Old English, Japanese Trail, Moorish, Egyptian,
Japanese Water, Arabian and Modern, and a number of borders and friezes (plates 82, 83). They
were all well received when first exhibited at the
Queen Victoria Golden Jubilee Exhibition in
1887.[55] The Anaglypta company continued to
prosper during the last decade of the century and
Dresser's Oriental-inspired designs dominated
their pattern books until as late as 1901. When they
were exhibited at the Glasgow International
Exhibition of that year a critic praised the 'touch
of the Orient', and singled out for particular commendation Dresser's pattern no. 298, entitled
Modern.[56] This was certainly one of his most successful Anaglypta designs and its Japanese lattice
effect became part of the repertoire of the Glasgow
style which emerged under Mackintosh's influence
(plate 82).

Henry Lightbown of Lightbown, Aspinall & Company in the late 1890s:

> I particularly remember one of the last occasions when the great man had returned from one of his frequent visits abroad to find inspiration, this time from Egypt, when most of his subjects were based on the Scarab, treated decoratively and conventionally.
>
> Lightbowns were permitted to buy some half-dozen of these (at what my father felt was an outrageous price) and I can still dimly see the strange shapes they presented to the wallpaper world of the day. I remember they were not successful in a commercial sense.
>
> My recollection of Dr. Dresser's appearance is not clear, but there was a tail-coat, a jove-like manner, a voice of authority and an aura.[57]

Cecil F. Tattersall, designer and author of *A History of British Carpets* (1934) and a pupil of Dresser's from 1894 until 1904, remembered Dresser as 'doing business with every firm manufacturing wallpapers and cretonnes, but when the Wallpaper Combine was formed (1899) he went to Germany and did extensive business with that country, which he visited at intervals.'[58]

Two wallpapers produced by the renowned Jean Züber Company of Rixheim in Alsace have recently come to light (plate 44). Annotated 'Dr. Dresser's designs' and dated 1903 and 1904, they were clearly produced for a market which by then was dominated by the Art Nouveau style, and testify to Dresser's position as a leader of fashion to the very end. His designs for Züber's were certainly his last works, for he died in the nearby city of Mulhouse in Alsace on 24 November 1904.

By the time of his death Dresser had designed a total of more than a hundred paperhangings, and made an enormous impact on the wallpaper industry in Britain, America and the Continent. His eminence in this field can perhaps be rivalled only by William Morris and C.F.A. Voysey.

Dresser retained his leading position in the wallpaper industry until the end of his life. Two letters from 1952 confirm this and provide us with a fascinating glimpse of Dresser in his last years. Allan Sugden recalled Dresser's visits to his grandfather

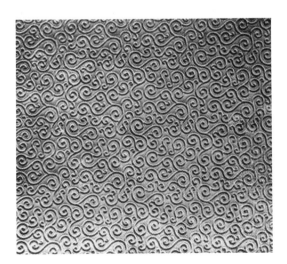

'Carpets'

The machine-made carpet industry expanded considerably during the Victorian period especially after the introduction of the power-driven Bigelow loom in the 1850s. Several new manufacturers were established and the Kidderminster factories produced double-cloth Brussels carpets and 'spool' Axminster rugs in competition with the Wilton worsted warp-face carpets.

Dresser rejected the naturalistic Victorian rug designs, and in 1862 focused attention on the geometrical and conventional Oriental patterns, which both Redgrave and Jones had recommended in the 1850s.[59] By the early 1860s carpet designers connected with the School of Design such as Jones, Matthew Digby Wyatt, and Dresser himself, had shown an interest in adapting the designs and structures of Oriental carpets.

In *The Art of Decorative Design* Dresser stressed that carpet design should be based on Oriental principles, and that carpets should serve as a background to the contents of the room. He advocated patterns that were based on the principle of radiating geometry, believing that this reflected the way that plants and flowers would be seen from above.[60] In *Principles of Decorative Design* he elaborated on these ideas and expounded his theories on colour:

> A carpet must be neutral in its general effect, as it is the background on which objects rest. Neutrality of effect is of two kinds. Large masses of tertiary or neutral colours will achieve its production, so also will the juxtaposition of the primary colours in small quantities, either alone or with the secondary colours, and black or white, but there will be this difference between the two effects – that produced by low-toned colours will be simply neutral, while that produced by primary colours will be 'bloomy' as well as neutral, and if yellows or reds slightly predominate in the intermingling of colours, the effect will be glowing and radiant.[61]

Nikolaus Pevsner confirmed that no less than 142 carpet designs of this type were supplied to John Crossley & Sons in 1871, and that 67 similar designs were sent to John Brinton Ltd in 1869.[62] These two Kidderminster companies were among the most famous carpet manufacturers in Britain and the only known commissioners of Dresser's carpet designs. Two Crossley patterns illustrated in *The Studio* in 1899 convey his individual style (plate 84). Most of his designs were laid out after the continuous radiating pattern, with marked scrolls or banded borders along the edges, which provided a 'frame' to the rug.

Dresser may well have been engaged as a designer by these companies as early as 1862, when he commented favourably on their exhibits at the London International Exhibition. The critic of the *Building News* referred to his designs for carpets

in 1865,[63] but none of these has been traced. Matthew Digby Wyatt's report of the Paris International Exhibition in 1867, however, provides a useful description of Dresser's early carpet designs:

> Dr. Dresser has been good enough to inform me that out of Messrs. Brinton & Lewis' collection the white-ground carpet with drab shadow and crimson arabesque scroll is intended for large rooms, where two-breadth designs are usually preferred, as giving greater scope for the artist's treatment of a massive subject in relief like this, of flowers and foliage, treated in self colours (ton sur ton) with heavy scroll-work to form the setting or panel-work of the whole.[64]

Dresser's art critic friend, George Augustus Sala, also recalled Dresser's achievements in his recollections of the Paris Exhibition:

> For some years past the taste and skill of Dr. Dresser has been put in requisition by some of the leading manufacturers both of England and the Continent, and both as designer of models of patterns, and as 'general art adviser', his talents have been of the very highest service to firms whose principals, as in the case of Messrs. Brinton & Lewis, combining capital and indefatigable enterprise, are laudably determined to bear Art as sedulously in view as they do industry; and who scorn, merely because a thing is 'sure to sell' and 'must find a market', to sow bad taste, broadcast and perpetuate ugliness.[65]

84
John Crossley & Sons carpet design. *The Studio*, Vol. xv, 1899, p. 108.

By 1871 the *Graphic Journal* ranked Dresser along-side his former tutors:

> The real competition is between the great ornamentists Sir Matthew Digby Wyatt, Mr. Owen Jones and Dr. Dresser. To the last-named must be awarded the palm. Seven large carpets from his design were sent [to the International Exhibition in London] by the manufacturers, Messrs. John Crossley & Sons. In two of these especially Dr. Dresser has made an advance for English art work. They are not copies, either in pattern, colouring, or character, but are English. Yet they achieve in great degree as art work what the quite dissimilar Eastern carpets already referred to do. There is entirety in the effect of the design, and fine colouring. That in which citron is the predominant tint is best. The next best is that facing the citron carpet, having a fine scroll pattern in blue of a good subdued tone, not like the garish blues now so plentiful in use.[66]

Recently two scroll patterns in Dresser's Japanese style have been located in the Patent Design Registry (plates 85, 86), and these may be the ones referred to in the article.

Dresser's carpet designs signalled the arrival of Japonism in the carpet industry. The *Furniture Gazette* endorsed these new 'Japanese designs', describing the colours as 'sage, olive, canary, or brown strewn with odd little figures, leaves and flowers in blue, red, and yellow'.[67] Similar designs produced by John Brinton & Sons and thought to be by Dresser have come to light, and clearly bear the mark of his taste for grotesque drollery and Japonism (plate 87).

In 1872 Dresser's designs for Crossley's were again recorded as highlights at the International Exhibition in London. The following contemporary description conveys some idea of their appearance:

> About a dozen or more specimens of various grounds, blue, green, dark purple, light purple, crimson, sky blue etc. The contrast of the arrangement of the colours in the patterns is very characteristic, being an admirable blending of richnesses, with effects of beauty . . . The borders of these carpets are clear and well drawn and all the masses of colours in the centre are so arranged as, so to speak, to define the border without cutting it out.[68]

85
John Crossley & Sons carpet design. 28 March 1871. Public Record Office, London.

Unfortunately, few of Dresser's carpet designs have been traced and yet another critic's description must suffice to give an impression of his work for John Brinton Ltd, shown at the Paris International Exhibition in 1878. There were eight different patterns:

> bright grass-green with yellow star-flowers, – geometric pattern of leaves, – multicoloured with brilliant gems of red, blue, yellow etc., – triangular patterns, – a green and blue carpet, – a green and yellow carpet with a wreath of

86
John Crossley & Sons carpet design. 6 March 1872. Public Record Office, London.

87
John Brinton & Co.
machine-woven Brussels
carpet. Attributed to
Dresser, c. 1874. Private
collection.

flowers for border on a dull white ground, – a carpet in Japanese style, with circles of drap and green, forming a trellis on blue, with over-running tendrils and flowers, – and finally one with a bunch of yellowish-white flowers on pale green, and a border of yellow flags on blue.[69]

Dresser expressed great admiration for Owen Jones's carpet designs,[70] which were highly influential, but Dresser's views on carpet manufacturing reached a wider section of the public. In 1876 he contributed a volume on *Carpets* to George Bevan's popular series entitled *British Manufacturing Industries*, which provided a historical survey of the carpet industry in the West and reiterated many of his earlier ideas.

Following Jones's death in 1874, the most fashionable models for carpet designs came from Dresser and William Morris. Morris began producing carpets in the 1870s, but from 1880 onwards he favoured the more exclusive hand-knotted 'Hammersmith' carpets made from his designs. Both Dresser and Morris intended to make Britain independent of carpets imported from the East, and under their influence the rug industry continued to expand during the late 1870s and 1880s.

Dresser's and Morris's carpets were soon distributed and copied in America, and their names were often used as descriptive adjectives, as in 'Dresseresque' and 'Morris style'. Dresser was the object of particular attention in 1873 after he had called the American taste in carpets the worst in the world.[71] That same year, probably as a result of his criticism, the American Government asked Dresser to provide a report on design 'applied to objects and to houses'.[72] This document has not yet been traced, but writers in the American carpet trade journals frequently referred to his criticism during the 1870s and 1880s. His condemnation of American rugs prompted manufacturers to take a close look at their products and some of them actually tried to improve standards.

In 1878 the *Carpet Trade Review* noted that 'the influence of Morris and Dresser had gone everywhere short of the Bannock region', and praised John Brinton's pattern in 'Dresser's own geranium leaf pattern'.[73] Two years later the journal reported:

> Some of our finest carpets are now got in fern patterns and leaflets. What is known at present in England as the Dresseresque designs, which represent fernery and leaves coloured in autumn hues, have just been introduced. The style is the outgrowth of one of Mr. Dresser's pet fancies – the 'flat character in decorative art'.[74]

None of these designs has been found, but they correspond to the Crossley carpets illustrated in *The Studio* in 1899 (plate 84).

By 1885 Dresser's ideas on carpets were seen by the *British Colonial and Manufacturing Journal* as a turning-point. Thanks to his efforts the rug trade had 'completely altered in pattern, design, and quality'.[75] Dresser, however, in an article in the same journal pointed out a retrograde tendency, namely the fashion for what he called 'Landscape Designs in Carpets':

> This strange reversion to a most debased form of art is the natural outcome of the changes which have been going on around us for some years past. We are getting almost as anxious for change as are the Americans, and in too many cases we seek novelty without for one moment considering whether the new is better or worse, or more appropriate or less so, than what is superseded.[76]

This misapplied naturalism had come into vogue under the influence of French allegorical and landscape designs, which remained popular in France and in America throughout the nineteenth century. Defenders of naturalism in Britain popularized these designs in the mid-1880s, and Dresser felt compelled to condemn the fashion. He was pleased to observe, however, that his conventional patterns were still produced and that a carpet made some sixteen years back had not been out of the loom for this entire period.[77] He was perhaps referring to one of the 67 patterns supplied to John Brinton Ltd in 1869.

Ironically, towards the end of his career Dresser became a victim of the industrial revolution for which he had pleaded so enthusiastically. The frantic search for novelty, which he had rightly warned against, led to increasing demand for change and for new techniques, and made Dresser and other instigators of design reform redundant. Perhaps the most acerbic critic of such tendencies was James M. Whistler, whose 'Ten O'Clock Lecture' in 1885 denounced the new class of people and artists 'who discovered the cheap and foresaw fortune in the facture of the sham'.[78] Whistler's and Dresser's dilemma over the merits of industrialism continued to provide subject for debate as the century drew to an end. In 1892 the *Journal of the Society of Arts* finally found against Dresser's carpet designs:

> Dr. Dresser also thoroughly mastered the technique of Brussels carpets, and produced a number of designs which complied with all the requirements of a floor covering, but their somewhat cast-iron character, and their want of variety prevented their permanent success.[79]

Dresser's stylized leaf, fern, floral, and scroll-work patterns which had remained in vogue for two decades had evidently outlived their popularity in the wake of industrial progress in the rug trade. Nevertheless, he had played a significant role in revitalizing the British and American carpet industry, and his designs had given considerable impetus to the movement for reform.

'Curtain Materials, Hangings and Woven Material Generally'

The principle of repetition and alternation of motifs in Dresser's textile designs was first discussed in *The Art of Decorative Design*, where he suggested a combination of geometrical units formed by curves and squares. Quadrangular, triangular, hexagonal, octagonal, circular, lozenge and cuspid motifs were analysed and broken down to form borders, frets, diapers and layered patterns of the kind admired by Dresser in Japanese ornamentation. A composite pattern of this kind was illustrated and recommended as being suitable for quilts and tablecloths (plate 88). In his *Development of Ornamental Art* Dresser stressed that the laws governing textiles were identical to those governing carpets generally, that is, the designs were based on a radiating symmetrical pattern. Hanging fabrics accordingly followed the rules laid down for wallpapers, namely a bilateral arrangement of themes.[80]

This arrangement had been followed by Dresser in his first textile designs for Liddiard's in 1853 (plate 11), and similar flower-sprig patterns were recommended in his 1862 publications. A number of stylized designs suitable for 'powdering' on a plain ground also occur in his sketchbook and pattern books. Several of these were adapted to the worsted-woollen and silk damask patterns he supplied to James W. & C. Ward and Norris & Company (later Warner & Company) in the late 1860s (plates 46, 47). These early Dresser textile designs appear to have much in common with Owen Jones's conventional patterns from the time, but they are sharper, crisper and more angular in contour, an effect frequently commended by Dresser. In his *Principles of Decorative Design* he lamented the general 'want of simple structure, want of simple treatment, want of simplicity of effect' in British textiles, and proposed simple and flat motifs such as circles, diapers, vertical and diagonal stripes as suitable for hanging fabrics, a sample of which shows a distinct Japanese effect (plate 89).

Dresser also believed that the patterns and colour-schemes should be adapted to suit the quality of the textile, so that rich and powerful patterns would be used for silk damasks, and simpler patterns for less costly materials. He followed these principles in his designs for James W. & C. Ward exhibited at the International Exhibition in London in 1871, some of which are reminiscent of Japanese textiles. Other designs reflect Dresser's admiration for Indian and Persian textiles (plate 47).

During the 1860s and 1870s Dresser was particularly active as a designer of silk and woollen damasks for James W. Ward, whose house he decorated in 1865. Some of these patterns were subsequently included in Dresser's books, and were clearly intended as study objects. Several of the Ward textiles display 'the broken diapers, irregular powderings and strange key patterns' which Dresser had admired in Japanese ornamentation.

Dresser was far ahead of his time in his assimilation of the structural qualities of 'surihaku' and 'katamigawara' patterns as they were called in Japan. Their layered composition of ground and superimposed motifs became a characteristic of his ornamentation, and can be seen in his advertising for Londos in 1873, and in some Ward textiles (plates 1, 19, 48, 90).

Godwin, Talbert and Day are among the other contemporary designers known to have produced Japanesque textile patterns during the 1870s, but none of their designs displays the vigorous sweep and supreme compositional balance which typify Dresser's work. These qualities are particularly apparent in some Dresser damasks produced by James W. & C. Ward, which show his adaptation of Egyptian, Japanese and other Oriental patterns (plates 1, 90). Three other Ward patterns from Dresser's hand at this time are very close to his contemporaneous designs for Minton's porcelain (plates 91, 147). The swooping wavelines and fishes later formed the basis of a similar design produced by F. Steiner & Company in the late 1890s (plates 45, 117).

Pre-dating Art Nouveau motifs by at least two decades, Dresser's damasks from the 1870s reflect the patterns which he admired in Japanese textiles:

They have the ground covered with fan-shaped panels, in which landscapes are wrought; and others have patterns of a wholly geometrical character. Then there are patterns formed of clouds, of storks, of insects, of pine leaves, of

89
Textile design from
Dresser's *Principles of
Decorative Design*, 1873,
fig. 91.

small diapers, of sailing boats, of bats, cobwebs, of fungi, of water, of feathers, of fire-flies, of sea-monsters, of broken diapers, irregular powderings, strange key patterns, rosettes, plaids, waved lines, and other elements too numerous to mention, even rain being used in some of their designs.[81]

James W. & C. Ward's log-books from the late 1880s onward contain numerous patterns which have been attributed to Dresser on stylistic grounds. We recognize his favourite Japanesque motifs with fans, owls etc. from 1886 and 1889 (plate 92), as well as the fan-shaped floral pattern similar to his pattern for Steiner's cretonnes (plate 118). Two other striking patterns in the Japanese and Moorish style, dated 1893 and 1895, resemble his designs for Lincrusta and Anaglypta wallcoverings from the same period (plate 71), and one of his last designs from 1901 displays the stylized water-lilies and trees he incorporated in contemporary designs for Minton and Jean Züber (plate 150). Roland Midgely, a former employee of Ward's, later confirmed that several Dresser patterns were in production until the beginning of this century.[82]

Dresser's daughter Nellie in an interview in 1952 mentioned that he did a few designs for Liberty & Company in 1882, and these may well have included patterns for the company's range of 'Lotus fabrics' launched that year.[83] These were clearly manufactured to cater for the Anglo–Japanese taste and several of the designs show typical Dresser motifs, notably his dragon pattern from

88
Textile pattern from
Dresser's *Art of Decorative
Design*, 1862, pl. v.

The Art of Decorative Design, which remained one of his favourite themes (plates 16, 124).

According to Nikolaus Pevsner, Dresser also supplied designs for lace patterns to Edward Cope & Company, and textile patterns to Barlow & Jones, Turnbull & Stockdale, and Tootal, Broadhurst & Lee, who merged with Wardle & Company in 1892.[84] Turnbull & Stockdale were renowned for their Anglo–Japanese patterns during the late 1880s and 1890s,[85] and these were probably designed by Dresser, but so far none of his work for the company has been located.

Following his tour of Japan, Dresser donated some sample books of textiles to the National Museum of Tokyo. This gift included thirteen lace curtains by Edward Cope's, and a number of tablecloths, bedspreads and cotton towels produced by Barlow & Jones and Tootal, Broadhurst & Lee. Regrettably these textiles have not been preserved but the records testify to his connection with these firms at the time.[86] Lace patterns sent to Edward Cope's in 1881 are included in the photographs from Dresser's account books taken by Pevsner in 1936, but these are too vague to provide a proper impression of his lace designs. However, some patterns in *Modern Ornamentation* (1886) show motifs based on geometrical and crystalline forms.

Tootal, Broadhurst & Lee's sample books from the late 1870s and 1880s have been preserved in the Bolton Museum, and contain patterns in the Japanese style which correspond to many of Dres-

90
Three James W. & C. Ward silk damask samples donated by the company to the Victoria & Albert Museum. c. 1875. Victoria & Albert Museum, London.

designs and colours. The same cloth is also made available for dressing-table covers' (plate 112).[87] This technique was probably inspired by the raised loops of Chinese carpets and Japanese appliqué patterns, which also formed the model for another novelty exhibited by the company in 1878:

> Messrs. Barlow & Jones have also produced curtains and coverlets in satin appliqué work and embroidery from charming designs by Dr. Dresser, using for their material unbleached cotton, which presents all the advantages of cheapness and durability, with solid and graceful appearance.[88]

Clearly the textiles were created in order to supplant the Japanese appliqué works which were in vogue at the time.

Among Dresser's most celebrated designs for Barlow & Jones were his Empire Quilt and Colombian Celebration Quilt produced to commemorate Queen Victoria's Golden Jubilee in 1887 and the 400th anniversary of Columbus' discovery of America in 1893. The Empire Quilt displays the heraldic devices of the British colonies, with the royal arms in the centre surrounded by seaweed wreaths, and the Star of India and the Prince of Wales' plumes in the corners. It was subsequently adopted for use at Windsor castle (plate 113).

ser's characteristic motifs, such as butterflies, crests, scrolls, bamboo and floral sprigs (plate 93). A pattern dated 1880 and signed C. D. displays birds in hawthorn branches, similar to his designs for stained glass at Bushloe House.

Dresser's first contact with Barlow & Jones was probably made around the time of the Paris International Exhibition in 1878, when the *Art Journal* praised his quilts as 'A great novelty in the art of weaving at the exhibition. The pattern (designed by Dr. Dresser) is produced by raised loops on a plain ground. These quilts are made in several

94
F. Steiner & Co. cretonne.
1902. Victoria & Albert
Museum, London.

95
F. Steiner & Co. 'Ladies
Smock' cretonne. 1902.
Victoria & Albert Museum,
London.

96
Linthorpe Pottery vase.
c. 1880. Maker's mark.
$6\frac{1}{10}$ in. high.

97
Opposite. Minton & Co. vase
no. 610. 1862. 10 in. high.
Minton Museum, Royal
Doulton Minton Co.,
Stoke-on-Trent.

98
Minton & Co. matchpots,
(left to right) nos. 1017, 618
and 1202. c. 1862–5.
$4\frac{1}{2}$–11 in. high. Royal
Doulton Minton Archive,
Stoke-on-Trent.

99
Minton & Co. porcelain jug
no. G 383 (April 1870) and
tableware nos. 1911 (June
1875) and 1716 (1873).
Private collection.

WHEN
THE
CHIEF
SHEPHERD
SHALL
APPEAR
YE SHALL
RECEIVE
A CROWN
OF GLORY
I PET.
V. 4

100
Minton & Co. art work for vase no. 1304. 1867. Royal Doulton Minton Archive, Stoke-on-Trent.

101
Opposite. Minton & Co. vases nos. 1342 (left) and 1356. Paris International Exhibition, 1867. Private collection.

102
Minton & Co. seau no. 1329
and vase no. 1348. 8 and
12 in. high. Minton
Museum, Royal Doulton
Minton Co.,
Stoke-on-Trent.

103
Opposite. Josiah Wedgwood
& Sons vase no. 1212.
Unglazed earthenware.
1867. $6\frac{1}{2}$ in. high. Private
collection.

104
Minton & Co. vases (left to
right) nos. 1379, 1380,
1382. 1868–9. c. 12 in. high.
Minton Museum, Royal
Doulton Minton Co.,
Stoke-on-Trent.

105
Minton & Co. vases
(clockwise from lower left)
nos. 1103, 1341, 1376, 1379,
1380, 1384, 1474, 1414,
1507. Private collection.

106
Watcombe Terracotta Co.
vases, jug and teapots.
Unglazed. Attributed to
Dresser, 1870. $5\frac{1}{2}$–11 in.
high. Private collection.

107
Old Hall Earthenware Co.
'Shanghai', 'Hampden' and
'Persian' plates; and jug.
c. 1884. Some marked with
maker's mark and
Dresser's facsimile
signature. Private
collection.

108
Ault Pottery (left to right)
nos. 328, 246, 263, 247, 248.
c. 1890–4. 8¾–28¼ in. high.
Reproduced from
Linthorpe shapes. Private
collection.

109
Linthorpe Art Pottery (left
to right) nos. 24, 138, 44,
140, 142, 141. c. 1879–80.
7¼–12 in. high. Private
collection.

110
Linthorpe Art Pottery
bowl and vases (left to
right) nos. 169, 301, 168,
424. c. 1879–80. 3¼–19¼ in.
high. Private collection.

111
Linthorpe Art Pottery
bowl with pierced and
relief decoration showing
orchids. c. 1880. 6 in. high.
Private collection.

The Colombian Celebration Quilt was exhibited at the Chicago World Fair in 1893:

It bears in the centre the American shield surmounted by thirteen stars of the original United States, and overshadowed by spreading palm branches; below is the American Eagle, bearing the arrows and olive branches in his claws. The upper border displays the arms of the state of Illinois, of which Chicago is the chief city, and the side borders the arms of Spain, under Ferdinand and Isabella, when Columbus discovered America . . . This unique and exquisite design is the work of Dr. Dresser, the eminent Art Designer.[89]

By the 1890s Dresser had become a household name in the British textile industry. His first tablecloth damask designs, produced by John Wilson & Sons, were launched in 1891. The *Art Journal* critic commented approvingly:

Flowers should be wholly or semi-conventionalised and the same holds good with animals, in dealing with which Dr. Dresser's designs for Messrs. Wilson and Sons have sometimes been specially able. One of this

designs is of owls, small birds, and butterflies, with the border's panelling formed of bamboo-canes and foliage. He usually displays a feeling for Japanese character, than which there can be no more appropriate. No. 9 shows the middle and narrow border of such a cloth, in which varied diapers prettily break, yet connect, the discs with bamboo, storks, and peony flowers (plate 114).[90]

The latter pattern, no. 9, shows Dresser's Japonism at its best, and it was subsequently used as an example of the Anglo–Japanese style in J.F. Blacker's *The ABC of Japanese Art*, published in 1911. F.T. Pigott in a series of articles on 'The Decorative Art of Japan' released in 1891 also recognized Dresser's importance for the 'Japanesy' fashion, which had 'come to be quite the thing', and referred the reader to suitable prototypes in Dresser's *Japan, its Architecture, Art, and Art-Manufactures*.[91]

The layered patterns in *Japan* greatly contributed to the reform of textile designs. One Japanese technique recommended by Dresser, of shading the ground from one colour to the other, inspired Warner's to produce similar silk damasks,

112
Barlow & Jones 'Terry Quilt'. *The Art Journal*, 1878, p. 151.

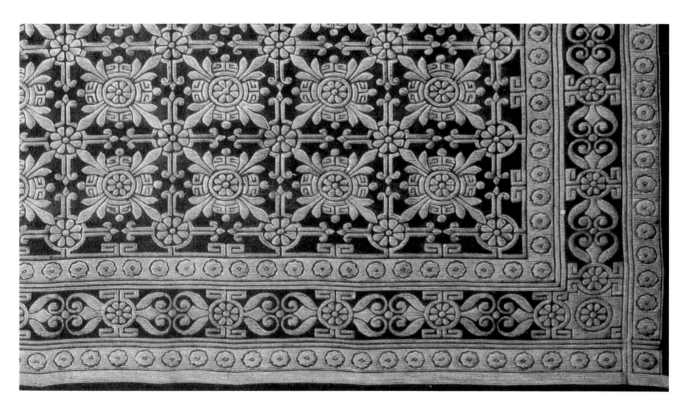

113
Barlow & Jones 'Empire Quilt'. Made for Queen Victoria's Golden Jubilee in 1887. *The Warehousemen & Drapers' Trade Journal*, 11 June 1887, p. 7.

114
John Wilson & Son damask pattern. *The Art Journal*, 1891, p. 182.

probably from Dresser's designs (plate 115). The superimposed clusters of flowers are close to his later design for Steiner's cretonnes (plate 94).

The Steiner cretonnes illustrated in *The Studio* article on Dresser in 1899 have generally been considered his last identifiable designs. One of them has been preserved in a private collection in Germany (plates 117, 118). Similar cretonnes included in Pevsner's article of 1937 appear to have been produced by the same company, and show the various changes of fashion which occurred in the last years of the century (plate 116). Some of these designs, however, seem to be less typical of Dresser and were perhaps designed by students in his studio. C.F. Tattersall, a pupil of Dresser's between 1894 and 1904, recalled that Dresser was mainly concerned with marketing and supervising, rather than with design, during this period.[92]

Few of Dresser's textiles for Steiner survive, but some were rescued by Barbara Morris for the Victoria & Albert Museum when the company went into liquidation in 1957. These samples have been traced in the Patent Office Design Registry, and some designs from 1902–3 incorporate Dresser motifs, such as the conventionalized Japanese Water and Ladies Smock cretonnes (plates 94, 95). The latter theme connects with his first textile design (plate 11), and shows his subdued colour scheme. Its sophistication places him on a par with Continental Art Nouveau designers.

Dresser's textiles and his surface ornamentation serve as telling documents in the debate over the appropriateness of ornamental design. Dresser argued that conventionalized and abstract patterns were to be preferred to the Victorian taste for allegorical and naturalistic imagery. Unlike many of his contemporaries he revered this type of ornamentation not just for its sheer attractiveness, but because of its formative effect on design and on interiors in general.

His overriding concern with the propriety of decoration has led to the preoccupation of many twentieth-century designers with minimal surface ornamentation.

115
Warner & Co. damask.
Company pattern book,
1891. Victoria & Albert
Museum, London.

116
Textile designs, probably
produced by F. Steiner &
Co. c. 1890–1904. Retailed
by Newman, Smith &
Newman. *The Architectural
Review*, Vol. 81, 1937,
p. 186.

117
Right. F. Steiner & Co.
cretonne. *The Studio*,
Vol. xv, 1899, p. 107.

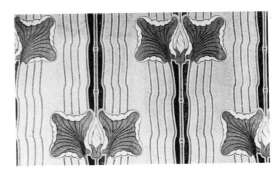

118
Page 116. F. Steiner & Co.
cretonne. *The Studio*,
Vol. xv. 1899, p. 109.

CERAMICS AND THE EXOTIC PERSPECTIVE

The nineteenth century witnessed an unprecedented interest in collecting and producing pottery and porcelain, which culminated in a virtual china mania in Britain during the latter part of Queen Victoria's reign. Extended trade facilities in the wake of colonialism had given rise to a taste for exotic pottery, which soon became the target of collectors and writers. By the middle of the century designers and manufacturers were exposed to a multitude of new art models from Greece, China, India, Japan and Persia, which sparked off a boom in ceramic production in Europe and America.

Dresser in his *Japan, its Architecture, Art and Art-Manufactures* said that he had been familiar with the Japanese Arita patterns from childhood.[1] It is uncertain whether he encountered Arita porcelain proper at this early stage, but he was clearly aware of the popular 'Japan' or 'Arita' patterns produced by well-known British manufacturers at the time. Some of the first porcelain made in Britain was in fact based on Japanese prototypes and by the 1840s the patterns had acquired a rich gilding and colouring which made a strong impression on the young Dresser. He may also have been aware of the presence of Arita porcelain in some of the most famous collections in Britain, as well as of the auction samples illustrated in Joseph Marryat's *Collections towards a History of Pottery and Porcelain* (1850), which was Dresser's sourcebook at the School of Design. Marryat was considered the greatest ceramic expert of his time and in 1853 he was engaged as adviser to the Museum of Ornamental Art (later the South Kensington Museum), whose acquisition policy he undoubtedly influenced.[2]

When the museum was founded in 1852 the Cole group had already bought several samples of Chinese and Japanese porcelain from the London dealer William Hewitt,[3] and the School's programme stated that: 'An educated designer for ceramic manufacture should at least have an adequate knowledge of what Japan, Meissen, Sèvres and Chelsea have already done.'[4] This policy was pursued by Dresser's tutor Octavius Hudson, whose lectures in 1854 dealt with Chinese and Japanese styles, and were illustrated by objects in the museum. Among these were certainly some Arita porcelain and other Japanese artefacts acquired from the Japanese sales exhibition in London in that year.[5]

The curator of the museum, John C. Robinson, was equally discerning in his appraisal of Japanese porcelain in 1855:

> The Japan porcelain is perhaps distinguished by a purer taste in design, the shapes of the pieces are simpler and more elegant than the Chinese, whilst in the painted decoration, grotesque or fantastic subjects are less affected, simple renderings of natural flowers and foliage, and elegant conventionalised floral ornaments, being very frequent. In colour, generally speaking, Japan porcelain is fuller and richer in effect than the Chinese.[6]

These qualities certainly appealed to Dresser, who around this time was beginning to advocate his art botany. Indeed his *Art of Decorative Design* popularized the concept of stylization found in Japanese lotus designs, which he considered 'the most exalted grade of ornament'.

The first comprehensive presentation of Japanese ceramics was at the International Exhibition in London in 1862, which featured Rutherford Alcock's collection. Dresser recalled having made no fewer than 80 drawings of the pieces exhibited.[7] The Japan section made a tremendous impact on British designers, including Dresser, whose lecture on 'The Prevailing Ornament of China and Japan' and articles on 'Japanese Ornamentation' (1863) constituted some of the first critical assessments of Japanese art in the West. He dealt at length with Japanese pottery, singling out for particular praise an eclipse-shaped vase and a bowl decorated with circular flower ornaments and crests, which

119–122
Four plate designs for
Minton & Co. c. 1871.
Royal Doulton Minton
Archive, Stoke-on-Trent.

influenced some of his own creations for Minton's in 1871 and for Linthorpe Art Pottery in about 1880 (plates 96, 119–122).

The Japanese fret, diaper and crest patterns illustrated in Dresser's articles recur frequently in his ceramic designs, and similar ornamentation was also featured in his books.

While the beauty of Japanese pottery and ornamentation acted as an important stimulus to the young Dresser's creativity, he also looked for inspiration to other exotic pottery, such as Greek, Egyptian and Islamic ware. In *The Art of Decorative Design* he quoted Semper's studies on Greek and Egyptian water vessels, which were perfectly suited for drawing water from the spring and from the river Nile respectively. This was the point of departure for Dresser's pronouncement that pottery 'should be perfectly adapted to meet all requirements of the work to which it was assigned, and that in the easiest and most simple manner'.[8] He considered such vital functional aspects as the position of handles and spouts, which should be determined by the observance of the point of gravity in the vessel. In this way the pot could be held with the least possible strain and without spilling the contents.[9] A cursory glance at Victorian jugs, and even at those produced today, suggests that this basic principle is constantly violated.

One of Dresser's main themes was the importance of finding the appropriate method of turning the material into functional and beautiful objects:

Clay is peculiarly fitted for being worked on the potter's wheel, as this mode of fabricating it into forms of utility is simple, and at the same time calculated to bring about the production of graceful forms, for here the influence of the attraction of the earth upon semi-plastic clay aids the potter in producing favourable results.[10]

This statement was accompanied by an illustration showing how the plastic clay had been extended and wrought into a funnel-shaped form with the help of the centrifugal force of the potter's wheel. Such shapes with or without a cavity base became Dresser's favourite vase forms. Clay as a material was highly valued by Dresser: it was inexpensive and could be coloured in the most sophisticated and enduring way, and it was 'susceptible of the highest art-finish, or the bold sketchy touch of the modeller's hand'.[11]

Dresser's progressive views were promoted in his writings, and in 1862 he particularly praised the Minton porcelain exhibited at the International Exhibition. During the 1840s and 1850s Minton's had produced designs by several of his tutors, such as John Bell, Henry Cole, Richard Redgrave, Gottfried Semper and John Simpson, and Dresser himself joined the company as a freelance designer in the early 1860s. Some of the designs he did for Minton's stand in 1862 have recently come to light and correspond with the drawings annotated 'Exhibition 1862' in his sketchbook, as well as with descriptions in his *Development of Ornamental Art*. Dresser in fact furnished many designs for the International Exhibition, and since he frequently commented on

his own creations without mentioning their provenance one may deduce that some 'very fine Persian vases, with larger forms in blue, and the smaller in two golds, and dull red' (plate 97), and 'two small elongated vases enriched with Chinese or Japanese ornament', originated from his studio.

Several of the borders were adapted from a border-sheet in his sketchbook (plate 123), and the dragon scroll is similar to that illustrated in *The Art of Decorative Design* (plate 124). This motif was also applied to Minton's vase no. 1073 some time during the early 1860s (plate 125), and presumably reflects one of Dresser's principal inspirational sources at the time. The triple-gourd shape (plate 97) was based on a Japanese vase illustrated on Plate 139 of Marryat's *History of Pottery and Porcelain* and indicates an early awareness of Japonism. Even more striking is the use of a rich cloisonné effect on porcelain, a technique discovered by the French ceramicist Eugène Collinot in 1861.[12] Dresser seems to have pioneered this technique in Britain, and Minton's 'cloisonné ware' became one of the firm's most popular products during the 1860s and 1870s.

A few more Dresser designs from this early period have been traced in Minton's archive, in particular a matchpot which corresponds to a drawing in his sketchbook marked 'Angular treatment of the herb-robert, semi-conventional' and 'Exhibition 1862'. This became a popular shape at Minton's and was reproduced with a variety of Dresser's cloisonné patterns for several decades. Another matchpot from 1862 was decorated with swastika patterns and borders, again from Dresser's sketchbook (plate 98), and identical borders also adorn an unusual bamboo-shaped vase. His jug and teapot incorporate similar bamboo effects, and were produced some time around the middle of the 1860s (plates 126, 127). The clean-cut shapes and angular handles, as well as the swastika patterns, appear to be derived from Japanese prototypes, and they can be compared to his later designs for electroplated silver.

Dresser's designs for Minton cloisonné patterns incorporated several of the Japanese ornaments he had recommended in 1863, such as stylized butterflies, beetles and grasshoppers, combined with angular scroll-work, borders, diapers and conventionalized botanical motifs. His Japonism often had a certain grotesqueness – frequently seen in Japanese art – and stood in sharp contrast to contemporary French Japonism creations, such as Félix Bracquemond's 'Service Rousseau', which

clearly preferred Minton's products to those of the French, and particularly applauded the brilliancy of their transparent enamel colours. The Japonist and critic Philippe Burty declared: 'None can come up to them [Minton's] in outline or in suitableness to their several uses.'[13]

By this time Dresser had become one of the most sought-after freelance designers at Minton's. His name was attached to a number of their products, and 'Dr. Dresser's style' became a household term. The majority of his patterns were adapted to new forms, but whether he actually designed Minton's shapes is not documented. His cloisonné patterns reveal a marked Oriental inspiration; clearly the Japanese enamels shown at the International Exhibition in 1862 had made a strong impression on him.

By the time of the Paris Exhibition of 1867 the technique of adapting enamel patterns to porcelain had been adopted by a number of Minton's designers, including Thomas Kirkby, John Henk and Charles Toft. The fashion soon spread to other British manufacturers, but few if any could compete with the brilliance and technical perfection of Minton's cloisonné ware, which has remained unsurpassed to this day.

Dresser's designs from Minton's stand in Paris in 1867 have all been located. They comprise twelve vases and some twelve different borders adapted for tableware and toiletware, and were

incorporated naturalistic motifs taken directly from Hokusai's Manga. This became clear at the Paris International Exhibition in 1867, which featured Bracquemond's service next to Dresser's Minton cloisonné ware. The international jury

124
Pl. XIV showing Chinese Dragon motif from Dresser's *Art of Decorative Design*, 1862.

125
Minton & Co. vase no. 1073
with Dragon pattern.
c. 1865. Minton & Co.
Shapebook, Royal Doulton
Minton Archive,
Stoke-on-Trent.

reproduced through several decades as 'Dresser's laurel' and 'Dresser's sprigs' (plate 130). The simplicity of the shapes can be compared to his later Linthorpe Art Pottery. Vase no. 1103 was first launched with a typical cloisonné pattern in about 1865–6. The exhibition version incorporates Dresser's unique stylized dog design, and most of his designs from 1867 display the grotesque drollery, frequently based on Japanese and other Oriental prototypes, which characterized much of his ornamentation from this time onward (plate 129).

Dresser's so-called pilgrim bottle for Minton's introduced a very beautiful shape, which he subsequently reproduced for Wedgwood's and for Linthorpe Art Pottery (plate 128). It was clearly based on some 'very fine flat shaped Japanese pilgrim bottles in cloisonné' shown at the International Exhibition in 1862.[14] His peacock-like bird grotesque was later replaced by stylized butterfly and angular scroll borders. The attractive Japonism butterfly decoration was executed in 23 different versions by Dresser and his pattern sheet provides an important source for identifying other Minton creations (plate 131). The motif was first included in two seaux shown by Minton's in Paris in 1867, and was successfully combined with Dresser's grotesque beetles and angular bulrushes (plate 133). This vigorous composition, referred to as 'Dresser's beetles' and 'Dresser's butterflies', remained one of his most popular designs for the company and for many years it adorned a wide variety of vases, tableware and toiletware (plate 99).

A number of Dresser vases were made

exclusively for the Paris International Exhibition in 1867 and preliminary patterns for some of them have been located in his sketchbook and pattern books (plates 100, 101, 132). The surprisingly ferocious chameleons and grasshoppers display his predilection for insect friezes. The grotesque grasshopper frieze was probably inspired by a Japanese vase with this motif in the Alcock collection.[15] Dresser subsequently discussed it in his *Japan, its Architecture, Art and Art-Manufactures* and illustrated a modified version as 'Old Bogey' in his *Principles of Decorative Design*.

Dresser's creations for Minton's in 1867 also featured some vases with lotus-scroll patterns freely adapted from Owen Jones's *Examples of Chinese Ornaments*, which was published in parts in 1866–7 (plates 102, 134). These shapes later received a variety of Dresser's patterns. The pilgrim bottle version, appropriately adorned with Japanese ladies on a turquoise ground, was presented by Dresser to the National Museum in Japan.[16] A cylindrical vase clearly influenced by Japanese brush vases was another popular Minton shape in the 1870s. The first sample featured Dresser's stylized leaf pattern, and is similar to his vigorous 'Truth, Beauty and Power' design for a Wedgwood vase executed in the same year (plates 136, 18).

Dresser probably began designing for Wedgwood's around this time, since his first designs for

126
Minton & Co. jug no. 618.
c. 1865. Minton & Co.
Shapebook, Royal Doulton
Minton Archive,
Stoke-on-Trent.

127
Minton kettle no. 619
c. 1865. Minton & Co.
Shapebook, Royal Doulton
Minton Archive,
Stoke-on-Trent.

tableware, toiletware and ornamental ware. The catalogue of the International Exhibition in London in 1871 lists 'five hanging vases' and 'three fish vases', which probably refer to Dresser's hanging pilgrim bottles of 1867 (plate 138). A jardinière majolica pattern, which again shows Dresser's predilection for stylized beetles and fishes, was registered with the Patent Office by Wedgwood's in 1872 (plate 139).

Dresser's output for Minton's was more extensive and better documented than his work for Wedgwood's. In the autumn of 1867 he launched a series of Japan-inspired vases decorated in the cloisonné style (production numbers 1379 to 1385) (plates 104, 105), and between 1868 and 1870 numerous of his designs were executed. Although showing Japonism and Oriental features, they are

them were registered with the Patent Office in the spring of 1867 and were certainly exhibited at the Paris Exhibition. A striking leafage border for tableware resembles the ones he designed for Minton's that year (plate 137), and a pilgrim bottle was decorated with similar grotesque motifs of cross-sections of flying cranes and flat fishes on alternatively turquoise, red and cane grounds (plate 103).

Although Wedgwood's executed a number of Dresser's designs during the late 1860s and 1870s, only a few of his works have been traced. However, the company's pattern and estimate books from the time record several Dresser borders, and 'Dresser's Bourbon sprigs' design was applied to

129
Minton & Co. art work for
vase no. 1103. c. 1866–7.
Royal Doulton Minton
Archive, Stoke-on-Trent.

all artistically modified versions of their prototypes (plate 28). A tripod vase (no. 1414) incorporating a mask-like scroll pattern reflects Dresser's fondness for this kind of grotesque motif, which recurs in a number of his subsequent Minton creations. Production nos. 1470 and 1471 reproduce Japanese shapes and display crest patterns lifted directly from Dresser's Japanese crest album (plates 105, 140). A pattern sheet with nineteen of Dresser's Japanese crests has been preserved in the Minton archive and, together with his butterfly sheet, is a valuable aid in identifying his designs (plate 142).

The intricate combination of funnel shapes in vase no. 1477 and three fan-shaped vases testify to Dresser's sense of form and his penchant for Japanese motifs of beetles, crabs, dragons, peacocks, lotus flowers and angular scrolls (plate 140). Their sparkling cloisonné patterns enhance the

128
Minton & Co. art work for
vase no. 1303. 1867. Royal
Doulton Minton Archive,
Stoke-on-Trent.

130
Opposite. Minton & Co.
plate borders. 1867. Royal
Doulton Minton Archive,
Stoke-on-Trent.

131
Minton & Co. art work
showing butterfly motifs.
c. 1867. Royal Doulton
Minton Archive,
Stoke-on-Trent.

132
Minton & Co. art work for
vase no. 1310. Paris
International Exhibition,
1867. Royal Doulton
Minton Archive,
Stoke-on-Trent.

shapes, and exemplify Dresser's dictum that 'the ornament must tend to emphasise the beautiful quality of the object and not destroy the form'.

In his 'Japanese Ornamentation' articles Dresser had observed that the 'true condition of the surface decorated' should be considered most

carefully,[17] and his tobacco caddy adorned with a cicada design admirably illustrates this principle (plate 141). Another Japanese technique introduced by Dresser was the high-relief insect and grotesque decorations, beautifully demonstrated in three vases with, respectively, birds' heads, beetles, and dragons (plate 28). These vases were shown at Minton's stands in Vienna in 1873 and in Paris in 1878 and attracted considerable attention. It is rare to find such imagination and sense of constructive decoration in the nineteenth century. In fact this type of design became highly popular during the first decade of the twentieth century and is characteristic of the Art Nouveau style.

During the early 1870s Dresser became involved in Minton's Art Pottery Studio (1871–5) at South Kensington, which was under the directorship of William S. Coleman and employed several famous designers. Among them was John Moyr Smith, who had been trained in Dresser's studio between 1867 and 1871. The Studio was supported by the South Kensington Museum and the School of Design and launched some of the first art pottery in Britain. Dresser's endorsement of such pottery in the opening year was certainly influential. In his *Principles of Decorative Design* he recommended the use of the potter's wheel in preference to 'the fancy moulds of plaster':

> I have before me some specimens of Japanese earthenware, which are formed of a coarse dark-brown clay, and are to a great extent without that finish which most Europeans appear so much to value, yet these are artistic and beautiful. In the case of cheap goods we spend time in getting smoothness of surface, while the Japanese devote it to the production of art-effect. We get finish without art, they prefer art without finish.[18]

Dresser had some Bizen and Seto Japanese ceramics in his own collection,[19] but his enthusiasm for such unpretentious earthenware was unheard of at the time. More readily collectable antiquarian Japanese porcelain had dominated the European market, and Dresser's unorthodox views pioneered a marked change in the collector's pursuits. He emphasized that 'Japan can supply the world with the most beautiful domestic articles that we can anywhere procure', and it was the domestic Japanese ceramics showing 'bold art-effects' rather than 'excessive finish' which served

136
Opposite. Minton & Co. art
work for vase no. 1376.
1867. Royal Doulton
Minton Archive,
Stoke-on-Trent.

137
Josiah Wedgwood & Sons
dinner-plate. 19 March
1867. Nikolaus Pevsner
Papers, Getty Center for
the History of Art and the
Humanities, Los Angeles,
California.

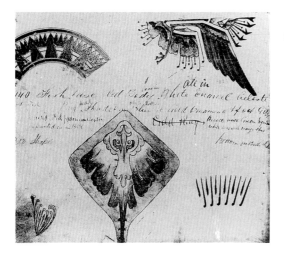

as models for Dresser's art pottery at Minton's and later at the Linthorpe Art Pottery.

George W. Rhead, a young apprentice at the Minton Studio and later co-author of *Staffordshire Pots and Potters*, recalled some of Dresser's work at this time:

Designs of a semi-humorous character, which, however, can scarcely be said fairly to represent his powers, which were very considerable. The

only example which remains in our memory is a small circular bottle with a flat surface, upon which was represented a rencontre of two cats on a garden wall, with a moon behind. . . .[20]

The 'semi-humorous' designs Rhead referred to have been preserved in the Royal Doulton Minton Archive. All are executed in the typical two-coloured style suitable for the Studio biscuit and underglaze colouring. They include the designs of cats meeting and parting, which were clearly inspired by Japanese studies of cats. This powerful design was adapted to Minton's pilgrim bottle vase (no. 1303), and exhibited at the London International Exhibition in 1871, together with a version of the 'enamelled birds' created for the same vase (plate 144). Dresser's designs for Minton's Art Pottery featured extensively at this exhibition, and included three seaux with 'grotesque ornament, frogs, flowers etc.', six cylindrical vases, and seven dinner plates.[21]

One of the frog designs has been preserved in the Minton archive; and the others were subsequently illustrated in the *Furniture Gazette* (plates 143, 145). Dresser repeatedly commended the frog motif. According to his daughter Nellie he had 'a thing about frogs'.[22] Indeed, the frog lent itself well to his so-called semi-humorous style. The six vases also incorporate animal and insect processions. A cat frieze entitled 'The Original Ethiopian Serenaders' and a configuration of bats called 'We are a Band of Brothers' harmonize perfectly with his Japanesque compositions of cranes, ducks, beetles, grasshoppers and other insects (plate 146).

The seven dinner plates show similar motifs of layered patterns, and incorporate ferocious cranes, beetles, crest patterns and stylized botanical elements (plates 119–122). Dresser's treatment of the Japanese system of interacting and overlapping patterns reveals his interest in schematization of form, a compositional technique which was to characterize his textile and wallpaper design (plate 152). This departure from orthodox decoration was typical of Dresser.

Some of Dresser's patterns for Minton's Art Pottery were also suited to textile patterns, and in fact two of his plates incorporating Japanese bamboo and 'autumn grasses' were adapted to his silk damask produced by James W. & C. Ward in the same year (plates 91, 147). Two striking Dresser patterns of cranes and other birds in the Oriental fashion were introduced in Minton's tiles in

140
Minton & Co. vases (left to right) nos. 1470, 1472, 1477. Late 1860s. Minton Museum, Royal Doulton Minton Co., Stoke-on-Trent.

1870, and were subsequently adapted to tableware and ornamental ware, some of which was produced at the Art Pottery Studio in London (plate 153). Several similar borders were executed at Minton's around this time (plate 148) and 'Dresser's Daisy and Butterfly' also adorned the frontispiece of his *Studies in Design* (plate 149).

In 1876 Dresser introduced a new range of production shapes at Minton's, with matching decorations in the cloisonné manner (plate 154). These inventive designs reflect some of his earlier shapes, such as the pilgrim bottle. Vases nos. 1904 and 1905 were adorned with a pattern entitled 'Night', featuring his favourite butterfly motif (plate 151). At the Philadelphia Centennial Exhibition in 1876 this cloisonné ware received international acclaim. Roger Soden Smith's report went so far as to place it on an equal footing with its Japanese prototypes:

141
Minton & Co. tobacco and tea caddies nos. 1471 and 1512. c. 5 in. high. Private collection.

'Fukihara and Minton, having run, so to speak, directly in competition, save in their designs, in the decoration of vases with cloisonné enamel' (plate 8).[23]

Encouraged by such recognition Dresser continued to adhere to this technique until at least 1886–7, when he designed a new series of shapes (Minton production numbers 2683–2705, 2774–2751, 2759–2760 and 2763). They combine several of the original forms he produced for Linthorpe Art Pottery some years earlier, and vases nos. 2683 to 2698 were also produced in biscuit with relief décor in the Japanese manner.

The 'Quick March' of cranes on vase no. 2692 shows another typical Japanese pattern (plate 157); the rest of the vases were adorned with decorations derived from various Oriental prototypes (plate 156). Vase no. 2763, for example, was inspired by a Japanese bronze candle-holder in Dresser's collection which was also reproduced by Benham & Froud (plates 155, 214). The layered floral pattern, produced in several different versions, was referred to as 'Dresser's chintz' motif in the Minton records (plate 158). His last recorded design for the company displays stylized waves, water-lilies and lotus flowers in his distinct Japonism style (plate 150). Avant-garde for their day, Dresser's designs for Minton's combine sophisticated artistic and industrial concepts in a way which still evokes admiration.

A similar combination of artistic and industrial techniques characterizes Dresser's designs for Linthorpe Art Pottery, Ault Pottery and Old Hall Earthenware Company. On stylistic grounds his

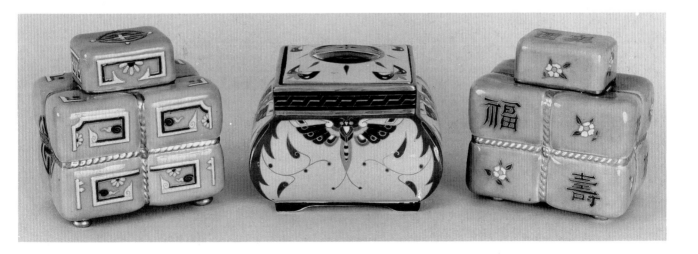

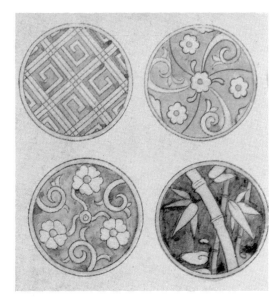

142
Minton & Co. art work
showing Japanese crest
patterns. Royal Doulton
Minton Archive,
Stoke-on-Trent.

144
Minton & Co. art work for
vase no. 1303. Dated 1871.
Royal Doulton Minton
Archive, Stoke-on-Trent.

143
Minton & Co. art work for
cylindrical vase. 1871.
Royal Doulton Minton
Archive, Stoke-on-Trent.

145
'Frog Frieze'. *The Furniture
Gazette*, 7 August 1880.
First produced by Minton &
Co. in 1871.

146
Minton & Co. art work
showing borders of
Japanese ducks, cranes,
beetles, grasshoppers and
various other insects. 1871.
Royal Doulton Minton
Archive, Stoke-on-Trent.

147
Minton & Co. art work for
two plates. *c.* 1875. Royal
Doulton Minton Archive,
Stoke-on-Trent.

148
Minton & Co. art work for
tableware. c. 1870. Royal
Doulton Minton Archive,
Stoke-on-Trent.

149
Minton & Co. art work
no. D. 2772 with 'Dresser's
Daisy and Butterfly'. 1876.
Royal Doulton Minton
Archive, Stoke-on-Trent.

150
Minton & Co. art work for
toiletware border. c. 1890.
Royal Doulton Minton
Archive, Stoke-on-Trent.

153
Opposite. Minton & Co. tile
with 'Dresser's tomtits'. 28
February 1870. Royal
Doulton Minton Archive,
Stoke-on-Trent.

151
Minton & Co. art work for
vase no. 1905. Royal
Doulton Minton Archive,
Stoke-on-Trent.

152
Minton & Co. art work for
tiles. c. 1871. Royal
Doulton Minton Archive,
Stoke-on-Trent.

name has also been linked with the Watcombe Terracotta Company. This pottery was founded in Torquay in 1869, using local terracotta clay, and continued in business until 1883.[24] Their products show distinct similarities with Dresser's designs for Minton's and Linthorpe's and occasionally incorporate ornamentation derived from his published works.

The square and angular teapots and jugs produced by Watcombe bear a close resemblance to Dresser's electroplate creations from the late 1870s, and one of their first products was a 'Japanese vase' taken directly from his *Principles of Decorative Design* (plate 106). This early unglazed Watcombe ware was called 'a triumph of the potter's art' by the American critic Arthur Beckwith in 1871, and set the pattern for similar pottery production in the United States.[25]

Some of the glazed Watcombe ware, which was introduced some time between 1875 and 1876, has motifs taken from Dresser's *Studies in Design*. The glazes were likened to Japanese glazes when shown at the Philadelphia Exhibition in 1876, and both the decorations and the shapes were frequently derived from Japanese prototypes and other exotic sources such as Greek, Egyptian and Islamic pottery (plate 159). A tray of Watcombe terracotta incorporating Dresser's typical stylized border and Japanesque bird motif was presented to the National Museum in Tokyo in 1876, and can still be seen there today.

The Old Hall Earthenware Company was founded in 1861, but it is uncertain when Dresser joined the firm. In 1884 he supplied a series of dinner-services named Persian, Shanghai and Hampden, which were produced as octagonal shapes and variously marked with Dresser's facsimile signature (plate 107). The services correspond with the ones described in *The Studio* article on Dresser as having a 'simple addition of hollows in the rim of the plate, such as a potter might make with his "thumb"'.[26] These were intended for salt, mustard and other condiments.

An Old Hall jug registered with the Patent Office in 1881 shows Dresser's unorthodox play with geometrical forms and is similar to a drawing he sent to Linthorpe that year (plates 161, 163). Other jugs and vases with distinctive Dresser patterns were also produced by the company in the 1880s, and further research on their production may shed new light on Dresser's specific designs (plate 5).

Much more is known about Dresser's produc-

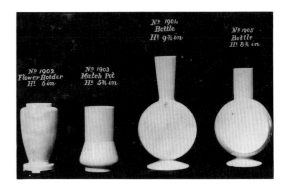

154
Minton & Co. vases nos. 1902–1905. Minton & Co. Shapebooks, Royal Doulton Minton Archive, Stoke-on-Trent.

tion for the Linthorpe Art Pottery, which was founded in Middlesbrough on Tees in August 1879.[27] Dresser had lectured on Japanese art in Middlesbrough in November 1878 and become friendly with John Harrison, the owner of the Sun Brick Works on the Linthorpe estate. Concerned at the high unemployment in the region, Dresser suggested to Harrison that brick clay could be more profitably adapted to pottery production. Thus the Linthorpe Art Pottery was established, under Harrison's directorship and with Dresser as art director and his assistant Henry Tooth as master potter. The venture was a great success. It provided employment for some hundred people and pioneered some of the first art ceramics in Britain.[28] Dresser later recalled that his first experiments at Linthorpe were inspired by Doulton's production of domestic salt-glazed stoneware,[29] but his sophisticated shapes and glazes far surpass Doulton's more commercial productions.

Linthorpe pottery was inexpensive and produced on a large scale, reaching production no. 4196 before the factory was closed down on John Harrison's death in 1889. The majority of the pieces bear mould numbers as well as the name LINTHORPE, together with Dresser's facsimile signature and Henry Tooth's initials. Some pots also carry the initials of the decorators: Fred Brown, William A. Burns, William Davidson, Sheldon Longbottom, Thomas Hudson, Lucy Worth and Richard W. Patey. Patey took over the works when Dresser and Tooth ceased their connection with the firm in 1882.[30] Dresser's signature seems to have been affixed to most shapes up to about no. 1700, but the fact that some pots are entirely unmarked and that his influence was felt even after 1882 has caused some confusion (plate 160). To further complicate the matter, Henry Tooth reproduced some of Dresser's shapes when

155
Minton & Co. art work for
vase no. 2763. c. 1887.
Royal Doulton Minton
Archive, Stoke-on-Trent.

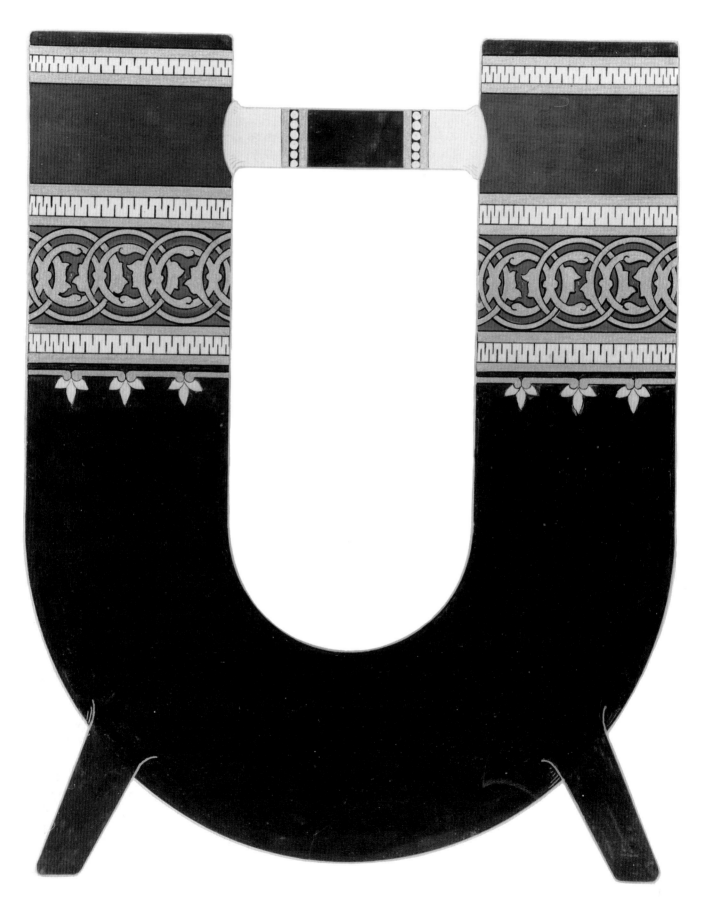

he founded the Bretby Art Pottery with William Ault in 1883, and Ault in turn acquired most of the Linthorpe moulds when these were publicly auctioned in July 1890.[31] Ault had set up his own pottery in 1887 and Linthorpe shapes with Dresser's signature impressed were soon put into production; some vases were painted in the faience manner by Ault's daughter Clarissa. Dresser was formally engaged by Ault in 1894, and the *Cabinet Maker* noted that 'in many of the forms there is evidence for Dr. Dresser's great knowledge of and predilection for Oriental models' (plate 108).[32] The Bretby and Ault potteries were acclaimed by contemporary critics and won several medals at international exhibitions, but they could not compete with the Linthorpe Art Pottery, which led the field in Britain during the 1880s.

Linthorpe Art Pottery gave concrete form to Dresser's belief that art can transmute the commonest materials into things of beauty, and convey 'the bold sketchy touch of the modeller's hand'. Their pots were first formed on the potter's wheel before receiving the finishing touches in a wooden mould. It was only after the first biscuit firing that painted decorations and glazing were applied, using such novel equipment as spray colour producers and gas ovens, said to have been the first in the country.[33] The essence of Dresser's Linthorpe pottery lay in its rich glazes, and its almost sculptural quality, which reveals his skill in creating shapes. The secret of the glazes was well guarded, but the materials seem to have been similar to those used in stained glass, mixed with flint or granite, which was ground for a week before it was ready for the glazing trough. Cornish clay and oxidate tints were then added and the colours were allowed to mingle in unusual, haphazard running patterns during the final firing, 'producing rich mottled and semi-translucent enamelled effects, very suggestive of some of the best methods of the Japanese', according to the *Art Journal's* critique of Linthorpe in 1880.[34]

The Linthorpe Art Pottery was launched at Dresser & Holme's sale room in London in November 1879. The *Furniture Gazette* critic welcomed it as 'A Novelty in Art Pottery'; he divided the pots into three main groups: about 150 samples of the plain-coloured ware, exemplified by a particularly beautiful double-gourd vase (plate 109), then the incised, pierced and relief pots (plates 110, 111), and lastly the ware 'enriched with bold paintings of flowers and birds in enamel colours' which appeared somewhat conventional,

156
Opposite. Minton & Co. art work for vase no. 2695. Royal Doulton Minton Archive, Stoke-on-Trent.

157
Minton & Co. art work for vase no. 2692. c. 1886–7. Royal Doulton Minton Co., Stoke-on-Trent.

'while in some few instances whimsical and grotesque shapes impart to them a Japanesque character' (plate 184).[35] Altogether there were some hundreds of pots. In the words of its trade brochure, Linthorpe Art Pottery offered the opportunity 'To people of moderate means, of possessing a vase or other objects equal in colour and decorative effect to the best Persian, Chinese, or Japanese productions, but at vastly less cost'.[36] Advertising material from the year 1880 confirms that these samples dominated Linthorpe's first range of production, which ran to about no. 400 (plate 162), but the models of Celtic, Egyptian, Greek, Mexican, Rhodean and Peruvian ceramics illustrated in Dresser's *Principles* also had a marked influence on his designs (plate 185).

The playful use of historicist sources is apparent in Dresser's sketches for Linthorpe Art Pottery dated 29 August 1881, which were photographed by Nikolaus Pevsner and are the only records extant (plate 163). They reveal the same daring combination of geometrical forms and angular handles as Dresser's metalware from the time, but it is uncertain whether all these eccentric shapes were put into production at Linthorpe. Some of the pots have been located, however, such as vase no. 827, which represents the middle range of his designs for Linthorpe (plate 186). From the same period are also some coffee and tea sets which are startling in their simplicity.

Contemporary commentaries compared Dresser's Linthorpe Art Pottery to Japanese ceramics,

158
Minton & Co. art work for border. c. 1887. Royal Doulton Minton Archive, Stoke-on-Trent.

159
Watcombe Terracotta Co. jugs and teapots. Glazed. Attributed to Dresser, c. 1875.

and indeed the two existing photographs of the Pottery show the walls hung with Japanese silks and pictures.[37] Although shapes and decorations were freely adapted from various historical sources, there is a marked tendency towards Japonism, and Dresser's studies of ceramics during his visit to Japan were of paramount importance for his Linthorpe creations. Probably the most influential source were the ceramics produced by Makudzu Kozan, whose 'Makudzu ware' was known as the most experimental pottery in Meiji Japan. One of the first Japanese artists to adapt Western techniques, Makudzu launched a complicated method of firing fifteen colours in one process beneath the glaze. When in Japan Dresser visited Makudzu's pottery and later described his celebrated glazes and relief techniques:

In most of his trials he used modelled flowers upon his vases. When I visited the pottery at Ota [near Tokyo] he was busily engaged upon some fine works of this character, as well as with the formation of large pots with which to delude the American buyer. But it was at the last Paris Exhibition that we saw this great potter in his strength; and he certainly showed himself as one of the giant ceramic workers of the world.[38]

160
Linthorpe Art Pottery
plate no. 1700. c. 1882. 6 in.
diam. Victoria & Albert
Museum, London.

Equally important for Dresser's creativity were his visits to the Awaji potters, whose products had been shown in the international exhibitions in Vienna in 1873 and in Philadelphia in 1876. He particularly liked their 'plain-yellow, brick-orange, full-green, and warm-purple' colours, and samples were acquired for Tiffany's and for Dresser's own collection, some of which inspired his first production for Linthorpe Art Pottery.

Dresser's observations on Japanese ceramics and pottery techniques in *Japan, its Architecture, Art and Art-Manufactures* were of great service to Linthorpe. A man of his own time, it was the contemporary and domestic ware above all which interested Dresser, but the ancient Japanese striated and running glaze techniques were also influential on his creations for Linthorpe and Ault.

Another source of inspiration were the Kyoto potters. Dresser praised the rustic wares of the Raku, Shigaraki and Iga potteries, and some coarse

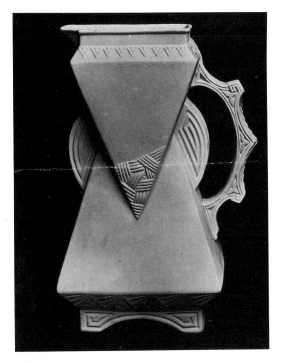

pottery with incised decoration produced by Mashimizu Zoraku. Rokubei Kiyomizu III's 'exceedingly crude' ware with 'a rich granite-like effect of colour, green, red, and black mingles' appealed to Dresser's taste, as well as Sawamura Tosa's 'crude heavy ware' decorated with 'curious rough leaves of the Buddhist lotus'.[39] This granite-like colouring and lotus leaves in relief are frequently found on Dresser's Linthorpe ware (plate 187).

Among other Japanese pottery acquired by Dresser for Tiffany's, and for his own collection, were the celebrated Banko, Shiba and Arita wares. He was also enthusiastic about the Mino pottery, whose domestic ware was 'rather like soap, being brown, grey and white mingled together in a tortuous and striated manner'. Certain documented Seto vases, such as the vase with 'fantastic frog scenes' which Dresser bought in Japan,[40] and other samples acquired by the South Kensington Museum from the Philadelphia Centennial Exhibition in 1876, inspired some of his most inventive Linthorpe vases (plate 188).

Dresser paid particular attention to the mottled Kishiu glazes, and these were adapted to his Linthorpe pottery. According to the *Pottery Gazette*: 'The "yellow mottle" was [just] such a perfect reproduction of a lost Japanese effect . . . A Japanese jar was under observation when the peculiar

blending of two colours on a background was noticed' (plate 6).[41]

Dresser's designs, however, were not slavish copies of Japanese prototypes. The similarities were striking and even baffled specialists but, as Robert Lee observed, the influence was a two-way affair:

It is interesting to note that the Japanese were large buyers of the products of Linthorpe. The love of such productions is probably inborn in this Eastern nation, world-famous craftsmen in such manufactures, and it was natural that the officers of Japanese steamers, coming regularly into the Tees for cargo, bought and were commissioned to buy considerable quantities of Linthorpe Ware, which were taken back to Japan where, presumably, much still remains. It has been stated, however, that some of these Japanese purchases of Linthorpe Ware have found their way back to Britain as Japanese Ware.[42]

The pottery expert Llewellyn Jewitt visited Linthorpe in 1880 and gave two accounts of the Pottery, which are included in his book, *Ceramic*

163
Opposite. Page from
Dresser's account book for
1881, showing designs for
Linthorpe Art Pottery.
Nikolaus Pevsner Papers,
Getty Center for the
History of Art and the
Humanities, Los Angeles,
California.

Sep. 3rd. Sent to J. Dixon + Sons. 6 Claret Jugs. 2 Ice Tongs 4 Spoons. 9 Toast Racks. 1 Toast Rack with Cruet. 1 Tea Set.

Art in Great Britain (1883). He was impressed by their production output and by the quality of the glazes:

> The peculiarity of this ware lies, of course, in the marvellous and never ending effect of the Linthorpe glaze, and the peculiar mode of treatment adopted in the preparation and arrangement of the colours . . . The gradation of tones, and the gradual blending and merging of one colour into another; the soft mossy or tufa-like appearance of some, and the close resemblance to harder materials in others; the richness, glow, and fullness of colour of this, and the subdued and aesthetic tints of those, are all equally pleasing to the eye.[43]

By 1882 interest in art pottery had developed to such an extent that the Royal Society of Art decided to arrange an exhibition of 'Modern English Pottery' featuring works by Brown-Westhead & Moores, Doulton, Maw, Minton, Wedgwood, Worcester and Linthorpe. Linthorpe ware appears to have been the highlight of the exhibition and was singled out for praise by the *Graphic Journal*:

> The great feature of the exhibition is a magnificent collection of the new Linthorpe Art Pottery, which more than any or even all the rest, emphasises the great advance which we Britishers have made in these matters during recent years. The collection consists of nearly every possible and useful ornamental object, from a flower-pot to a Tazza, from the humble water-bottle to the stately vase. But its interest consists not so much in its variety, though that is noteworthy enough, as in the extraordinary beauty of its colours and the

brilliance of its glazes. It is not too much to say that this Linthorpe Ware is quite a new feature in European pottery, for in depth, richness, variety, and glorious beauty of colour it is only matched by the splendid wares of the East.[44]

Linthorpe Art Pottery created a name for itself in its day, and achieved world-wide fame at the international exhibitions in Calcutta in 1883 and in New Orleans in 1884, when Dresser's designs were still in production. However, the later pots are marked by a certain stiffness in shape and excessive overall incised decorations, which Dresser would never have sanctioned, and the pottery fell into decline in the late 1880s.

Dresser's focus on art products, and in particular his work for Linthorpe Art Pottery, helped to raise the status of pottery. From being a functional commodity it came to be considered art proper. Pottery items became collectable objects and were integrated into the aesthetic interior as decorative elements. When the Linthorpe Pottery went into liquidation in 1889 the *Pottery Gazette* mourned its passing and described it as 'almost the pioneer in the way of inexpensive pottery'.[45] It surpassed its many competitors in both design and execution and there is no doubt that Dresser and his Japanese-inspired creations were instrumental in its success:

> At the time Linthorpe Pottery was established the influence of Japan on English decorative art was very great. Dr. Dresser having constituted himself the high priest of the cult, it is to be expected that where he has any influence, Japanese style and decorations would play a considerable part. This was the case of Linthorpe Pottery. . .[46]

METALWORK
SIMPLICITY
AND
FUNCTION

Dresser designed some of the most forward-looking metalwork to emerge from the nineteenth century, and it has aptly been compared to the twentieth-century products of the Wiener Werkstätte and the Bauhaus. There is the same geometrical simplicity and contained functional feel, but Dresser's style is more organic and reflects his studies of plant and animal forms. He was particularly concerned with the economic use of costly metals, and with constructional honesty, even to the extent of exposing the rivets.

His first recorded metalwork products from 1865 were regarded as progressive novelties and clearly challenged the elaborate naturalism and historicism prevalent in Victorian silver objects, which were falling out of favour:

> It is gratifying to hear that an effort is about to be made by an influential house to get rid of them, and to replace them by something better. Messrs. Elkington have long had in preparation a class of goods for these purposes, from designs by Dr. Christopher Dresser, and which, in point of manufacture, will come between the costly beaten work and the meretricious common ware which, dignified by the general denomination of 'plate', have been accustomed to adorn the tables of our middle class at many a surburban villa.[1]

The *Building News* critic was referring to Dresser's first designs for Elkington's electroplated silver. The company had registered a patent for the gilding of metal objects using electrolysis in 1840. Dresser had praised their techniques and designs in 1862,[2] but he probably did not supply designs for them until the mid-1860s. His connection with the firm has erroneously been dated to about 1873,[3] but even a cursory examination of the Elkington pattern books, although these are incomplete, would indicate an earlier date. His clean-cut shapes are easily distinguishable in the company's records from about 1866–7 and comprise a tea-kettle, a centre-piece and a tripod sugarbowl. The kettle resembles his designs for Minton's of the mid-1860s (plate 126), and rudimentary sketches of the centre-piece and sugarbowl appear in his sketchbook from that time (plate 14). The beads in the sides of the sugarbowl had a functional purpose according to Dresser's *Principles of Decorative Design*: 'Instead of forming a vessel throughout of thick metal, we may construct it from a thin sheet of silver, but in order that it possess sufficient strength we must indent one or more beads in its side.'[4] (See cover illustration.)

Dresser's review of the Paris Exhibition revealed that he found much to admire in Japanese metalwork and that he particularly liked the Japanese bronze teapots. He tried to persuade English manufacturers to produce tea-services in bronze, but was unsuccessful.[5] His sketchbook contains drawings of kettles and 'sugar basins of bronze' with beads on the sides and angular legs (plate 14). These were reproduced in his 'Principles of Decorative Design' articles of 1871 and fulfil his demand for steadiness and functionalism.[6] They may well have been produced in electroplate by Elkington's to match Dresser's Japan-inspired teapot of 1867, but they have not been traced in the company's early records and occur only in a pattern book of 1885.

164
Elkington & Co. enamel
doorplate. 3 February 1866.
Public Record Office,
London.

Dresser's sketchbook has remained a major source for identifying some of his unknown metalware, and contains a number of specifications for teapots, enamel work, and even door furniture, which was probably produced by Elkington's in the late 1860s and during the 1870s. The company's first cloisonné doorplates were in fact registered with the Patent Office in 1866, and show distinct Dresser features, such as scroll and entrelac motifs similar to those included in his Jeffrey wallpapers of 1867 (plate 164).

Although no other enamel designs by Dresser

for Elkington's have been found, he was most certainly involved in its first production of cloisonné ware shown at the Paris International Exhibition in 1867, and described as 'quiet and discreet'.[7] Dresser had admired similar qualities in Japanese enamels,[8] and he illustrated several enamel patterns in his 'Japanese Ornamentation' articles of 1863, but he was more of an instigator than a promoter of the fashion. Elkington's cloisonné became highly popular in the 1870s and 1880s, but most of their designs have been attributed to the firm's art directors, Leonard Morel-Laudeil and Antoine Wilms.

Dresser's first metalware was mainly in electroplated silver, a medium which met his requirement for inexpensive materials. A tureen in the Elkington pattern books from 1869 reveals his predilection for simple shapes, straight legs and angular handles, which became the principal characteristics of his metalwork designs (plate 165). The severely geometric form of the tureen, stripped of all ornament, is surprising for its time and established Dresser's highly personal style.

Dresser's admiration for Japanese teapots and other cooking vessels clearly inspired his original metalwork, and his review of the Vienna International Exhibition in 1873 expressed regret that 'while the kettle is an object of use in every house in the land, we have to go to Japan to learn how to make one as it should be'.[9] He marvelled at the variety of materials and eccentric shapes used in Japanese metalwork, and he was particularly intrigued by the exposure of rivets and joints of various metal belts. The 'square kettles and round kettles and polyhedric kettles' shown in Vienna provided the impetus for several of his teapots produced by Elkington's in 1885 (plates 166, 167, 168). A number of them, and some of the claret jugs designed in the same year, incorporate belt-like formations and exposed constructions, and show an almost organic sense of form and texture (plate 169). The attention to functional details such as substructures, handles and spouts was unexpected for the 1880s, but was typical of Dresser's metalwork. His sources were certainly the Japanese art metalwork imported by Londos and Dresser & Holme in the 1870s, but above all he was inspired by the objects he studied during his tour of Japan in 1876–7 (plate 22).

During his stay in Japan Dresser had the rare privilege of inspecting the Imperial collections in the 'Shosoin' treasure-house in Nara and in the Imperial palace in Kyoto. He profited greatly from

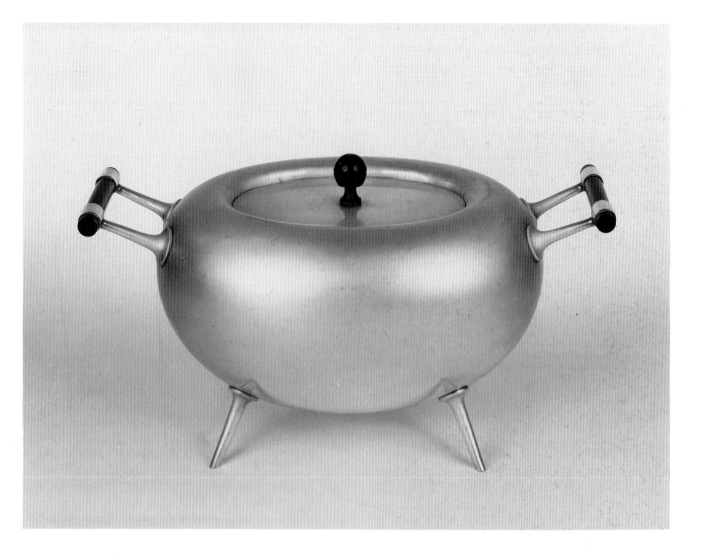

the guidance of the director of the National Museum, Machida Hisanari, who was a connoisseur of Japanese metalwork and pottery. In his book on Japan, Dresser recalled the splendour of the repoussé and damascene works shown to him in Nara. He was particularly struck by the beauty of a modest water-jug whose spout was raised to the top of the orifice and covered by a flat lid, and by a heater for saké.[10] These objects inspired some of his first heating vessels and decanters for Elkington's and Hukin & Heath in 1879–84 (plates 169, 170, 190). Perhaps even more striking is the similarity between some of the undecorated metal objects in the Shosoin and Dresser's own designs, such as the tureen and ladle produced by Hukin & Heath in 1880 (plates 171, 172). These designs show the 'breadth of treatment, simplicity of execution, and boldness of design'[11] which Dresser had praised in Japanese metalwork.

165
Elkington & Co. electroplated tureen no. 12780, with ebony handles. Dated 1869. 8 in. high. Private collection.

It was this simplicity rather than the elaborate encrusting and mixture of metals (mokumé) which influenced Dresser's electroplate designs, and his creations are far removed from the imitative reproductions which soon became popular in Britain. British Assay laws prevented the use of mixed metals amalgamated or combined with gold or silver, and Dresser avoided all but the simplest material and decorations in his designs. His almost aggressively smooth finish and unexpected forms have no precedent in Western tradition of design, and in *Principles of Decorative Design* he condemned contemporary pastiches and looked to the East for new models:

Modern European silversmiths have fallen into the error (an error now prevailing wherever art can be applied to any object) of making their works of a pictorial, rather than an ornamental,

166
Elkington & Co.
electroplated teapots
nos. 16611 and 16675.
Maker's mark and date
cipher for 1885. $4\frac{1}{4}$ in. high.
Fine Art Society, London.

167
Opposite. Elkington & Co.
electroplated teapot
no. 17912 with stand.
Maker's mark and date
cipher for 1885. $11\frac{1}{4}$ in.
high. Private collection.

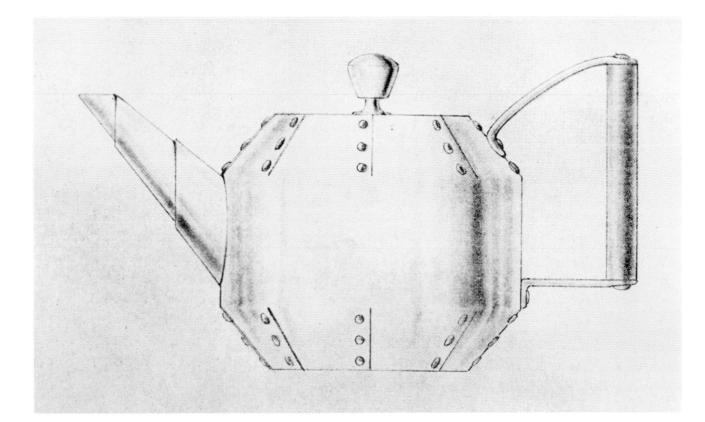

168
Elkington & Co.
electroplated teapot.
c. 1888. *The Studio*, Vol. xv,
1899, p. 111.

169
Elkington & Co.
electroplated claret jugs
(left to right) nos. 16594,
17558 and 17556. 14 April
1885. $8\frac{1}{2}$–10 in. high.
Maker's mark and date
cipher.

170
Elkington & Co. 'Komai'
patterned tea-set in solid
silver. 1884–5. Private
collection.

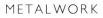

171
Hukin & Heath
electroplated tureen and
ladle, with ivory handles.
Marked 'Designed by Dr.
C. Dresser'. 28 July 1880.
9 in. diam. Private
collection.

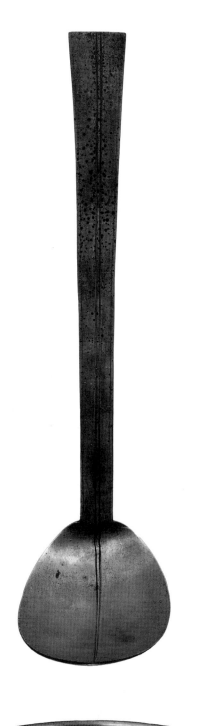

172
Japanese bronze bowl and ladle. 17th century. Shosoin National Treasure House, Nara, Japan.

character – an error the Arabians, Indians, and Japanese never perpetrate, whose works in metal are unsurpassed by any, and equalled by few.[12]

Dresser's marked bias in favour of the Japanese was noted by the *Art Journal* critic when Hukin & Heath launched their Dresser designs in 1879:

Their Art adviser and guide is Dr. Dresser, under whose educated taste and practical experience they have procured a large collection of singularly excellent Art works, vast improvements on the 'have beens' of earlier times and fully meeting all requirements in the present state of Art progress. They have done this without increasing the cost of such articles, supplying ample evidence of the principle long ago advocated by The Art Journal, and in a measure adopted as its motto, that 'beauty is cheaper than deformity.' We have examined with very great satisfaction the articles to which we direct public attention, and it is our duty to accord to them a high praise, not only to co-operate with the able and liberal manufacturers, but to encourage others to do likewise. So much is public taste advancing among all classes, poor as well as rich, that ere long 'a thing of beauty' only will be found in all our factories and shops . . . They have acted under the advice of a competent Art teacher – there are few better – and they ought to, as they surely will, reap a productive harvest from the seed so skilfully planted and cultivated. The works of their own special trade are those we admire most; many of them are positive studies of grace combined with the useful – simplicity and purity in form with readiness of application to the purposes to which they are to be applied. Messrs. Hukin & Heath reproduce several of the Persian and Japanese Art works with accuracy unsurpassed – perfect copies indeed – by the electric process; such specimens, being selected for reproduction by Dr. Dresser, are of course always beautiful examples of Art.[13]

J.W. Hukin and J.T. Heath had registered their trademark in 1875, and Dresser was involved in some of their first productions. Pevsner noted that Dresser had sent some admirable designs for cruets to the company in October 1877,[14] but these were not entered in the Patent Office Design Registry until 31 July and 8 October 1878 (plate 173). They were part of the new range introduced by Dresser

Hukin & Heath
electroplated cruet set
with glass containers.
Designed in 1877 and
registered with the Patent
Office Design Registry on
31 July 1878. Nikolaus
Pevsner Papers, Getty
Center for the History of
Art and the Humanities,
Los Angeles, California.

174
Hukin & Heath
electroplated tea-set
no. 1888. Marked
'Designed by Dr. C.
Dresser'. 6 May 1878. 7$\frac{1}{2}$in.
high. Private collection.

between 10 April 1878 and 9 May 1881, comprising all kinds of domestic electroplate from cruets, tea-sets, glass-stands, egg-boilers, toast-racks, to decanters etc. Most of these early works were marked 'Designed by Dr. C. Dresser' (plate 174), but subsequent designs were more often unmarked and Dresser continued his connection with the company even after it changed its name to Heath and Middleton (1887).

Preliminary drawings for some of these items have been preserved in Dresser's sketchbook, notably drawings of the kettles, egg-boilers and other objects produced by Hukin & Heath in May 1878. Japanese influence and concern with functional aspects are particularly apparent in three tea-sets registered with the Patent Office on 26 March 1879 (plates 175, 176, 177). Their crest patterns and foliage decorations in the Japanese style provide an elegant alternative to Dresser's usual smooth surfaces. The strict geometrical shapes, straight legs, spouts and angular handles bring to mind the polyhedric Japanese vessels Dresser had admired in Vienna in 1873. A range of cruets, condiment sets, glass-stands and toast-racks produced in 1878 and based on similar geometrical shapes (plates 178, 191) were perhaps inspired by Japanese metal and lacquer stands. Strangely they also bring to mind the fences, railings and temple-gates (torii) which Dresser had studied while in Japan.

175
Hukin & Heath solid silver
tea and coffee sets with
incised Japanese crest
decorations. Marked
'Designed by Dr. C.
Dresser'. 26 March 1879.
5–8in. high. Private
collection.

176
Hukin & Heath
electroplated tea-set
no. 2103, with incised
Japanesque decoration.
Marked 'Designed by Dr.
C. Dresser'. 19 October
1879. Tokyo National
Museum of Modern Art.

177
Hukin & Heath
electroplated picnic tea-set
nos. 2109 and 2110. Marked
'Designed by Dr. C.
Dresser'. 19 October 1879.
Private collection.

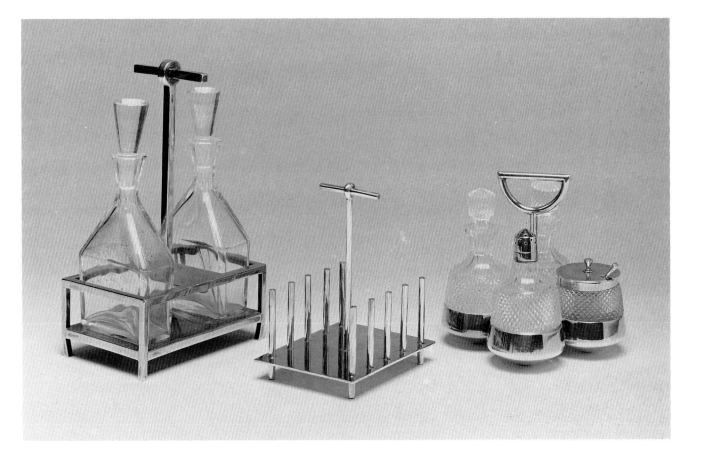

178
Hukin & Heath
electroplated cruet sets
and toast-rack (left to
right) nos. 1953, 1987 and
2239. Marked 'Designed by
Dr. C. Dresser'. 8 October
and 12 November 1878.
5¼–8in. high. Fine Art
Society, London.

179
Elkington & Co.
electroplated cruet sets
nos. 17286 (left) and 17282.
28 March 1885. 5–7 in. high.
Fine Art Society, London.

A similar set of designs was supplied to Elkington's in 1885 (plate 179).

The glass containers included in Dresser's electroplate were probably produced by the Tees Bottle Company of Middlesbrough, which is known to have supplied 'artistic glass' to the Art Furnishers' Alliance between 1880 and 1883.[15] Even more original was the glass incorporated in Dresser's decanters produced by Hukin & Heath between 9 October 1879 and 9 May 1881 (plate 190). A preliminary drawing for one such vessel appears in his sketchbook, together with a centre-piece annotated 'all dishes and the entire frame to revolve' (plate 180), which was registered with the Patent Office Design Registry on 9 May 1881. A set of toast-racks incorporating similar atom-like joints suggestive of Dresser's scientific interests (plate 181) was also registered at that time.

Equally ahead of their time are some egg-coddlers and spoon-warmers from 1884–5, showing Dresser's typical 'crow's feet' and Japanesque straight handles (plate 182). A tankard with a bamboo handle and lacquer decoration, produced by Hukin & Heath, was based on a Japanese vessel imported by Dresser & Holme (plate 199). A similar tankard was also produced by Elkington's at

180
Opposite. Hukin & Heath
centre-piece with revolving
dishes, shape no. 2508.
Attributed to Dresser. 9
May 1881. 10¼ in. high.
Private collection.

this time, probably from Dresser's design.[16] Dresser's penchant for Japanese metalwork clearly inspired the extreme simplicity of his designs for Hukin & Heath, especially his last works for them dated 1892–4, which include a set of elongated decanters (plate 200), a candle-holder and a tea-set, all of which are unsigned (plates 201, 202, 203).

Perhaps more than any other Victorian designer, Dresser mastered the clean-cut and simple vernacular suitable for mass production, and his designs provided exemplary models for the reform movement among British metalworkers. However, his output in this field was probably too revolutionary and at times was regarded as rather eccentric. This was certainly the case with a range of radical designs supplied for James Dixon & Sons in 1879, which were produced in a very limited number both in pure silver and in electroplate. They reflect Dresser's fascination with polyhedric Japanese tea-kettles and include three tea-sets, six tea-kettles and a decanter (shape nos. 2272–2281) and six sugarbowls (nos. 131–6), all marked with his fac-simile signature. Dixon's 'Costing-book' of 1879 has disappeared, but photographs of the book taken in 1972 remain a useful source of identifying Dresser's designs.

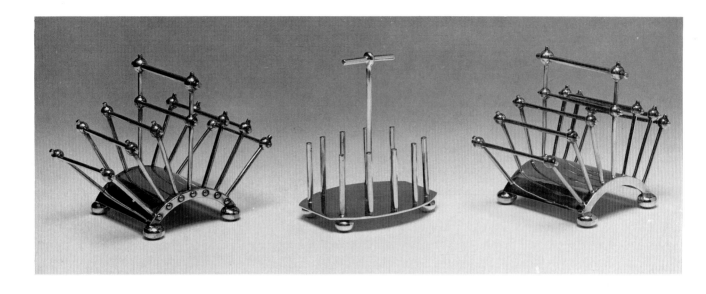

These quasi-geometric shapes show his progressive ideas at their best and look forward to the designs of the twentieth century. Tea-set no. 2272 brings to mind Dresser's dissections of plant forms (plate 204), whereas nos. 2273 and 2278 are strictly geometrical and based on drawings in his sketchbook (plate 205). Another spherical tea-set was produced by Elkington's in 1885. This innovative shape was perhaps one of Dresser's most popular silver designs. Teapot no. 2274 was called 'English Japanese' in Dixon's catalogues (plate 206); and no. 2276, a pleasing wheel-shaped teapot, was probably based on 'a remarkable wheel-formed Japanese teapot' which was sold at Sotheby's in July 1879 and attracted widespread admiration

181
Hukin & Heath
electroplated toast-racks
(left to right) nos. 2556,
2566 and 2655. 1881. 5in.
high. Fine Art Society,
London.

182
Hukin & Heath
electroplated egg-coddlers
and spoon-warmer with
ebony handles, (left to
right) shape nos. 2693, 2857
and 2887. 8in. high. Fine
Art Society, London.

(plate 207).[17] The angularity and constellation of forms in shape nos. 2274 and 2280 constitute some of the most original designs that ever emanated from Dresser's studio (plates 206, 208). All combine mechanical skill with an artistic merit unsurpassed by any of Dresser's contemporaries.

Shirley Bury, who examined the Dixon archive in 1962, was amazed by Dresser's knowledge of industrial processes. She listed some 37 of his designs in production between 1879 and 1882,[18] including decanters (production nos. 2546 to 2259), cruet sets (nos. 2393–2396) and a conical tea-set (plate 209).

Nikolaus Pevsner illustrated some of the original drawings for toast-racks, claret jugs, spoons, ice

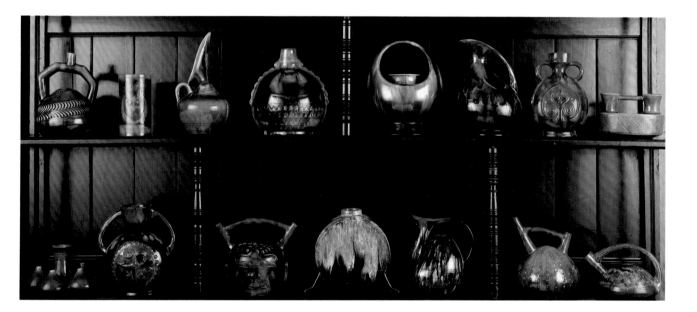

183
Page 161. Linthorpe Art
Pottery tea caddy with
Japanese dragon and wave
pattern in relief. *c.* 1880.
9¼ in. high. Private
collection.

184
Opposite. Linthorpe Art
Pottery vase no. 439 and
plate painted with flowers.
Private collection.

185
Linthorpe Art Pottery
vases (left to right)
nos. 330, 337, 296, 331, 347,
312, 335, and (above) 227,
175, 346, 248, 228, 341, 336,
314. *c.* 1880. 5¾–18¾ in.
high. Private collection.

186
Linthorpe Art Pottery (left
to right) nos. 602, 890, 576,
646, 639, 827. c. 1881. 3¾–
11¼ in. high. Private
collection.

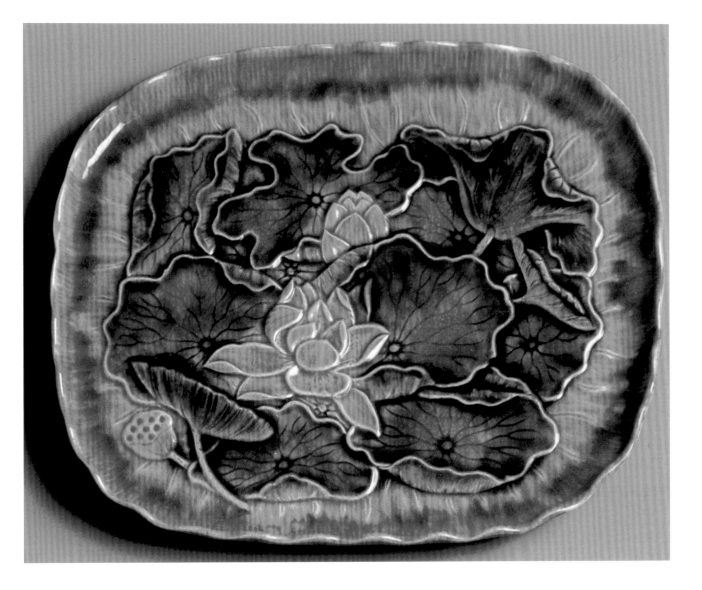

187
Linthorpe Art Pottery tray
no. 441 with relief
decoration in the Japanese
style. c. 1880

188
Linthorpe Art Pottery nos.
246, 178, 424, and frog bowl
from Dresser's own
collection c. 1880.
5¼–12¼ in. high. Private
collection.

189
Opposite. Schemes for
interior decoration, dado,
frieze, filling, cornice and
ceiling papers from
Dresser's *Principles of
Decorative Design*, 1873,
pl. II.

190
Hukin & Heath glass and
electroplated decanters
with drinking glasses
no. 2105 (19 October 1879)
and no. 2509 (9 May 1881).
3½–11 in. high. Fine Art
Society, London.

191
Opposite. Hukin & Heath
condiment set no. 1936.
Marked 'Designed by Dr.
C. Dresser'. 11 April 1878.
Fine Art Society, London.

192
Benham & Froud brass and
copper trays and kettles.
c. 1882–5. Private
collection.

193
Richard Perry, Son & Co.
'Kardofan' candle-holder.
30 October 1883. 11 in.
high. Private collection.

194
Clutha glass made by James
Couper & Sons. c. 1883.
$3\frac{1}{2}$–16 in. high. All marked
'Clutha designed by C.D.
Registered', with Liberty's
lotus flower trademark.
Private collection.

195
Opposite. Clutha glass
produced by James Couper
& Sons. 1880. 4–24 in. high.
Some marked 'Clutha
designed by C.D.
Registered', with Liberty's
lotus flower trademark.
Private collection.

196
Opposite. Clutha 'solifleur'
glass vase made by James
Couper & Sons. *c.* 1883.
10 in. high. Marked 'Clutha
designed by C.D.
Registered', with Liberty's
lotus flower trademark.
Private collection.

197
Stained-glass skylight in
Bushloe House entrance
hall, Leicester. *c.* 1880.

199
Hukin & Heath bamboo
tankard with electroplated
fittings and lacquer
decoration in Japanese
style, shape no. 2936. 1888.
6½ in. high. Private
collection.

198
Opposite. Stained-glass
window in Japanese style in
Bushloe House, Leicester.
1880.

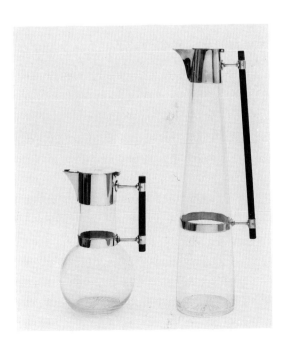

200
Hukin & Heath decanters
with electroplated fittings
and ebony handles.
Attributed to Dresser,
1892. 10–17in. high. Private
collection.

tongs, and tea and coffee sets Dresser sent to James Dixon & Sons in 1881 (plate 163). A number of these items have been found in recent years. Daring in their day with their inventive geometrical shapes, they still seem revolutionary (plates 210, 211). Indeed, Pevsner called Dresser one of the 'Pioneers of Modern Design'.

Dresser's designs for brass, copper and cast iron objects formed an essential element of his artistic interiors. The range of his designs included candle-holders, kettles, trays, coalboxes in mixed metals, cast iron furniture, stoves, andirons and fireplace surrounds. The nineteenth century has been called 'the new iron age' – a reference to the Industrial Revolution – and indeed, without iron and the new machinery the making of goods in brass, copper and other metals could never have reached such a high level of production. In the first part of the century copper was largely employed for utilitarian and kitchen articles, but in the 1860s it was replaced by enamelled iron. This reduced the risk of copper poisoning, and was better suited to modern gaslight fittings and other decorative art objects. Designers were quick to adapt brass, copper and iron to new purposes, and the increased import of mixed metal objects from the East, and especially from Japan, soon made its impact. By the 1870s objects made of iron, copper and other metals had become a colourful part of the aesthetic interior.

Dresser is known to have replaced 'the fireplaces, gas and other fixtures' when he decorated the interiors of Allangate Mansion in 1870. The drawing room is described as having been lit 'by means of delicately designed standards of polished brass copied from Grecian temple lamps'.[19] Such a lamp, produced by Benham & Froud, was illustrated in *The Studio* article on Dresser, and may well have originated from as early as 1870 when Dresser is first mentioned in connection with the firm (plate 212). However, other objects illustrated in the article were made for the Art Furnishers' Alliance's show of 'works in iron, brass and mixed metals' and date from 1882.[20]

Photographs of the Benham & Froud objects have been preserved among the company's papers now in the Chubb archives (plate 213), and it has been suggested that some of them were produced by Chubb's, but Dresser in fact supplied only metal hinges, locks and safes to this company. Several of the Benham & Froud items show the belt-like formation of various metals and the exposed rivets Dresser praised in Japanese metal-

work, and one of the candle-holders was an almost exact replica of one he brought back from Japan in 1877 (plate 214 and frontispiece).

Other designs for Benham & Froud, such as a sophisticated brass and copper coffee pot, and an egg-shaped ewer with a looped handle, reveal Persian and Moorish inspiration (plates 192, 215). The combination of geometrical shapes and the strange angularity of the spouts are characteristic of Dresser. A Japan-inspired brass and copper kettle with

201
Hukin & Heath electroplated candle-holder with stopper and ebony handle. 1894. 8½ in. high. Metropolitan Museum of Art, New York.

a wrought-iron stand (plate 216) was described by Pevsner as having a 'Pre-Art Nouveau rhythm'.[21] Indeed, many of Dresser's designs contain elements which were to achieve prominence around the turn of the century. Dresser generally preferred the use of the less expensive cast iron, but in *Principles of Decorative Design* he suggested the use of wrought iron – previously reserved for outdoor gates, railings and other fixtures – in interior decoration.[22] This was to launch a fashion for artis-

202
Hukin & Heath
electroplated tea-set with
stand and burner.
Attributed to Dresser,
1894. 5–10 in. high. Private
collection.

tic ironwork lamps and kettles in British homes.

In *Principles* Dresser had recognized the high quality of repoussé, damascene and inlaid metalwork produced in Arabia, India and Japan, and endorsed the Japanese fashion for inlaying silver and brass in copper.[23] His book on Japan paid considerable attention to these sophisticated techniques: 'In no country in the world has damascening been carried on to such perfection as in Japan . . . Damascening, chasing, hammering, inlaying, and combining metals are means by which they achieve effects, as well as by careful use of textures.'[24]

Dresser's intricate inlaid trays and plaques produced by Benham & Froud combined brass, copper, lead and electroplate, rather than silver, because British Assay laws forbade the mixture of silver or gold with base metals (plate 192). These delicate works in the Japanese style were probably made for the Art Furnishers' Alliance exhibition

in 1882, but he had previously produced repoussé panels for Benham & Froud coalboxes in 1878 (plate 217). One critic praised six Benham & Froud coalboxes – called Sutton, Victoria, Marlborough, Kingston, Richmond and Negron – 'from the fertile pen of our old friend Dr. Dresser', to whom he attributed much of the firm's success over the last decade:

No firm has done more to adorn the chimneypiece with art work than Messrs. Benham & Froud Ltd. They were the first among those who saw the opportunity, and used it, to lift the coal-box and the fitments of the grate from the decrepitude into which they had, some years ago, fallen. Taking only the coal-box, which is our present concern, it is wonderful what has been evolved from the garish, meretricious, and really dreadful things of the last generation (plate 218).[25]

203
Hukin & Heath
electroplated kettle with
wicker handles. Attributed
to Dresser, 1895. 8¼ in.
high. Private collection,
Australia.

204
James Dixon & Sons silver
teapot, shape no. 2272. 25
November 1880. $4\frac{1}{2}$ in.
high. Private collection.

205
James Dixon & Sons
electroplated teapots with
ebony handles, nos. 2273
and 2278. 25 November
1880. $4\frac{1}{2}$–$5\frac{1}{2}$ in. high. Fine
Art Society, London.

206
James Dixon & Sons
electroplated teapot with
ebony handle, shape
no. 2274. 25 November
1880. c. 9 in. high. Fine Art
Society, London.

207
James Dixon & Sons
electroplated teapot with
ebony handle, no. 2276. 25
November 1880. 5 in. high.
Württembergisches
Landesmuseum, Stuttgart.

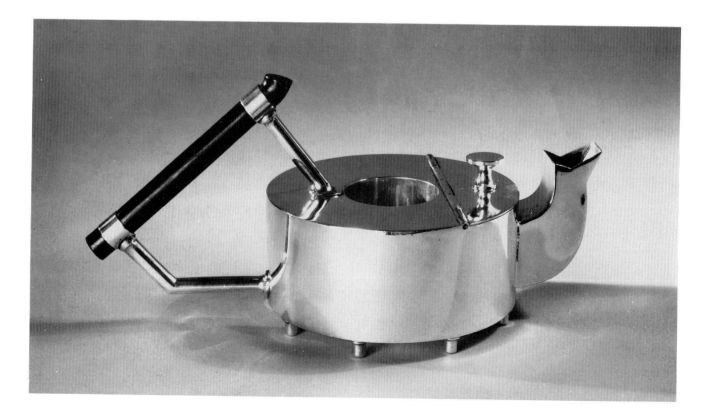

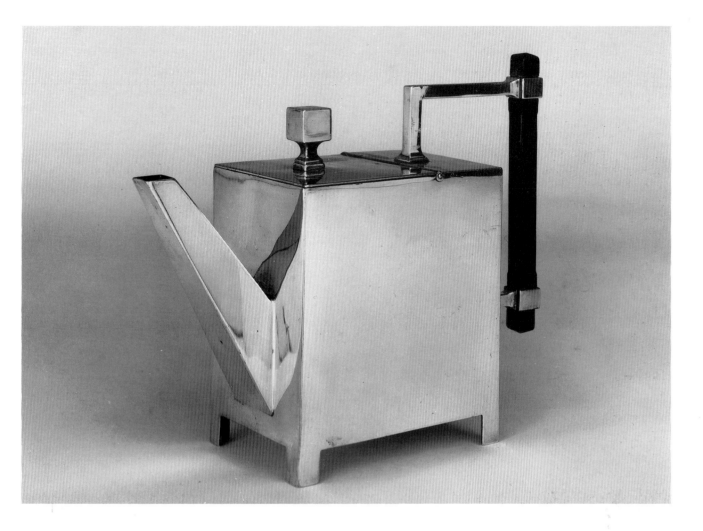

208
James Dixon & Sons tea-
kettle with ebony handle,
no. 2280. 25 November
1880. 9 in. high. British
Museum, London.

209
James Dixon & Sons
electroplated teapot with
ebony handle, shape
no. 2294. 1881. 8½ in. high.
Private collection.

210
James Dixon & Sons
electroplated toast-rack
with ebony handle, shape
no. 963. 25 November
1880. Fine Art Society,
London.

211
James Dixon & Sons
electroplated toast-racks,
shape nos. 67, 65, and 66.
Signature and date cipher
for 1880. $5\frac{1}{2}$ in. high. Fine
Art Society, London.

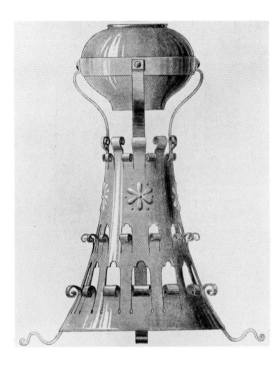

212
Benham & Froud lamp in
copper and brass. Probably
made about 1870. *The
Studio*, Vol. xv. 1899, p. 112.

213
Benham & Froud candle-
holders, trays and kettles in
brass and copper. c. 1882.
Chubb & Sons Archive,
London.

214
Japanese brass and copper
objects acquired by the
South Kensington Museum
from Londos & Co. and
from Dresser's widow.
Victoria & Albert Museum,
London.

215
Benham & Froud copper
and brass ewer with looped
handle. c. 1882–5. 11 in.
high. Private collection.

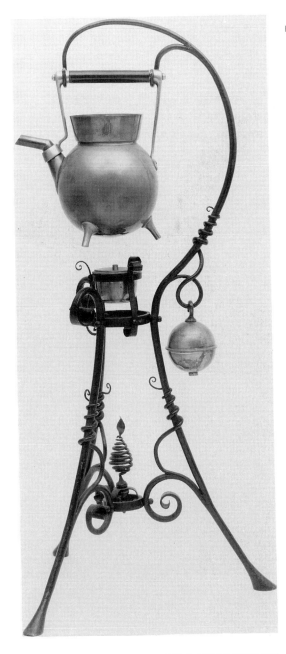

216
Benham & Froud brass and
copper kettle with ebony
handle and wrought iron
stand and burner. c. 1885.
Total height c. 32 in.
Private collection.

218
Benham & Froud wooden
coalbox 'Richmond', with
metal decoration. *The
Furniture Gazette*, 1
October 1886, p. 347.

217
Benham & Froud wooden
coalbox with repoussé
panel in Japanese style.
1878. Public Record Office,
London.

219
Richard Perry, Son & Co.
tinned iron ewer in red and
black, with looped handle.
Marked 'Dr. Dresser's
design'. Probably produced
in 1876. 14 in. high. Private
collection.

220
Richard Perry, Son & Co. spun copper jug with electroplated bands and ebony handle. Marked 'Dr. Dresser's design'. c. 1876–80. 9 in. high. Private collection.

dating seems primarily to be affixed to the Kardofan candle-holder registered and retailed by Arthur Liberty in 1883 (plate 193). This popular candle-holder was produced in large numbers and frequently tinted in Liberty's so-called 'aesthetic colours' – turquoise, red, yellow and green. It may have been created by Dresser exclusively for Arthur Liberty, and the daring combination of hemispherical forms prefigures the purity of the Cymric silver and Tudric pewter designed by Archibald Knox, who may have been a student of Dresser's.[26] These Gaelic or Celtic-sounding products, like Dresser's 'Clutha' glass, were devised to cater for the resurgence of nationalism in art, but their names were entirely spurious and probably invented by Liberty's.

Dresser's designs for Richard Perry, Son & Company are all based on a sophisticated play with geometrical forms such as the square, triangle,

222
Richard Perry, Son & Co. brass candle-holder. Marked 'Dr. Dresser's design'. 1880s. Private collection.

Dresser was among the first designers in Britain to promote the use of these colourful metalwork objects in interiors. His designs for the Wolverhampton firm Richard Perry – famous for its japanned and tinned iron, a fashionable product during the early nineteenth century – included some pleasing tinned iron ewers and candle-holders, as well as works in brass and copper (plates 219, 220). Some of these items, however, are marked with conflicting registration numbers for 20 January 1876 and 30 October 1883. The latter

hexagon, cone and sphere, which are frequently contrasted and bound together by a straight or curved handle (plates 221, 222). Devoid of excess ornamentation these clean-cut shapes exemplify Dresser's tenets of constructional honesty and purity. Above all, they convey his concern with creating objects which were 'capable of giving pleasure to the poor man – if appreciative – who may possess it, as well as the rich'.[27] *The Studio*, which showed many of his works in brass and copper in 1899, emphasized the 'strenuous efforts of Mr. Dresser to raise the national level of design, not by producing costly bric-a-brac for millionaires, but by dealing with products within the reach of the middle classes, if not the masses themselves.'[28]

221
Richard Perry, Son & Co. tinned iron candle-holder in red and black, with stopper and wooden handle. Marked 'Dr. Dresser's design'. 20 January 1876. 5¼ in. high. Private collection.

ART GLASS AND THE LUMINOUS MATERIAL

The nineteenth century was a period of great industrial and artistic expansion, and there was an increasing interest on the part of both manufacturers and collectors in the glass of the ancient world – Egyptian, Islamic, Roman and particularly Venetian – leading to a revival of earlier styles and techniques. The emergence of this new glass, frequently called aesthetic or art glass, can be compared to that of art pottery. It developed from the simple formation of the material per se but led to ever more surface embellishing, and to the production of so-called fancy glass in the latter part of the century.

Art glass stood in sharp contrast to the popular lead crystal and cut glass which had been so criticized by John Ruskin. He believed that cut glass violated the molten nature of the material and advocated a revival of Venetian glass methods.[1] Other arbiters of design reform such as Dresser, Charles L. Eastlake and William Morris[2] championed this revival, and in their time Venetian glass was imported in quantities and provided a valuable source of inspiration.

Dresser was one of the first writers on design to acknowledge the contemporary progress in glass-making under Venetian influence. His *Development of Ornamental Art in the International Exhibition* of 1862 devoted an entire chapter to 'Glass for Decorative and Household Purposes'. He praised the 'exceeding advantage of the simplicity of treatment' apparent in the glass exhibited by James Powell & Company and by J. Lobmeyr of Vienna, and endorsed the 'rapid progress' in glass-making which, he said, stemmed from a renewed respect for the molten material:

It will be found that whenever the true susceptibilities of a material are sought out, and the endeavour is to produce beauty by the mode of working which is most befitting to the peculiar mode in which the material is worked, that the manufacture progresses in art.[3]

Few if any materials, maintained Dresser, lent themselves more readily to this purpose than glass and clay, and he stressed the similarity between the glass blower's rotating of the pipe and the potter's work at the wheel. Both methods involved the most appropriate recognition of natural laws and brought about shapes that were beautiful, simple and functional. Indeed it was this kind of scientific interest which inspired Dresser to launch a set of principles conducive to the development of art pottery and art glass in Britain. They were first treated as fully fledged subjects in his articles on 'Principles of Decorative Design' in 1871. Here he had expressed admiration for the complicated scientific techniques which underlie the working of glass – later to materialize in his own glass designs. In accordance with the doctrines of art furniture and art pottery he voiced a preference for bold artistic effects, rather than excessive finish, in the production of glass. He cited his sources of inspiration as Greek, Roman and Venetian prototypes and recommended only a limited use of cutting and engraving, stressing the importance of appropriate working methods: 'Glass has a molten condition as well as a solid state, and while in the molten condition it can be blown into forms of exquisite beauty . . . for the operation of gravitation and similar forces upon plastic matter is calculated to give

223
Clutha glass vase with four
small handles. Green
streaked with blue. 1880.
Victoria & Albert Museum,
London.

beauty of form.'[4] An illustration of a simple hock-bottle, described as a mere elongated bubble, 'with the bottom portion pressed in so that it may stand, and the neck thickened by a rim of glass being placed around it' led Dresser to the consideration of fitness of purpose, which was one of his favourite topics. His set of principles on bottles and decanters were much ahead of their time and have remained pertinent to this day:

> A bottle is only intended to be filled once, whereas a decanter will have to be filled many times; and a bottle is formed so that it may travel, while a decanter is not meant to be the subject of long journeys. . . . All objects which are meant to be refilled many times should have a funnel-shaped mouth, but if a bottle had a distended orifice it would not be well adapted to transport. . . As most decanters are intended to hold wine, the brilliancy of which is not readily apparent when that portion of the vessel which contains the liquid rests immediately upon the table, it is desirable to give to the vessel a foot, or in other words, raise the body of the decanter so that light may surround it as fully as possible.[5]

In order to fulfil all the practical requirements for such domestic glass vessels, Dresser repeated his dictum that spouts and handles should be placed in accordance with the centre of gravity. The illustrations of jugs and decanters in *Principles* were used as practical examples of his argument (plate 224).

Dresser is known to have designed a number of similar glass containers for his electroplate-mounted decanters, cruets and condiment sets produced by Elkington's, James Dixon & Sons and Hukin & Heath from about the late 1870s onwards, and he may well have been engaged in glass-making when he published his articles on glass in 1871. Numerous drawings of decanters and bottles in his sketchbook from about 1861 to 1875 suggest that this was the case, but until recently the makers have remained unknown.

The bottles and containers for his electroplate designs, however, were almost certainly produced by the Tees Bottle Company of Middlesbrough on Tees. The scant information available about this company confirms that it had a depot in London by 1879,[6] and that in 1880 it launched its 'new artistic glass' at the opening of Dresser's Art Furnishers' Alliance in New Bond Street, London.[7] The Tees Bottle Company supplied a

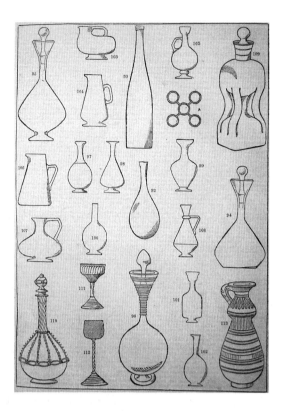

224
Glass shapes from *The Technical Educator*, Vol. II, 1871, p. 25.

number of goods to the Alliance between 1880 and 1883, and Dresser may well have instigated the contact when he visited Middlesbrough in 1878. We know that most of the goods marketed by the Art Furnishers' Alliance were designed by its art director, Dresser, and we may therefore surmise that he was the master of the 'new artistic glass' made by the Tees Bottle Company.

Dresser's major contribution to the production of art glass stemmed from his understanding of the technical aspects of glass blowing. His acquaintance with novel techniques of manufacturing made him aware of wholly new colours and textures, and in *Principles of Decorative Design* he describes the aesthetic appeal of coloured glass:

> Glass is capable of assuming the most delicate of shades, of appearing as a soft, subtle, golden hue of the most beautiful light tertiary green, lilac, and blue and indeed, of almost any colour . . . A dinner table requires colour. Let the cloth be pale buff, or cream-colour, instead of white; and the glass water-vessels of very pale, but refined and various tints; and the salt-cellars, if of glass, also coloured, in a tender and befitting manner, and a most harmonious effect will be produced.[8]

In this way Dresser prepared the way for art glass, just as he had earlier paved the way for art furniture, art pottery and art interiors. His own designs for Clutha glass, produced by James Couper & Sons of Glasgow, are typified by a daring use of colours combined with hand-blown and industrial manufacturing techniques.

Brian Blench, the authority on James Couper's glass, recently suggested that Dresser first became interested in the company's production of St Mungo glass, which was a Venetian-inspired material used by stained-glass artists in the 1860s and 1870s. He believes that Dresser's Clutha glass was made some time in the late 1870s or early 1880s.[9] The subtle colouring of St Mungo glass does indeed accord with Dresser's theories on stained glass, and his windows for Allangate Mansion and Bushloe House may well incorporate this material.

St Mungo glass was in fact used by Dresser's student, John Moyr-Smith, in his interiors for Stirling's library, built in Glasgow in 1865, but sadly these have been destroyed.[10]

It has proved impossible to pinpoint the date of the first production of Clutha glass, but Blench's hypothesis seems reasonable. Dresser's daughter Nellie provided the date of 1880 for two pieces of Clutha glass from her father's collection donated to the Victoria & Albert Museum in 1952 (plate 223). She also said that her father made a few designs for his friend Arthur Liberty's company in 1882.[11] Among these were certainly the Clutha glass vases retailed by Liberty's from about this time (plate 194), and described as 'Decorative, Quaint, Original and Artistic'.[12]

Liberty was a main shareholder in the Art Furnishers' Alliance and took over many of its products, including Dresser's Clutha glass, when it went into liquidation in 1883. Arthur Liberty had recognized the potential of the Alliance and of Dresser's designs, and he appears to have organized his own company after much the same pattern in 1883, when he opened his Furnishing and Decorating Studio.[13] Dresser's Kardofan brass candle-holder and his Clutha glass were among Liberty's most popular products and exemplify the purity of form which was to characterize the Liberty style during the first part of the twentieth century.

It has been suggested that the name Clutha was derived from the Gaelic word for 'cloudy', but in fact it was probably invented by Liberty's, as were the names of Dresser's Kardofan candle-holder

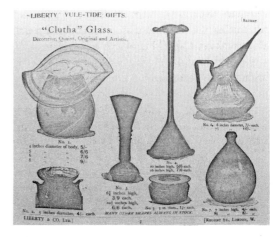

225
Clutha glass made by James Couper & Sons in Liberty's 'Yule-Tide Gifts Catalogue', 1895.

and Archibald Knox's later Cymric silver and Tudric pewter. As noted in the previous chapter, these Gaelic or Celtic-sounding names were intended to promote the idea of a national art. Clutha glass was in fact frequently set in Tudric pewter during the late 1890s.

The Clutha glass retailed by Liberty's was marked with the company's lotus flower trademark and bore the words 'Clutha, Designed by C.D. Registered' (plate 225). A few pieces with James Couper & Sons' mark have been traced but, confusingly, most samples appear without marks. Some of these unmarked ones have been identified among the goblets and jugs photographed by Nikolaus Pevsner from Dresser's account book for 1881 (plate 163).

Clutha glass is deliberately bubbled and streaked in daring shades of colour. Dresser's favourite 'greenery-yallery' scheme seems to prevail, but secondary and tertiary colours of amber, lilac, purple, pink, turquoise etc. were also incorporated separately or in a perfect fusion of tints.

During the 1870s methods were developed in Britain whereby vessels with several colours could be made. The technique, which involved the infusion of coloured particles into the glass while it was exposed to heat, gave a seemingly faulty disposition of colour, causing patches or streaks of different tints (plate 194). Dresser was among the first designers to adapt the technique, and his Clutha glass frequently displays irregular patterns in lighter and darker shades, and occasionally the multi-colour effect of 'solifleur' (plate 196). More regular combed and spiral patterns were also produced (plate 226), but the seminal importance of Clutha glass was that it reproduced Roman and

Venetian aventurine and murrhine effects by permeating the coloured glass with irregular metallic streaks or foils. This gave it a jewel-like brilliance which had not previously been seen in Britain. The technique rapidly became popular and earned Clutha glass an international reputation (plate 227). A kind of bubbled, speckled and frosted Clutha glass with lustre patches in the antique fashion was a late product of the company. It was probably introduced by the Glasgow architect-designer George Walton, who replaced Dresser as chief designer at Couper's in 1896, but continued to produce the kind of glass and shapes popularized by Dresser.

There are as many shapes as there are colours in Dresser's Clutha glass, and no two pieces are identical. Frequently characterized by attenuated necks with furled or wavy rims, Dresser's vases have been compared to his dissections of flowers, and clearly some of the shapes owe much to his artistic botany (plate 228). Others relate to his ceramic designs, for instance the twisted vase inspired by Japanese Tamba pottery and the Pre-Colombian-shaped Clutha bottle illustrated in *The Studio* in 1899.

Tall-necked Japanese, Persian and Indian water-sprinklers acquired by the South Kensington Museum in the 1870s and 1880s also inspired some of Dresser's elongated and slightly bent vase-necks (plate 227), while others again reveal his penchant for the Oriental gourd and ninepin shapes (plate 195). His jugs incorporate the angular handles which predominate in the designs photographed by Pevsner in 1937 (plate 163). In some cases, a decorative effect of horizontal trailing is applied to his vases (plate 229).

The machine which enabled these glass threads to be applied to the vessel had been patented by William J. Hodgetts in 1876, and Dresser's Clutha glass demonstrates his delight in such inventions. Conceived in an antiquarian spirit, but revealing novel techniques, colours and textures, Clutha glass was soon produced on a solid commercial footing, providing an impetus to the production of much late nineteenth-century art glass.

Sowerby's art glass was exhibited next to Clutha glass at a special show organized by the Art Furnishers' Alliance in 1882. The show attracted considerable attention in the art press and the critic of the *Cabinet Maker* announced:

A new kind of glass of English manufacture which in point of artistic merit and originality

226
Page 194. Clutha 'green' glass vase with spiralling grooves, produced by James Couper & Sons. 9 in. high. Marked 'Clutha designed by C.D. Registered', with Liberty's lotus flower trademark. Private collection.

227
Page 195. Clutha 'amber' glass vase with metallic foils in murrhine technique, made by James Couper & Sons. 19¼ in. high. c. 1883. Marked 'Designed by C.D. Registered', with Liberty's lotus flower trademark. Victoria & Albert Museum, London.

promises to rival the finest examples of the old Venetian glass-blowers. The specimens on view will be large and important decorative works, which are in no degree imitative, but have a character essentially original as regards design and treatment and are far more improving than the examples of glass-blowing with which we have hitherto been familiar.[14]

Some of the first Clutha and Sowerby art glass measured up to 65 centimeters in height, and their shapes, colours and textures show distinct similarities. It has been suggested that Dresser was involved with Sowerby's production, but he was probably more of an inspiration than an instigator.[15]

It was around this time that William Morris first expressed his views on art glass. He was certainly well aware of the Clutha and Sowerby art glass and his recommendation of plain hand-blown glass with 'specks and streaks' seems to echo Dresser's. Morris never designed any art glass himself, but he probably inspired Philip Webb to create the plain and simple table glass which was produced by James Powell & Sons and retailed by Morris, Marshall, Faulkner & Company.[16]

The simplicity of Webb's glass in fact matched that of Dresser's Clutha glass, and set the pattern for Powell's subsequent glass production, such as the pale green glass designed by Thomas Graham Jackson and Harry Powell's 'art nouveau' glass, which featured regularly at the Arts and Crafts Exhibitions.[17] Clutha glass was shown next to Powell's at these exhibitions and the two were frequently compared by the critics. This kind of glass was deemed to be the result of individual craftsmanship rather than the product of commercial industry, hence the generic term art glass.[18] Plain and simple art glass was in considerable demand during the 1880s and 1890s, and the designer Lewis F. Day in his articles on 'Victorian Progress in Design' noted that it was 'in the graceful forms of blown glass that our recent advance is most evident'.[19] The expansion of the cut-glass industry, however, frequently inhibited this progress, and in 1882 the *Pottery Gazette* told its readers: 'The age of plain glass is gone or going, and cut and engraved glass is fast coming in again, in spite of Dr. Dresser and Oscar Wilde.'[20]

There was certainly a revival of interest in some of the more elaborate types of glass production and decoration in the late 1880s, but the soundness of Dresser's principles and the success of his Clutha

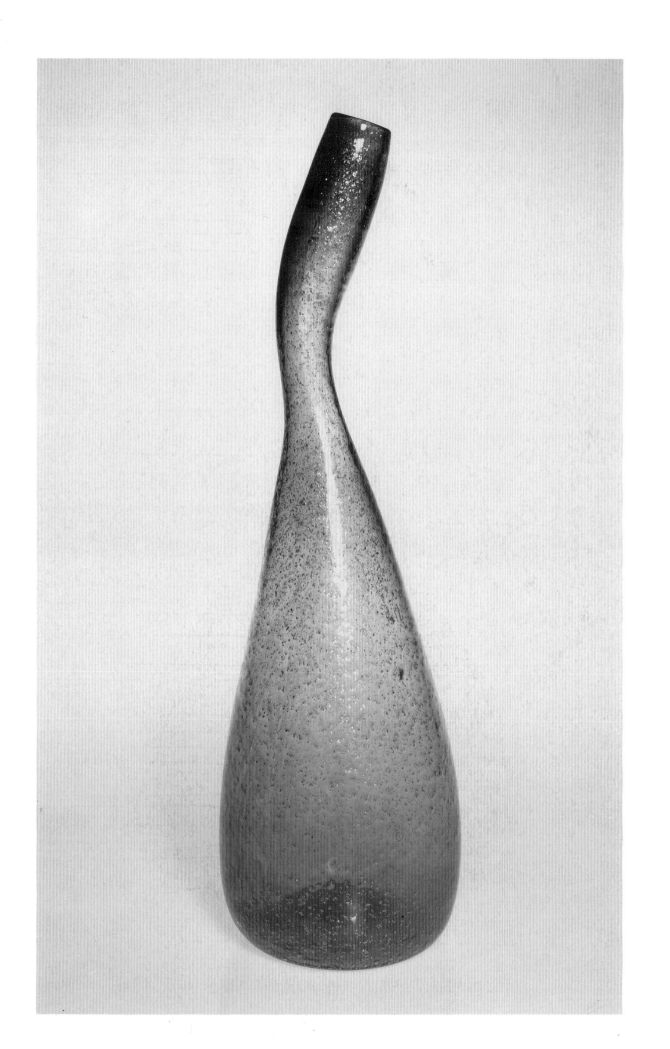

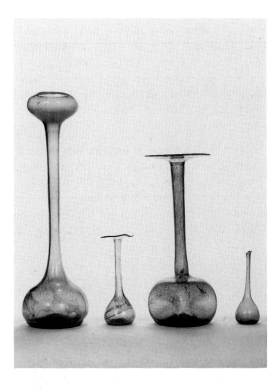

228
Clutha glass vases with
aventurine streaks made by
James Couper & Sons.
c. 1883. 5–16¾ in. high. All
marked 'Designed by C.D.
Registered', with Liberty's
lotus flower trademark.
Private collection.

glass windows in the figurative style. This revival of an old art was greeted with enthusiasm and soon inspired Dresser and other British artists to experiment with innovative patterns and techniques. Dresser's interest had also perhaps been kindled by his tutor Octavius Hudson, who in the 1840s had catalogued a number of medieval stained-glass cathedral windows.[22]

Dresser's principles were governed by his belief in two-dimensionality and in stylized ornamental forms, which led him to reject much of the figural and religious character of Pre-Raphaelite stained glass:

> A window should never appear as a picture with parts treated in light and shade. The foreshortening of the parts and all perspective treatments, are best avoided, as far as possible. I do not say that the human figure, the lower animals, and plants must not be delineated upon window glass, for on the contrary, they may be so treated as not only to be beautiful, but also to be a consistent decoration of glass; but this I do say, that many stained windows are utterly spoiled through the window being treated as a picture, and not as a protection from the weather and as a source of light. If pictorially treated subjects are employed upon window glass, they should be treated very simply, and drawn in bold outline without shading, and the parts should be separated from each other by varying their colours.[23]

Thus, according to Dresser, even a design for stained glass embraced practical aspects. He decreed that 'strong colours should rarely be used in windows'. In fact he advocated the same colour scheme which he had employed in his Clutha glass: 'Tints of cream yellow, pale amber, light tints of tertiary blue, blue-grey, olive, russet, and other sombre or delicate hues, enlivened by small portions of ruby or other full colour'.[24]

The stained-glass patterns illustrated in *Principles of Decorative Design* show the schematic stylization which characterizes much of Dresser's ornamentation. Two of the designs were derived from the patterns of frost on a window pane in winter and are reminiscent of his designs from the late 1860s (plate 230). In 1870–1 a similar pattern was incorporated in his stained glass for Allangate Mansion, later included in his *Modern Ornamentation* (plate 232). This kind of abstract formal design, maintained Dresser, represented what stained glass 'may advantageously be'. He also

glass continued to play an important role in British glass-making. It may well have prompted Thomas Webb & Sons to produce a similar range of art glass called 'Old Roman', which in 1888 led to a complaint from James Couper's alleging deliberate copying and infringement of their copyright.[21] Certainly under Dresser's influence British glassware attained an expressive character, which was based on the consistency of molten glass and the varying refraction of colour and light, a similar effect to that obtained in stained glass.

Dresser devoted a whole chapter to stained glass in his *Principles of Decorative Design*. Seeking historical precedents, he looked back to the medieval techniques and methods advocated by Pugin, Ruskin and Morris. These disciples of the art of the Middle Ages had discarded the painted windows of later times, and returned to the use of flat areas of coloured glass bounded by dark lead lines.

The Gothic designs of Pugin were highly popular in the 1850s but by the 1860s Morris is known to have been experimenting with a different kind of stained-glass production. He encouraged his friends Edward Burne-Jones and Ford Madox Brown to realize the new ideas, and towards the end of the decade Morris, Marshall, Faulkner & Company launched its Pre-Raphaelite stained-

229
Clutha glass vase made by
James Couper & Sons.
c. 1883. 13½ in. high.
Marked 'Designed by C.D.
Registered', with Liberty's
lotus flower trademark.
Private collection.

the aim of letting light into the room, but stained glass was also used for decorative purposes in his interiors. At Allangate Mansion for instance he inserted four stained-glass medallions of female heads personifying morning, noon, evening and night on the wall between the drawing-room windows:

> These medallions are so arranged that whilst during the daytime they are lit up from without in the same manner as ordinary stained glass windows, in the evening they can be illuminated by means of powerful gas jets fixed behind, with extremely novel and charming effect.[27]

This ingenious scheme thus focused attention on the tinted glass even at night, and provided warmth and colour to otherwise barren areas of the interior. In fact Dresser pioneered this kind of decorative

illustrated some borders and centre squares of glass, which could be combined with plain windows (plate 231). The same conventionalized and spiky leaves featured in his skylight windows for Bushloe House (plate 197). Dresser particularly recommended stained glass as a means of brightening the sombre atmosphere of Victorian halls and corridors which, wrote an American writer, 'only need colored glass to throw a charm over the entire interior, the depth of the hall giving that vista which so appropriately terminates in the play of light and color'.[25] Dresser's distinctly linear and ornamental stained glass differed fundamentally from the more figural and naturalistic windows created by the Pre-Raphaelites and by his student John Moyr Smith. The latter adhered to Dresser's Japonism, but his style is far more floriated and pictorial.[26]

Even Dresser's Anglo-Japanese stained-glass windows were created according to his principles, with the centre panels in subdued colours surrounded by borders highlighted by small strips of primary colours. The centre panels often incorporated owls and other birds, as well as butterflies and fishes, combined with flowers and leaf patterns, and resemble motifs used by Dresser in other media (plate 198).

Primarily, Dresser's windows were created with

230
Stained-glass window pattern in Dresser's
*Principles of Decorative
Design*, 1873, fig. 183.

Fig. 152.

Fig. 151.

Fig. 147.

Fig. 149.

Fig. 150.

Fig. 153.

Fig. 148.

Fig. 154.

use of stained glass in the aesthetic interior, and his various schemes for its application were a natural development of his emphasis on the integration of the different forms of art in a single setting. Like his schemes for rooms decorated in various colours and styles, his stained-glass windows were also designed to match specific types of interiors.

Dresser's views on stained glass gained considerable popularity in the later 1870s and during the 1880s. His ideas even reached America through the work of Charles Booth, a stained-glass artist from Liverpool who emigrated to New York in 1875.[28] Booth's writings and designs adhered remarkably closely to those of Dresser, and he and Louis Comfort Tiffany became the main instigators of the stained-glass fashion in the United States.

Dresser and Tiffany had met at the Philadelphia Exhibition in 1876, and Tiffany soon embraced many of Dresser's ideas. The large collection of Japanese artefacts which Dresser collected for Tiffany's on his visit to Japan included numerous window enamel screens, referred to as 'glass screens' in the catalogue.[29] Dresser claimed to have introduced Japanese window enamels to the West,[30] and their luminous quality evidently inspired his own designs, as well as the first Japanesque stained-glass windows created by Tiffany in 1877–8.

The two friends, Dresser and Tiffany, played a key role in popularizing artistic stained glass, and it soon became an all-consuming interest in America and Britain. An American critic in 1882 described the transformation which had taken place:

> Many years ago stained glass windows would have suggested to the vulgar mind a dim religious light, but modern fashion decides that light transmitted through colour is pleasanter and more artistic than the full glare of the white light of the day and so . . . handsome houses today are all more or less decorated in it.[31]

Dresser's principles on glass and stained glass achieved widespread acceptance through his association with Tiffany, who in the 1890s also began producing 'favrile glass', which seems to have been inspired by Dresser's Clutha glass. Drawings of Clutha glass from *The Studio* article on his work (1899) have recently been discovered

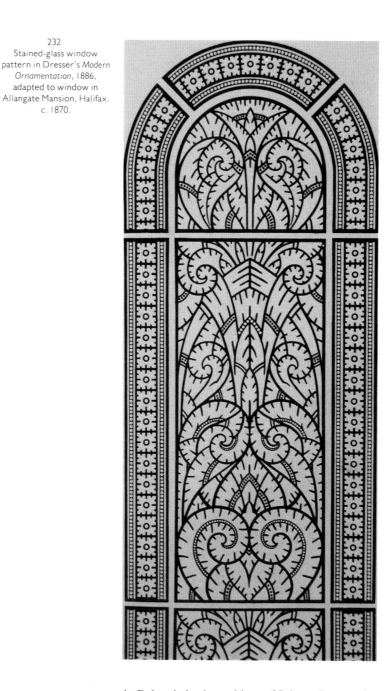

232
Stained-glass window pattern in Dresser's *Modern Ornamentation*, 1886, adapted to window in Allangate Mansion, Halifax. c. 1870.

231
Opposite. Stained-glass window patterns in Dresser's 'Principles of Decorative Design', *The Technical Educator*, 1871, p. 25.

in Bohemia in the archives of Johann Loetz, who around 1900 produced a highly popular Art Nouveau glass similar to that of Dresser's.[32] Clearly Dresser's art theories and his prodigious output of designs for art glass, stained glass, art furniture, pottery, metalware and surface patterns had an enormous impact and met with international acclaim during the last part of his life and for long into the twentieth century.

NOTES

ABBREVIATIONS FOR SOURCES
REFERRED TO IN THE NOTES

A & JHC   *Artist and Journal of Home Culture*
AJ   *The Art Journal*
Art   Dresser, *The Art of Decorative Design*, London 1862, published also as articles in *The Building News*, 1861, pp.997–8, 1862, pp.8–9; and in *The Planet*, 1862, pp.123–35.
'Art Manufactures'   Dresser, 'The Art Manufactures of Japan', *Journal of the Society of Arts*, 1878, pp.169–78.
BMG   *The British Mercantile Gazette*
BN   *The Building News*
'Botany'   Dresser, 'Botany as Adapted to the Arts', *The Art Journal*, 1857, pp.17–20, 53–5, 86–8, 109–11, 249–52, 340–2; 1858, pp.37–9, 237–9, 293–5, 333–5, 362–4.
CM   *Cabinet Maker and Art Furnisher's Journal*
Development   Dresser, *Development of Art in the International Exhibition*, London 1862.
DPA   Department of Practical Art
DSA   Department of Science and Art
'Eastern Art'   Dresser, 'Eastern Art and its Influence on European Manufacture', *Furniture Gazette*, 1874, pp.89–90, 111–12, 136–7, 159–160, 183–4; and in *Journal of the Society of Arts*, XXII, 1874, pp.211–21.
FG   *The Furniture Gazette*
HF & D   *The House Furnisher and Decorator*
'Hindrances'   Dresser, 'Hindrances to the Progress of Applied Art', *Journal of the Society of Arts*, XX, 1872, pp.435–43, 513.
'Industrial Exhibition'   Dresser, 'Art and Industrial Exhibitions', *The Building News*, 1865, p.212.
Japan   Dresser, *Japan and its Architecture, Art and Art-Manufactures*, London 1882.

'Japanese Ornamentation'   [Dresser], 'Japanese Ornamentation', *The Builder*, 1862, pp.308–9, 364–5, 423–4 (published anonymously).
JDA   *Journal of Decorative Art*
JSA   *Journal of the Society of Arts*
Modern   Dresser, *Modern Ornamentation*, London 1886.
NAL, V & A   National Art Library, London, Victoria and Albert Museum.
'New System'   Dresser, 'On a New System of Nature Printing', *Journal of the Society of Arts*, V, 1857, pp.285–304.
'Ornamentation'   Dresser, 'Ornamentation considered as High Art', *Journal of the Society of Arts*, XIX, 1871, pp.217–26, 352.
'Paris Exhibition'   Dresser, 'The Paris Exhibition 1867', *The Chromolithograph*, 1867–8, pp.12–13, 18–19, 36–7, 51, 82–3, 97–8, 112–13, 124–5, 138–9, 154–5, 167–8, 178–9.
PG   *Pottery Gazette*
'Prevailing'   Dresser, 'The prevailing ornament of China and Japan', *The Building News*, 1863, pp.387–8.
'Principles'   Dresser, 'Principles of Decorative Design', *The Technical Educator*, 1870–2.
Principles   Dresser, *Principles of Decorative Design*, London 1873
PRO   Public Record Office
'Production'   Dresser, 'On the Production of Ornament under Quasi Inspiration', *Warehousemen and Drapers' Trade Journal*, 1875, p.341.
RDMA   Royal Doulton Minton Archive
RDMM   Royal Doulton Minton Museum
Studies   Dresser, *Studies in Design*, London 1875–76.
V&A,MR   Victorian & Albert Museum Registry
V&A,NR   Victorian & Albert Museum Nominal Registry
'Works'   Dresser, 'The Works of Owen Jones', *Furniture Gazette*, 1874, pp.1054–5.

INTRODUCTION

1 'Ornamentation', p. 352.
2 V&A, NR, Nellie Dresser interview, 1 April 1952.
3 Dresser's D.Phil. certificate, 14 September 1859, Universitätsarchive, Jena, Ms.no. 364.
4 'The Work of Christopher Dresser', *The Studio*, Vol. XV, 1899, p. 104.
5 *The Builder*, 1904, p. 610.

CHAPTER ONE

1 Alf Bøe, *From Gothic Revival to Functional Form*, Oslo 1957, pp. 45–53.
2 *Art*, pp. 15 and 144.
3 Henry Cole Miscellanies III, Draft Reports of the Select Committee on the School of Design, 1847–9, p. 6, NAL, V&A.
4 Michael Darby, 'Owen Jones and the Eastern Ideal', D.Phil. thesis, Reading University, 1974.
5 'Works', p. 1265.
6 'Ornamentation', p. 221.
7 *Japan*, preface.
8 Henry Cole, *Art-Manufactures collected by Felix Summerly, shewing the Union of Fine-Art with Manufacture*, London 1847, p. 1.
9 Henry Cole Miscellanies III, op. cit., p. 18.
10 *JSA*, Vol. 23, 1875, p. 512.
11 *Official Descriptive and Illustrated Catalogue of the Great Exhibition*, Vol. I, London 1851, p. 1418.
12 'Prevailing', p. 387.
13 Owen Jones, *Doctrines of the Department of Practical Art*, London 1852, p. 28.
14 Henry Cole, *Lectures on the Result of the Great Exhibition*, London 1852, p. 112.
15 DSA, *Report of the Exhibition of the Works sent from various Schools of Ornamental Art in May 1852*, London 1852, p. 20.
16 DSA, *First Annual Report*, London 1854, p. 355.
17 'Ornamentation', p. 222.
18 Stuart Durant, 'Christopher Dresser,

botanist, designer and writer', M.Litt. thesis, Royal College of Art, London 1973, pp. 122–3.
19 DPA, *First Annual Report*, London 1853, p. 217.
20 *Art*, preface.
21 'Ornamentation', p. 224.
22 DSA, *Second Annual Report*, London 1855, p. 153.
23 DSA, *Minute Books*, 17 June 1855, PRO (E.D.28/4-110).
24 Ibid., 17 June 1854, PRO (E.D.28/2-182) and Dresser's Botanical Diagrams, V&A, Prints & Drawings, Box 230, nos. 3925–3996.
25 DSA, *Third Annual Report*, London 1856, p. 46.
26 DSA, *Minute Books*, 23 August 1855, PRO (E.D.28/4-110).
27 'New System', p. 285.
28 'Botany', p. 364.
29 *Art*, p. 184.
30 *Studies*, p. 3.
31 'Production', p. 341.
32 Dresser letter, dated 6 October 1861, Greater London Record Office (A/RSA/16 E.1–15, nos. 116a & b).
33 *Art*, p. 1.
34 Ibid., p. 25.
35 Ibid., p. 177.
36 Ibid., p. 14.
37 Ibid., pp. 34–40.
38 Charles Baudelaire, *Œuvres Complètes*, Paris 1923, pp. 92–4.
39 Op. cit., p. 48.
40 Ibid., p. 49.
41 Ibid., p. 98.
42 Ibid., pp. 140–3.
43 Ibid., p. 16.
44 Ibid., p. 189.
45 *Development*, p. 29.
46 Ibid., p. 24.
47 Ibid., pp. 31–2.
48 *The Athenæum*, 1862, p. 183.
49 *AJ*, 1862, p. 179.

50 Walter Hamilton, *The Æsthetic Movement in England*, London 1882; and Elisabeth Aslin, *The Æsthetic Movement*, London 1969; Gillian Naylor, *The Arts and Crafts Movement*, London 1974.
51 *Art*, p. 169.
52 Ibid., p. 169.
53 Ibid., p. 164.
53 William Morris, *The Collected Works*, XXII (1910–15), p. 77.
54 Elisabeth Aslin, *The Æsthetic Movement*, London 1969, pp. 52–78.
55 'Industrial Exhibitions', p. 212.
56 Matthew Digby Wyatt, *On the Arts of Decoration at the International Exhibition at Paris*, Vol. III, London 1868, p. 2.
57 'Paris Exhibition', p. 12.
58 'Principles', 1870, pp. 120–1.
59 *Art*, p. 185.
60 'Principles', 1870, p. 152.
61 Ibid., p. 151.
62 Ibid., p. 121.
63 'Principles', 1873, p. 17.
64 'Ornamentation', p. 220.
65 Ibid., p. 352.
66 'Hindrances', pp. 436–7.
67 *BN*, 1866, p. 361.

CHAPTER TWO

1 *The Gentleman's Magazine*, Vol. 95, 1825, p. 259.
2 British Museum, Index to Minutes, Vol. V, 12 November 1859.
3 *Official Descriptive and Illustrated Catalogue of the Great Exhibition*, London 1851, Vol. III, p. 714.
4 Willem van Gulik, 'The von Siebold Collection and its Ethnological Importance', *Bonner Zeitschrift für Japonologie*, band III, Bonn 1981, pp. 271–83.
5 *Catalogue du Musée Chinois et Japonais*, Paris 1840.
6 V&A, MR, nos. 33–34, 48–49, 50–51 and 689/1852.

7 DSA *Minute Books*, 20 April 1854, PRO (ED.28.2/no. 105).

8 *Edinburgh Review*, CXII, 1861, p. 45.

9 *Art*, p. 147.

10 Rutherford Alcock, *Catalogue of Works of Industry and Art sent from Japan to the International Exhibition*, London 1862.

11 *Christie's Auction Catalogues*, 15 May and 1 December 1862.

12 G. C. Williams, *Murray Marks and his Friends*, London 1919, pp. 13–43, and Alison Aburgham, *Liberty's, A Biography of a Shop*, London 1975, pp. 18–34.

13 William Burges, 'The Japanese Court in the International Exhibition'. *The Gentleman's Magazine*, September 1862, pp. 243–54.

14 Ibid., p. 224.

15 *Development*, pp. 90 and 146.

16 *JSA*, 1857, p. 291.

17 John Leighton, 'On Japanese Art', *JSA*, 1863, p. 596, and privately printed in leaflet form.

18 Dresser, 'The Prevailing Ornament of China and Japan', *BN*, 22 May 1863, pp. 387–8, and 'Japanese Ornamentation', *The Builder*, 1863, pp. 308–9, 364–5, and 423–4.

19 Godwin's Sketchbooks, n.d., V&A, Prints & Drawings (Ms.A.123c, p. 8).

20 'Prevailing', p. 388, and 'Japanese Ornamentation', pp. 364–5 and 423–4.

21 'Japanese Ornamentation', p. 365.

22 Ibid., p. 308.

23 Op. cit.

24 Ibid., p. 424.

25 'Art Manufactures', p. 169, and Dresser's 145 drawings of Japanese Ceramics, V&A Museum (D.397–541/1905).

26 *The Reader Magazine*, 1863, pp. 501–3, 536–8, and 1865, p. 691.

27 Widar Halén, 'Christopher Dresser and the Cult of Japan', D.Phil. thesis, Oxford 1988, pp. 99–109.

28 'Paris Exhibition', 1868, p. 112.

29 Ibid., 1867, p. 12.

30 Philippe Burty, 'Le Mobilier Moderne', *Gazette des Beaux-Arts*, tome 24, 1868, pp. 27–8.

31 Charles Locke Eastlake, *Hints on Household Taste*, London 1868, p. 173.

32 Yamada Chisaburo, ed., *Japonisme in Art*, Tokyo 1980, pp. 59–64.

33 Ibid., p. 65.

34 *BN*, 1869, p. 527.

35 Matthew Digby Wyatt. 'Orientalism in European Industry', *Macmillan's Magazine*, XXI, 1870, pp. 551, 556.

36 Jacob Falke, 'Chinese and Japanese Art and its importance for Modern Art Industry', *The Workshop*, 1870, pp. 321–4.

37 *The Builder*, 1872, p. 257.

38 *AJ*, 1872, p. 293.

39 *Transactions of the Asiatic Society of Japan*, Tokyo/London 1872–1968.

40 *Official British Report of the International Exhibition of 1871*, London 1872, p. 8.

41 *Tokyo Exhibition Society Journal* (Kaigai Hakurankai Hanpo Sando Shiryo), I, Tokyo 1928, p. 77.

42 *HF & D*, 1873, p. 40.

43 *Official Guide to the International Exhibition of 1873*, London 1873, p. 37.

44 *FG*, 1878, X, p. 75.

45 *PG*, 1883, p. 68.

46 *The Times*, 27 April 1874, p. 9(e).

47 *British Museum Letterbook* 1875, no. 5327.

48 *HF & D*, 1873, p. 40.

49 *In Pursuit of Beauty, Americans and the Æsthetic Movement*, exhibition catalogue, Metropolitan Museum, New York 1986, p. 193.

50 Minton & Co.'s exhibition album for the Vienna Exhibition in 1873, Royal Doulton Minton Archive, Stoke-on-Trent (Ms. 1469).

51 William P. Blake, *Report on Ceramic Art at the Vienna Exhibition in 1873*, New York 1875, p. 14.

52 'Eastern Art', p. 111.

53 Ibid., p. 136.

54 Ibid., p. 159.

55 Uyeno Naoteru, *Japanese Arts and Crafts in the Meiji Era*, Tokyo 1958, p. 114.

56 *The Alexandra Palace Guide*, 1875, p. 7.

57 *The Alexandra Palace Guide*, 1879, p. 9.

58 Robert Lee, 'A Forgotten Yorkshire Pottery, Linthorpe Ware', *Heaton Review*, no. 7, Bradford 1934, pp. 37–41.

59 Alison Aburgham, *Liberty's, A Biography of a Shop*, London 1975, p. 22.

60 *AJ*, 1874, p. 14.

61 Dresser, 'Art Museum', *The Penn Monthly*, pp. 117–26.

62 *New York Times*, 6 May 1877, p. 10, cutting in Tiffany & Co. scrapbook, Tiffany Archive, New York.

63 *In Pursuit of Beauty*, exhibition catalogue, Metropolitan Museum, New York 1986, p. 255.

64 *FG*, 1876, p. 255.

65 Roger Soden-Smith, *Ceramics at the Philadelphia Exhibition in 1876*, London 1876, p. 278.

66 *The Builder*, 1878, p. 213.

67 *Japan*, preface.

68 *The Japan Mail*, 11 January 1877, p. 16.

69 Lady Thomas Brassey, *Voyage in a Sunbeam*, London 1878, p. 342.

70 *Japan*, pp. 214–15.

71 *Naimusho Nishi* (Report of the Ministry of the Interior), 1877, Tokyo National Archive, Ms. 2a-10-2025, and *Tokyo National Museum Centennial Catalogue*, Tokyo 1973, pp. 136, 151–6.

72 *Japan*, p. 353.

73 *Tokyo National Museum Acquisition Catalogue and Miscellanies*, Vol. II, 1880, no. 28.

74 V&A Museum (D.397–541/1905) and Tiffany & Co. Archive, New York.

75 *Japan*, p. 154.

76 British Museum (Ms. 2919-5/1/1913) and V&A Museum (DJ. 104-1905, DJ. 76-1905, and DJ. 161-68-1965).

77 Ibid., p. 108.

78 Ibid., p. 144.

79 Ibid., p. 210.

80 Ibid., p. 344.

81 *Dresser Collection of Japanese Curios selected for Messrs. Tiffany Co.* (to be sold at auction by Leavitt, Auctioneers), New York, 18 June 1877.

82 *In Pursuit of Beauty*, exhibition catalogue, Metropolitan Museum, New York 1986, pp. 186–9.

83 *Philadelphia Evening Bulletin*, 9 June 1877.

84 *The Graphic*, 20 April 1877.

85 Joe Earle, 'The taxonomic obsession, British collectors and Japanese objects 1852–1896', *The Burlington Magazine*, XXVIII, 1981, pp. 864–73.

86 *The World*, 21 April 1877.

87 Correspondence between Dresser and George A. Sala, dated 4 July and 28 December 1877, The Brotherton Library, University of Leeds, and Dresser, 'Art Manufactures', 1878, p. 169.

88 'Art Manufactures', p. 169.

89 *FG*, 1878, p. 277.

90 Dresser, 'Is the Rage for Queen Anne Over', *The Cabinet Maker*, 1880, I, pp. 17–19.

91 Dresser, 'Japanese Woodwork', *The Builder*, 1878, p. 654.

92 Dresser, 'Works from Japan', *The Builder*, 1878, p. 969, and Model ceilings in the V&A Museum, entry nos. 390 and 391-1905.

93 *FG*, XII, 1879, p. 22.

94 *PG*, 1883, p. 435.

95 Register of the Art Furnishers' Alliance Co., 10 February 1882, PRO, London (BT.2670, no. 14236).

96 Dresser, *Principles of Art with Preparatory Remarks upon the Objects and Practical Aims of the Art Furnishers' Alliance Limited*, London 1881.

97 *CM*, 1880, p. 64.

98 *CM*, 1881, p. 1.

99 Elisabeth Aslin, *The Æsthetic Movement*, London 1969, pp. 125–6.

100 *A & JHC*, 1881, pp. 217–18.

101 'The Works of Christopher Dresser', *The Studio*, XV, 1899, p. 104–14.

102 Mervyn Levy, *Liberty Style*, London 1986, p. 39.

103 Dresser, 'Japanese Art Workmanship', *Furniture Gazette*, XVII, 1882, pp. 223–9.

104 *Catalogue of a Loan Collection of Oriental Art at the Corporation Galleries*, Glasgow 1882.

105 *PG*, 1882, p. 1023.

106 *Edinburgh Review*, CLVII, 1883, pp. 509–18.

107 *New York Times*, 17 December 1882, p. 6.

108 Rutherford Alcock, *The Capital of the Tycoon*, 1863, p. 279.

109 *Arts and Crafts Essays by members of the Arts & Crafts Exhibition Society*, London 1903, pp. 28–33.

110 *FG*, XIX, 1883, p. 55.

111 *JDA*, 1884, p. 494.

112 Dresser, 'Some Features of Japanese Architecture and Ornamentation', *The Architect*, 1884, pp. 384–6.

113 *CM*, 1885, p. 181.

114 *JSA*, XXXIV, 1886, pp. 1204–15, 1231–42 and 1254–75.

115 Yamada Chisaburo, ed., *Japonism in Art*, Tokyo 1980, p. 261.

116 *AJ*, 1885–6.

117 Joe Earle, op. cit., pp. 864–73.

118 Edward Morse, *Japanese Homes and their Surroundings*, Boston 1886, p. 316.

119 *BA*, XXV, 1886, p. 157.

120 *The Builder*, LII, 1887, p. 492.

121 *JDA*, 1904, p. 127.

122 *AJ*, 1887, pp. 185–202.

123 *JSA*, XXXVII, 1889, pp. 694–7.

124 Arthur Liberty, 'The Industrial Arts and Manufacture of Japan', *Journal of the Society of Arts*, XXXVIII, 1890, pp. 673–86, and Charles Holme, 'Japanese Pottery', *The Art Journal*, 1892, pp. 154–8.

125 Charles Holme, *Catalogue of Japanese Art*, Warrington Museum, 1890, preface.

126 *AJ*, 1889, p. 330.

127 *Kunstgewerbeblatt*, 1892, pp. 1–3.

128 *The Builder*, 1904, p. 610.

CHAPTER THREE

1 Nikolaus Pevsner, 'Art Furniture of the Eighteen-Seventies', *Architectural Review*, CXI, 1952, pp. 43–50.

2 'Principles', 1870, pp. 311–13, 376–8, 403–6.

3 *CM*, 1880, I, p. 1.

4 *Art*, p. 18.

5 *Development*, p. 90.

6 *The Builder*, 1862, p. 185.

7 'Allangate, Halifax' in *Castles and Country Houses in Yorkshire*, (compiled from *The Bradford Illustrated Weekly Telegraph*), Bradford 1885, n.p.

8 Ibid.
9 *The Architect*, 1876, pp. 4–5.
10 'Paris Exhibition', p. 12.
11 *Principles*, 1873, p. 59.
12 'Eastern Art', p. 213.
13 *CM*, 1 July 1881, p. 1.
14 *Japan*, p. oo.
15 *Chodo Zue*, (1804) a book of furniture designs, Wellcome Institute, London.
16 *Catalogue of Art Furniture to be sold by Auction by Thurgood & Martin*, London, 24 August 1884.
17 *A&JHC*, 1882, p. 354.
18 *FG*, XVIII, 1882, p. 218.
19 *CM*, IX, 1888, p. 85.
20 *Development*, p. 157.
21 Owen Jones, *Lectures on the Result of the Great Exhibition*, 1852, p. 291.
22 'Paris Exhibition', p. 19.
23 'Ornamentation', p. 225.
24 *Principles*, 1873, p. 145.
25 Ibid., p. 70.
26 *BMG*, 1878, p. 217.

CHAPTER FOUR

1 *Development*, p. 57.
2 *Principles*, p. 13.
3 *Development*, p. 60.
4 *Art*, p. 16.
5 Dresser, *The Decoration of Ceilings*, London 1868, doctrines 23–24.
6 *Principles*, p. 77.
7 *FG*, XIII, 1880, p. 251,
8 *JDA*, 1905, p. 17.
9 John Crossley & Co. Correspondence with Dresser, dated 23 August 1871 to 18 March 1873, Halifax, West Yorkshire Archive (Ms.c.300/172).
10 *JDA*, 1884, p. 474 & fig. 476.
11 *The Decoration of Ceilings*, op. cit., Doctrine 21.
12 *Artistic Houses*, Vol. I, 1880, pp. 138–9.
13 'The Work of Christopher Dresser', *The Studio*, Vol. XV, 1899, p. 110.
14 *Development*, pp. 49–50.
15 *BN*, 1865, p. 916.
16 DSA, *Catalogue of the Exhibition of Art-Manufacture*, London 1858, no. 667.
17 *AJ*, 1860, p. 378.
18 *The Builder*, 1861, p. 258.
19 *Development*, p. 38.
20 List of Creditors to the Art Furnishers' Alliance, 23 February 1887, London, PRO Company Liquidation Files, W. 188.
21 Dresser, 'The Decoration of Flat Surfaces', *Building News*, 1864, p. 366.
22 *BN*, 1864, p. 315.
23 *BN*, 1867, p. 905.
24 *The Builder*, 1867, p. 362.
25 Matthew Digby Wyatt, *On the Arts of Decoration at the International Exhibition at Paris*, London 1868, Vol. III, pp. 11–17.
26 'Paris Exhibition' (1867), p. 36.
27 *Principles*, pp. 83–93.
28 Elisabeth Aslin, *Edward W. Godwin*, London 1986, pp. 13–14.
29 *Castles and Country Houses of Yorkshire* (compiled from *The Bradford Illustrated Telegraph*), Bradford 1885, n.p.
30 *Principles*, pp. 90–1.
31 *Studies*, p. 3.
32 Op. cit., p. 6.
33 Op. cit., p. 39.
34 Op. cit., p. 37.
35 Jeffrey & Co. log-book, 1875–6, Arthur Sanderson & Sons Archive, London.
36 *The Times*, 27 April, p. 9e.
37 *British Museum Letterbook*, 1875, no. 5327, dated Teheran 22 April 1875.

38 Nikolaus Pevsner, 'Christopher Dresser, Industrial Designer', *Architectural Review*, Vol. 81, 1937, pp. 183–6.
39 *JDA*, 1884, IV, p. 472.
40 Allan Sugden and John L. Edmondson, *A History of English Wallpaper 1609–1914*, London 1925, pp. 168–254; and Pevsner, op. cit., p. 185.
41 List of Creditors to the Art Furnishers' Alliance, 23 February 1887, London, PRO Company Liquidation Files, W. 188.
42 Arthur Sanderson & Sons Costing-books, 1900–4, Arthur Sanderson & Sons Archive, London.
43 Carl Graff, 'Der Anglo–Japanische Stil des 19.Jahrhunderts', *Österreichische Monatschrift für den Orient*, XI, 1885, pp. 39–41.
44 *FG*, XIII, 1880, p. 163.
45 Lewis F. Day, 'Victorian Progress in Applied Design', *The Art Journal*, VII, 1887, pp. 185–202.
46 Jean Lahore, *L'Art Nouveau*, Paris 1901, p. 36.
47 Constance Harrison, *Woman's Handiwork in Modern Homes*, New York 1881, p. 136.
48 *Art Amateur*, Vol. 13, 1885, p. 33.
49 *A&JHC*, 1882, p. 258.
50 V&A NR, letter from Chubb & Son, 7 May 1952, Ms.55/4583.
51 *Japan*, p. 151.
52 *JDA*, XXV, 1905, p. 66.
53 *JDA*, XXV, 1905, p. 67.
54 *JDA*, IX, 1891, p. 66.
55 *JDA*, VII, 1887, p. 97.
56 *JDA*, XXI, 1901, pp. 175–81.
57 V&A NR, letter from Allan V. Sugden, dated 22 March 1952.
58 V&A NR, letter from Cecil F. Tattersall, dated 6 September 1952.
59 *Development*, pp. 65–80.
60 *Art*, p. 143.
61 *Principles*, p. 101.
62 Pevsner, op. cit., p. 184.
63 *BN*, 1865, p. 916.
64 Wyatt, op. cit., p. 27.
65 George A. Sala, *Notes and Sketches of the Paris Exhibition*, Paris 1868, p. 278.
66 *The Graphic*, 1871, p. 519.
67 *FG*, 1874, p. 509.
68 *Warehousemen & Drapers' Trade Journal*, I, 1872, p. 111.
69 Ibid., 1878, p. 245.
70 Dresser, 'The Works of Owen Jones', *Furniture Gazette*, 1874, pp. 1054–5.
71 *Principles*, p. 104.
72 *FG*, 1874, p. 184.
73 *The Carpet Trade Review*, 1878, pp. 92–3.
74 Ibid., 1880, p. 223.
75 *British Colonial and Manufacturer Journal*, 1885, February Supplement, p. 1.
76 Ibid., 1885, p. 2.
77 Ibid., 1885, p. 2.
78 James M. Whistler, *Ten O'Clock Lectures*, London 1885, pp. 12–13.
79 *JSA*, Vol. 42, 1892, p. 434.
80 *Development*, pp. 101–4.
81 *Japan*, p. 441.
82 V&A NR, letter from Ronald D. Simpson and Roland Midgley, dated 23 June 1951 (Ms.52/638).
83 V&A NR, interview with Nellie Dresser, dated 1 April 1952.
84 Pevsner, op. cit., p. 185.
85 *AJ*, 1887, p. 201.
86 *Tokyo National Museum Acquisition Catalogue*, II, no. 7, Tokyo National Museum Archive.
87 *AJ*, 1878, p. 189.

88 *The Illustrated Paris Universal Exhibitor*, 1878, p. 353.
89 *Warehousemen & Drapers' Trade Journal*, 1893, pp. 23–5.
90 *AJ*, 1891, p. 179.
91 *The Builder*, LXI, 1891, pp. 288–323.
92 V&A NR, letter from Cecil F. Tattersall, dated 6 September 1952.

CHAPTER FIVE

1 *Japan*, preface and p. 392.
2 DSA *Minute books*, August 1853, PRO (E.D.28.2.no.221).
3 John C. Robinson, *Catalogue of the Museum of Ornamental Art at Marlborough House*, London 1854, pp. 10–11.
4 Henry Cole, *Miscellanies*, III, p. 16, dated 31 March 1852, NAL, V&A.
5 DSA, *Minute Books*, list of Japanese articles dated 20 April 1854, PRO London (E.D.28.2.no.105).
6 John C. Robinson, *Catalogue of the Museum of Ornamental Art at Marlborough House*, London 1855, p. 50.
7 'Art Manufactures', p. 177.
8 *Art*, pp. 129–33.
9 Ibid., pp. 134–7.
10 Ibid., p. 138.
11 *Principles*, p. 117.
12 Albert Jacquemart, 'Les Beaux-Arts et l'Industrie', *Gazette des Beaux-Arts*, XI, 1861, p. 507.
13 Philippe Burty, *Chefs d'Œuvre des Arts Industriels*, Paris 1867, p. 121.
14 *Christie's Auction Catalogue of the Remi Schmidt & Co. Collection*, 1 December 1862, lot 97.
15 *Christie's Auction Catalogue of Sir Rutherford Alcock's Collection*, 9 June 1898, lot 475.
16 *Catalogue of the Tokyo National Museum*, Tokyo 1976, no. 1430.
17 'Japanese Ornamentation', p. 364.
18 'Principles', 1871, p. 343.
19 *Christie's Auction Catalogue of Dr. Christopher Dresser's Collection*, 18 April 1905, lot 19.
20 George W. Rhead and Frederick A. Rhead, *Staffordshire Pots and Potters*, London 1906, p. 360.
21 *Official Catalogue of the International Exhibition*, London 1871, nos. 4222, 4293 and 4326.
22 V&A NR, Nellie Dresser letter, dated 1 April 1952.
23 Roger Soden Smith, *Ceramics at the Philadelphia Exhibition*, London 1876, p. 31.
24 Watcombe Terracotta Co. registered September 1869 and liquidated 1883, London, PRO Company Files (BT.31.1487/4568).
25 Arthur Beckwith, *Report on Pottery at the London International Exhibition*, New York 1872, p. 88.
26 'The Work of Christopher Dresser', *The Studio*, Vol. XV, 1899, p. 112.
27 Robert Lee, 'A Forgotten Yorkshire Pottery, Linthorpe Ware', *The Heaton Review*, Bradford 1934, pp. 37–40.
28 Ibid.
29 *JSA*, 1880, p. 356.
30 Robert Lee, op. cit.
31 *CM*, 1890, p. 27.
32 *CM*, 1894, p. 335.
33 *PG*, XL, 1915, pp. 849–53.
34 *AJ*, 1880, p. 53.
35 *FG*, 1880, p. 334.
36 Malcolm Haslam, *English Art Pottery 1865–1915*, Woodbridge 1975, p. 96.
37 Jonathan R. A. Le Vine, *Linthorpe Art*

Pottery Exhibition Catalogue, Billingham Art Gallery, Middlesbrough 1970, p. 13.
38 *Japan*, p. 287.
39 Ibid., pp. 368–414.
40 Ibid., pp. 278, and *The Dresser Collection of Japanese Curios and Articles Selected for Messrs. Tiffany & Co.*, New York 1877, no. 177.
41 *PG*, 1915, XL, pp. 849–53.
42 Robert Lee, op. cit., pp. 37–8.
43 Llewellyn Jewitt, 'Ceramic Art', *The Reliquary*, XXI, 1881, p. 58, and XXIV, 1883, pp. 113–14.
44 *Graphic Journal*, 1882, p. 63.
45 *PG*, 1889, p. 447.
46 *PG*, 1915, XI, pp. 849–53.

CHAPTER SIX
1 *BN*, 1865, p. 916.
2 *Development*, pp. 171–2.
3 Adrian Tilbrook, 'Christopher Dresser's Designs for Elkington & Co.', *Journal of the Society of Decorative Arts*, no. 9, 1985, pp. 23–8.
4 *Principles*, p. 136.
5 'Paris Exhibition', p. 18.
6 *Principles*, pp. 135–9.
7 *BN*, 1867, p. 905.
8 'Eastern Art', 1873, p. 143.
9 Op. cit., p. 136.
10 *Japan*, 1882, pp. 100–8.
11 Ibid., p. 426.
12 *Principles*, p. 138.
13 *AJ*, 1879, p. 222.
14 Nikolaus Pevsner, 'Christopher Dresser, Industrial Designer', *Architectural Review*, Vol. 81, 1937, pp. 183–6.
15 *Prospectus of the Art Furnishers' Alliance Co.*, London 1880, p. 4.
16 Elkington & Co. Pattern books, Vol. 13, no. 17147, November 1888, London, NAL, V&A.
17 *The Times*, 15 July 1879, p. 4d.

18 Shirley Bury, 'The Silver Designs of Dr. Christopher Dresser', *Apollo*, December 1962, pp. 766–70.
19 'Allangate Mansion, Halifax', *Castles and Country Houses of Yorkshire*, Bradford 1885.
20 *CM*, 1882, p. 204.
21 Nikolaus Pevsner, op. cit., pp. 184–5.
22 *Principles*, pp. 144–52.
23 Ibid., p. 142.
24 *Japan*, 1882, p. 422.
25 *CM*, 1886, p. 103.
26 Adrian Tilbrook, *The Designs of Archibald Knox for Liberty & Co.*, London 1976, pp. 16–17.
27 *Principles*, p. 145.
28 Op. cit., p. 110.

CHAPTER SEVEN
1 John Ruskin, *The Stones of Venice*, London 1851–3, Vol. 2, p. 392.
2 Charles Lock Eastlake, *Hints on Household Taste*, London 1868, p. 227, William Morris, 'The Lesser Arts of Life', *Lectures on Art Delivered in Support of the Society for the Protection of Ancient Buildings*, London 1882, p. 197.
3 *Development*, p. 117.
4 'Principles', 1871, p. 24.
5 Ibid., p. 26.
6 David M. Tomlin, 'A Nineteenth Century Glasswork – The Tees Bottle Company', *Cleveland and Teeside Local History Society Bulletin*, Middlesbrough on Tees 1979, pp. 12–16.
7 *Prospectus of the Art Furnishers' Alliance Co.*, London 1880, p. 4.
8 *Principles*, pp. 131–2.
9 Brian Blench, 'Christopher Dresser and his Glass Designs', *Annales du 9ième Congres de l'Association Internationale pour l'histoire du Verre*, Nancy 1985, pp. 345–59.
10 *BN*, 1865, p. 312.

11 V&A, NR, Nellie Dresser interview, 1 April 1952, and letter dated 4 April 1952.
12 Barbara Morris, *Liberty Design, 1874–1914*, London 1989, pp. 70–1.
13 Widar Halén, 'Christopher Dresser and the Cult of Japan', unpublished D.Phil. thesis, Oxford 1988, pp. 278–9.
14 *CM*, 1882, p. 204.
15 *PG*, 1 May 1882, p. 464.
16 Barbara Morris, *Victorian Table Glass and Ornaments*, London 1978, pp. 175–7.
17 Ibid., pp. 178–83.
18 *Catalogue of Arts & Crafts Society Exhibition*, London 1890, no. 271, and 1903, p. 156.
19 Lewis F. Day, 'Victorian Progress in Applied Design, *Art Journal Royal Jubilee Number*, June 1887, pp. 185–202.
20 *PG*, 1 December 1882, p. 00.
21 Barbara Morris, *Victorian Table Glass*, op. cit., p. 184.
22 V&A, National Art Library, Octavius Hudson papers.
23 *Principles*, p. 153.
24 Ibid., p. 155.
25 Mary Gay Humphreys, 'Colored Glass for Home Decoration', *Art Amateur*, no. 5, June 1881, pp. 14–15.
26 John Moyr-Smith, *Ornamental Interiors*, London 1887.
27 'Allangate Mansion, Halifax', *Castles and Country Houses in Yorkshire*, Bradford 1885.
28 Charles Booth, *Modern Surface Ornament*, New York 1877, and *The Art Worker Magazine*, February 1878.
29 *The Dresser Collection of Japanese Curios and Articles Selected for Messrs. Tiffany & Co.*, New York, 1877, no. 177.
30 *Japan*, p. 152.
31 *Crockery and Glass Journal*, Vol. X, 1882, p. 19.
32 Research undertaken by Jan Mergl, Institute for the History of Arts of the Czechoslovak Academy of Science, Prague, Czechoslovakia.

DRESSER'S MANUFACTURERS

Alexandra Palace Co., London (artistic director 1873 until *c.* 1880).
Allan, Cockshut & Co., London, wallpapers, 1878 onward.
Anaglypta Co., Lancaster and London, linoleum wall coverings, 1887 to 1894 (acquired by Potters of Darwen, now Crown Paints).
Art Furnishers' Alliance Co., London (artistic director 1880–2).
Ault Pottery, Swadlincote, reproduced Dresser's Linthorp shapes from 1886 onward (Dresser formally engaged 1892–1900).
Barlow & Jones, Bolton and Manchester, quilts and textiles, 1878–1900.
Benham & Froud Co., London, metalwork, 1873–93.
Bretby Art Pottery, Burton-on-Trent, reproduced Dresser's Linthorpe shapes, 1883–90.
Brinton & Lewis, Kidderminster (partnership dissolved in 1870. later John Brinton & Co.), tufted and chenille Axminster and Brussels carpets, 1867–*c.* 1900.
Catto & McClary, London, wallpapers, 1864–71 (bought by Wylie & Lockhead of Glasgow in 1871).
Chubb & Son, London, metal fixtures, locks and furniture, 1878–83.

Couper, James & Sons, Glasgow, 'Clutha glass', *c.* 1880–96.
Coalbrookdale Co., Coalbrookdale, cast iron, 1867–87.
Cooke, William, Leeds (merged with Trumble in 1886), wallpapers, 1866–90.
Cope, Edward, Ltd, Nottingham, lace, 1877 onward.
Crossley, John, & Sons, Halifax, Brussels, Wilton and Axminster carpets, 1871 onward.
Deakin & Moore, Birmingham, metalwork, 1880s.
Dixon, James, & Son, Sheffield, silver and electroplate, 1870s and 1880s.
Dresser & Holme, later Holme & Co. (director 1878–82).
Elkington & Co., Birmingham, silver and electroplate, 1865–90.
Essex & Co. (formerly Knowles & Essex), wallpapers, 1887 onward.
Hardman & Co., Birmingham, ironmongers, 1870s.
Hukin & Heath, Birmingham/London (later Heath & Middleton 1887–1909), electroplate silver, 1877–1900.
Jackson & Graham, London, carpets, 1858 (organized Japanese exhibition in 1877).
Jeffrey & Co., London, wallpapers, 1867–87.

Knowles, Charles, & Co., London (Knowles & Essex until 1887), wallpapers, 1894–5.
Lewis, John, & Co., Kidderminster (Brinton & Lewis until 1870), Axminster and Brussels carpets, 1870s.
Liberty & Co., London, textiles and metalwork, 1882–3.
Liddiard & Co., retailers Hargreaves Brothers, London, textiles, 1853.
Lightbown, Aspinall & Co., Manchester, wallpapers, 1880s.
Line, John, & Co., Reading and London, wallpapers, 1880s.
Linthorpe Art Pottery, Middlesbrough, 1879–82 (Dresser's shapes reproduced until the liquidation of the company in 1889).
Londos & Co., London (artistic adviser 1873–83).
Minton & Co., Stoke-on-Trent, porcelain, 1862–90.
Minton's Art Pottery, London, pottery, 1871–5.
Newman, Smith & Newman, London, rollerprinted cottons, 1896 onward.
Norris, Charles, & Co., London, silk damasks, 1860s and 1870s (taken over by Warner & Sons in 1885).
Old Hall Earthenware Co. Ltd, Hamley, Staffordshire, pottery, 1880s.

Perry, Richard, Son & Co., Wolverhampton, metal-work, 1876–83.
Potter, Charles & William, Darwen (called Potters of Darwen, now Crown Paints), wallpapers, 1876 onward.
Sanderson, Arthur, & Son, London, wallpapers, 1880s until 1904.
Scott, Cuthbertson & Co., London, wallpapers, 1860–87.
Steiner, Frederic, & Co., Lancashire, 1890s until 1904.
Tees Bottle Co., Middlesbrough, probably glass, 1878 until 1880s.
Tootal, Broadhurst, Lee & Co., Bolton and Manchester (Wardle, Tootal, Broadhurst, Lee & Co. in 1892), textiles, 1877 onward.
Torquay Terracotta Co. Ltd, Torquay. Dresser probably designed for them between 1875 and 1899.
Turnbull & Stockdale, Lancashire, textiles, 1880s.
Walton, Frederick, & Co., Lancaster and London, wallpapers, linoleums and linoleum wall coverings, Lincrusta Walton, 1874 onward.
Ward & Cope, Nottingham (later Edward Cope Ltd), lace, 1876 until 1880s.
Ward, J. W. & C., Co., Halifax, silk and wool damasks, 1865–1904.
Wardle, Tootal, Broadhurst, Lee & Co., Bolton, textiles, 1892 onward.
Warner & Sons, London, silk damasks, 1880s and 1890s.
Watcombe Pottery Co., Torquay, 1869–80.
Wedgwood, Josiah, & Sons, porcelain, 1867 onward.
Wilson, John, & Sons, London, damasks, 1890s.
Wilson & Fennimore Co., Philadelphia, US, wallpapers, 1876–7.
Woollams, William, & Co., London, wallpapers, 1858–87.
Wylie & Lockhead, Glasgow, wallpapers, 1871–3.
Züber, Jean, & Co., Rixheim, Alsace, France, wallpapers, 1899–1904.

BIBLIOGRAPHY

1. ARTICLES AND BOOKS BY CHRISTOPHER DRESSER

'The relation of science to ornamental art', *Royal Institution Proceedings*, II, 1857, pp.350–2.
'On a new system of nature printing', *Journal of the Society of Arts*, V, 1857, pp.285–304.
'Botany as adapted to the Arts', *The Art Journal*, 1857, pp.17–20, 53–4, 86–8, 109–11, 249–52, 340–2; 1858, pp.37–9, 237–9, 293–5, 333–5, 362–4.
'Contributions to Organographic Botany, Linnean Society', MSS.5.B.230. London 1858.
'Botany as applied to the Fine Arts and Manufactures', *Journal of the Society of Arts*, VIII, 1859–60.
The Rudiments of Botany, Structural and Physiological, London 1859, 2nd edn 1860.
Unity in Variety as Deduced from the Vegetable Kingdom, London 1859, 2nd edn 1860.
'On the morphological import of certain vegetable organs', *Transactions of the Edinburgh Botanical Society*, VI, 1859, pp.321–2.
'On the stem or axis as the fundamental organ in the vegetable structure', *Transactions of the Edinburgh Botanical Society*, VI, 1860, pp.432–4.
Popular Manual of Botany, Edinburgh 1860.
'The art of decorative design', *The Building News*, 1861, pp.997–8, and 1862, pp.8–9.
'The art of decorative design', *The Builder*, 1862, pp.185–6.
'On decorative art', *The Planet*, 1862, pp.123–35.
The Art of Decorative Design, London 1862.
Development of Ornamental Art in the International Exhibition, London 1862.
'The prevailing ornament of China and Japan', *The Building News*, 1863, pp.387–8.
'Japanese Ornamentation', *The Builder*, 1863, pp.308–9, 364–5, 423–4. Published anonymously.
'Art foliage', *The Building News*, 1865, pp.307–8.
'Art and industrial exhibitions', *The Building News*, 1865, p.212.
'The Paris Exhibition 1867', *The Chromolithograph*, 23 November 1867–15 February 1868, pp.12–13, 18–19, 36–7, 51, 82–3, 97–8, 112–13, 124–5, 138–9, 154–5, 167–8, 178–9.
The Decoration of Ceilings, privately printed, London 1868.
General Principles of Art, Decorative and Pictorial, with hints on colour, its harmonies and contrasts, privately printed, London 1868, and Pennsylvania 1877.
'Principles of design', *The Technical Educator*, Vols I–IV, 1870–2; pp.49–51, 87–90, 120–1, 151–3, 191–2, 221–3, 229–31, 277–9, 311–13, 376–8, 403–6; Vol. II, pp.24–6, 56–8, 87–9, 119–21, 151–4, 191–2, 248–50, 280–1, 312–13, 327–9, 375–7; Vol. III, pp.24–6, 49–50, 104–5, 145–6, 215–17, 79–82, 360–1; Vol. IV, pp.23–5 (published in book form as *Principles of Decorative Design*, London 1873).

'Ornamentation considered as high art', *Journal of the Society of Arts*, XIX, 1871, pp.217–26, 352.
'Hindrances to the progress of applied art', *Journal of the Society of Arts*, XX, 1872, pp.435–43, 513.
Principles of Decorative Design, London 1873.
'Good taste in house furnishing', *Furniture Gazette*, 1874, pp.10, 37–8, 61–2, 86–7.
'Eastern art and its influence on European manufacture', *Furniture Gazette*, 1874, pp.89–90, 111–12, 136–7, 159–60, 183–4; *Journal of the Society of Arts*, XXII, 1874, pp.211–21.
'A retrospective glance at the Vienna exhibition', *Furniture Gazette*, 1874, pp.277–8, 304.
'The grotesque in decorative art', *Furniture Gazette*, 1874, p.329.
'On colour', *Furniture Gazette*, 1874, pp.352–3, 376, 539.
'The expression of Egyptian ornament', *Furniture Gazette*, 1874, p.479.
'Fitness and beauty', *Furniture Gazette*, 1874, p.484.
'The works of Owen Jones', *Furniture Gazette*, 1874, pp.1054–5.
'On the true principles of art as applied to the manufacture of jet ornaments', *Whitby Times*, 23 October 1874, and *Furniture Gazette*, 1874, pp.1264–5.
'On the production of ornament under the influence of quasi-inspiration', *Warehousemen and Drapers' Trade Journal*, 1875, p.341.
Studies in Design, London 1875–6.
Carpets (in the series *British Manufacturing Industries*, ed. G. Phillips Bevan), London 1876.
'Art Industries', 'Art Museums', 'Art Schools', *The Penn Monthly*, 1877, pp.21–3, 117–26, 215–20.
'Notes on four Japanese ceilings', Victoria & Albert Museum, National Art Library, Mss.86.E.E.3.(1878). Published in *The Builder*, 1878, p.969.
'The art manufactures of Japan', *Journal of the Society of Arts*, 1878, pp.169–78.
'Japanese woodwork', *The Builder*, 1878, p.654.
'Works from Japan', *The Builder*, 1878, p.696.
'Is the rage for Queen Anne over?', *The Cabinet Maker*, I, 1880, pp.17–19.
'Art in our homes', *Furniture Gazette*, XIII, 1880, pp.269, 287, 305, 387, 419, 435.
'The decoration of ceilings', *Furniture Gazette*, XIII, 1880, pp.181–2.
'Propositions', *Furniture Gazette*, XIII, 1880, pp.90–2.
Principles of Art with Preparatory Remarks upon the Objects and Practical Aims of the Art Furnishers' Alliance, London 1881.
Japan its Architecture, Art and Art-Manufactures, London 1882.
'Japanese art workmanship', *Furniture Gazette*,

XVII, 1882, p.264.
'Some features of Japanese architecture and ornament', *The Architect*, 1884, pp.384–6.
'Landscape designs', *British and Colonial Manufacturer*, 1 January 1885, supplement, pp.2–3.
'The decoration of our homes', *The Art Amateur*, New York 1885, Vol. 13, pp.14–16, 33, 35 and Vol. 14, pp.110–12.
Modern Ornamentation, London 1886.

2. GENERAL SOURCES

Adburgham, Alison, *Liberty's, A Biography of a Shop*, London 1975.
The Aesthetic Movement and the Cult of Japan, Fine Art Society, London 1972.
Anscombe, Isabelle, *Arts and Crafts in Great Britain and the U.S.A.*, London 1978.
——, 'Knowledge is Power, The designs of Christopher Dresser', *The Connoisseur*, May 1979, pp.54–9.
Aslin, Elizabeth, *The Aesthetic Movement, Prelude to Art Nouveau*, London 1969.
——, *E. W. Godwin, Furniture and Interior Decoration*, London 1986.
Batkin, Maureen, *Wedgwood Ceramics 1846–1959*, London 1980.
Blacker, J. F., *Nineteenth-Century English Ceramic Art*, London 1911.
Blench, Brian J. R., 'Christopher Dresser and his glass designs', *Annales du 9ème congres de l'Association Internationale pour l'histoire du Verre*, Nancy 1985, pp.345–9.
Bøe, Alf, *From Gothic Revival to Functional Form*, Oslo 1957.
Bracegirdle, Cyril, 'Linthorpe, the forgotten pottery', *Country Life*, 29 April 1971.
Bromfield, David, 'The art of Japan in later nineteenth century Europe, Problems of art criticism and theory', unpublished PhD thesis, University of Leeds, 1977.
Bury, Shirley, *Victorian Electroplate*, London 1971.
——, 'The silver designs of Dr. Christopher Dresser', *Apollo*, December 1962, pp.766–70.
Castles and Country Houses in Yorkshire, anonymous (from *Bradford Illustrated Weekly Telegraph*), Bradford 1885, n.p.
Clark, Sir Kenneth, *The Gothic Revival*, London 1929, new edn 1962.
Cole, Henry, *Lectures on the Result of the Great Exhibition*, London 1852.
Collins, Michael, *Christopher Dresser 1834–1904*, Exhibition Catalogue, Camden Arts Centre, London 1979.
——, *Towards Post-Modernism, Design since 1851*, London 1987.

Cook, Clarence, *What shall we do with our walls?*, New York 1880.

Cooper, Jeremy, *Victorian and Edwardian Furniture and Interiors*, London 1987.

Crawford, Alan, *C. R. Ashbee, Architect, Designer and Romantic Socialist*, London 1986.

Crook, J. Mordount, *William Burges and the High Victorian Dream*, London 1981.

Crook, J. Mordount (ed.), *The Strange Genius of William Burges, Art-Architect, 1827–1881*, National Museum of Wales, Cardiff 1981.

Culme, John, *Nineteenth Century Silver*, London 1977.

Darby, Michael, 'Owen Jones and the Eastern ideal', unpublished PhD thesis, Reading University, 1974.

Darby, Michael, *The Islamic Perspective*, London 1983.

Dennis, Richard, and John Jesse, *Christopher Dresser 1834–1904*, Exhibition Catalogue, Fine Art Society, London 1972.

Durant, Stuart, 'Aspects of the work of Dr. Christopher Dresser (1834–1904), botanist, designer and writer', unpublished M.Litt. thesis, Royal College of Art, London 1973.

Dyce, William, *The Drawing Book of the Government School of Design*, London 1842, new edns 1846 and 1854.

Earle, Joe, 'The taxonomic obsession, British collectors and Japanese objects 1852–1896', *The Burlington Magazine*, XXVIII, 1986, pp.864–73.

Eastlake, Charles Locke, *Hints on Household Taste*, London 1868.

——, *A History of the Gothic Revival*, London 1872.

Edis, Robert W., *Decoration and Furniture of Town Houses*, London 1881.

Eidelberg, Martin, 'Bracquemond, Delâtre and the discovery of Japanese prints', *The Burlington Magazine*, CXXIII, 1981, pp.221–7.

Evett, Elisa, *The Critical Reception of Japanese Art in Late Nineteenth Century Europe*, Michigan 1982.

Gaunt, William, *The Aesthetic Adventure*, Oxford 1945.

Girouard, Mark, *Sweetness and Light. The Queen Anne Movement 1860–1900*, Oxford 1977.

——, *The Victorian Country House*, Oxford 1971, new edn London 1979.

Godden, Geoffrey, *British Pottery and Porcelain 1780–1850*, London 1963.

——, *British Pottery*, London 1974.

Gombrich, E. H., *The Sense of Order, a study in the psychology of decorative art*, Oxford 1979.

Greysmith, Brenda, *Wallpaper*, London 1976.

Grønwoldt, Ruth (ed), *Art Nouveau Textile-Dekor um 1900*, Stuttgart 1980.

Halén, Widar, 'Christopher Dresser and Japan Observed', *Journal of the Society for the Study of Japonisme*, no. 4, Tokyo 1984, pp.11–26.

——, 'Christopher Dresser, Designpionjær', *Svensk Form Magazine*, no. 4, Stockholm 1987, pp.8–13.

——, 'Christopher Dresser and the Cult of Japan', unpublished D.Phil. thesis, Oxford 1988.

——, 'The Dresser pattern books from Charles Edward Fewster's Collection', *Journal of the Decorative Arts Society*, Vol. 12, 1988, pp.2–9.

Hamilton, Walter, *The Aesthetic Movement in England*, London 1882.

Haslam, Malcolm, *English Art Pottery 1865–1915*, Woodbridge 1975.

Heskett, John, *Industrial Design*, London 1980.

Honour, Hugh, *Chinoiserie, The Vision of Cathay*, London 1961.

——, *Goldsmiths and Silversmiths*, New York 1971.

Honour, Hugh, and John Fleming, *The Penguin Dictionary of Decorative Arts*, New York 1977, new edn 1989.

Hughes, G. B., *Victorian Pottery and Porcelain*, London 1967.

——, *Modern Silver*, London 1967.

Impey, Oliver, *Chinoiserie, The Impact of Oriental Styles on Western Art and Decoration*, Oxford 1977.

Impey, Oliver, and Malcolm Fairley, 'The change in Japanese ceramics', *Meiji, Japanese Art in Transition*, Exhibition Catalogue, Haags Gemeentsmuseum, Leiden 1987, pp.21–6.

In Pursuit of Beauty, Americans and the Aesthetic Movement, Exhibition Catalogue, Metropolitan Museum, New York 1986.

Ishida, Tametake, *Dresser Hokoku (Dresser Report)*, Tokyo 1877.

Japonisme, Exhibition Catalogue, Galeries Nationales du Grand Palais, Paris 1988.

Jones, Joan, 'Dr. Christopher Dresser and the Minton connection, Botanist, artist, designer', *Journal of Audiovisual Media in Medicine*, 1988, Vol. 11, pp.14–16.

Jones, Owen, *The Doctrines of the Department of Practical Art*, London 1852.

——, *The Grammar of Ornament*, London 1856.

——, *Examples of Chinese Ornament*, London 1866–7.

Joppien, Rüdiger, *Christopher Dresser, Ein Viktorianischer Designer*, catalogue, Kunstgewerbemuseum, Cologne 1981.

Lee, Robert, 'A forgotten Yorkshire pottery, Linthorpe Ware', *Heaton Review*, no. 7, Bradford 1934, pp.37–41.

Leighton, John, *On Japanese Art*, privately printed, London 1863, n.p.

Le Vine, Jonathan, *Catalogue of Linthorpe Pottery Exhibition*, Billington Art Gallery, Middlesbrough 1970.

Levy, Mervyn, *Liberty Style*, London 1986.

Lowry, John, 'The rise of the Japanese vogue', *Country Life*, 1958, pp.752–3.

Lucie-Smith, Edward, *The Story of Craft*, Oxford 1981.

——, *A History of Industrial Design*, Oxford 1983.

MacCarthy, Fiona, *A History of British Design 1830–1970*, London 1972.

Madsen, Stephen Tschudi, 'Viktoriansk Decorative Kunst', *Nordenfjeldske Kunsitindustrimuseums Arbok, 1952* (Trondheim), pp.9–92.

——, *Sources of Art Nouveau*, Oslo 1956, reprinted 1976.

Marryat, Joseph, *Collections towards a History of Pottery and Porcelain*, London 1850, new edn 1857.

Moreland, Arthur, 'Linthorpe, a forgotten English pottery', *The Connoisseur*, 1914, pp.85–8.

Morris, Barbara, *Victorian Embroidery*, London 1962.

——, 'Textiles', *The Encyclopedia of Victoriana*, London 1975.

——, *Victorian Table Glass and Ornaments*, London 1978.

——, *Inspiration for Design, the Influence of the Victoria and Albert Museum*, London 1986.

——, *Liberty Design 1874–1914*, London 1989.

Morris, William, *Collected Works of William Morris*, Vols I–XXIV, London 1910–15.

Morse, Edward, *Japanese Homes and their Surroundings*, Boston 1886.

Moyr-Smith, John, *Ornamental Interiors*, London 1887.

Mucha, Alphonse A., *Documents Décoratifs*, Paris 1902.

——, *Formenwelt aus dem Naturreiche*, Leipzig 1904.

Muthesius, Hermann, *Der Kunstgewerbliche Dilettantismus in England*, Berlin 1900.

——, *Das Englische Haus*, Vols I–III, Berlin 1904–8.

Naylor, Gillian, *The Arts and Crafts Movement*, London 1971.

Parry, Linda, *Textiles of the Arts and Crafts Movement*, London 1989.

Pevsner, Nikolaus, *Pioneers of the Modern Movement from William Morris to Walter Gropius*, London 1936.

——, 'Christopher Dresser, Industrial Designer', *The Architectural Review*, LXXXI, 1937, pp.183–6.

——, *Academies of Art, Past and Present*, Cambridge 1940.

——, *Matthew Digby Wyatt*, Cambridge 1950.

——, 'Art Furniture', *The Architectural Review*, CXI (London), 1932, pp.43–50.

Pointon, Marcia, *William Dyce, a Critical Biography*, Oxford 1979.

Pugin, Augustus N. W., *Floriated Ornament*, London 1849.

Redgrave, Richard, 'Importance of the study of botany to the ornamentist', *Journal of Design*, 1849, pp.147–51, 178–85.

——, *Supplementary Report on Design*, London 1852.

Rhead, George W. and Frederick A., *Staffordshire Pots and Potters*, London 1906.

Robinson, John Charles, *The Treasury of Ornamental Art*, London 1852.

——, *Catalogue of the Museum of Ornamental Art*, London 1854 and 1855.

Rose, Peter, 'William Arthur Benson; a pioneer designer of light fittings', *Journal of the Decorative Arts Society*, Vol. 9, 1985, pp.50–7.

Rowland, Kurt, *History of the Modern Movement*, London and New York 1973.

Ruskin, John, *The Collected Works of John Ruskin*, 39 vols, London 1903–12.

Sala, George Augustus, *Notes and Sketches of the Paris Exhibition*, London 1868.

Schmutzler, Robert, *Art Nouveau-Jugendstil*, Stuttgart 1962.

Schaefer, Herwin, *The Roots of Modern Design*, London 1970.

Semper, Gottfried, *Wissenschaft, Industrie, und Kunst, Betrachtung der Schluss de Londoner Industrie-Ausstellung*, Braunschweig and London 1852.

——, *Der Stil in den Technischen un Tektonischen Kunsten*, I–II, Braunschweig 1860–3.

——, 'Practical Art in Metal and Hard Materials, its Technology, History and Style', 1853, Victoria & Albert Museum. Ms.86. N.54.

Shioda, Makato, *Catalogue of Japanese Ceramics*, Tokyo and Philadelphia 1876.

Sugden, Alan Victor, and John Edmondson, *History of English Wallpapers 1509–1914*, London 1925.

Sullivan, Michael, *The Meeting of Eastern and Western Art*, London 1973.

Sutton, Denys, *James McNeill Whistler*, London 1966.

——, 'Japonaiserie for ever, the Gouncourts and Japanese Art', *Apollo*, 1984, pp.59–64.

——, 'Cathay, Nirvana, and Zen', *Apollo*, 1966, pp.148–57.

Talbert, Bruce J., *Gothic forms applied to Furniture, Metal Work and Decoration for Domestic Purposes*, Birmingham 1867.

——, *Examples of Ancient and Modern Furniture, Metal Work, Tapestries, Decorations etc.*, London 1876.

Tattersall Cecil E., *A History of British Carpets*, London 1934.

Terry, Ellen, *The Story of My Life*, London 1908.

Tilbrook, Adrian, *The Designs of Archibald Knox for Liberty & Co.*, London 1976.

——, 'Christopher Dresser's designs for Elkington & Co.', *Journal of the Society of Decorative Arts*, no. 9, 1985, pp.23–8.

—— (ed.), *Truth, Beauty, and Design, Victorian and Edwardian and later decorative art*, Exhibition Catalogue, Fisher Fine Art Gallery, London 1986.

Uyeno, Naoteru, *Japanese Arts and Crafts in the Meiji Era*, Tokyo 1958.

Vaughan, William, *German Romanticism and English Art*, London 1979.

Victorian and Edwardian Decorative Arts, Exhibition Catalogue, V & A Museum, London 1952.

Victorian and Edwardian Art, The Hanley-Read Collection, Catalogue, Royal Academy, London 1972.

Wakefield, Hugh, *Victorian Pottery*, London 1962.

Watanabe, Toshio, *Early Japonisme in Britain 1850–1870*, unpublished PhD thesis, Basel University, 1983.

——, 'The Western Image of Japanese Art in the late Edo Period', *Modern Asian Studies*, XVIII, 1984, pp.667–84.

Wichmann, Siegfried (ed.), *Weltkulturen und Moderne Kunst*, Exhibition Catalogue, Haus der Kunst, Munich 1972.

——, *Japonismus, Ostasien-Europa. Begegnungen in der Kunst des 19. und 20. Jahrhunderts*, Herrsching 1980, English edn London 1981.

'The Work of Christopher Dresser' (anonymous), *The Studio Magazine*, Vol. XV, 1899, pp.104–14.

Wyatt, Sir Matthew Digby, *Industrial Arts of the Nineteenth Century*, London 1851–3.

——, *Metalwork and its Artistic Design*, London 1852.

——, *On the Arts of Decoration at the International Exhibition at Paris, consisting of reports to the British Government in class XV Decoration, class VXIII Carpets and Tapestries, class XIX Paper Hangings*, I–III, London 1868.

——, 'Orientalism in European Industry', *Macmillan's Magazine*, XXI, 1870, pp.551–66.

Yamada, Chisaburo (ed.), *Decorative Arts of Japan*, Tokyo 1964.

——, (ed.) *Dialogue in Art, Japan and the West*, London 1976.

——, (ed.) *Japonisme in Art. An International Symposium*, Tokyo 1980.

Yokoyama, Toshio, 'Japan in the Victorian Mind, 1850–1880. A study of stereotyped images of a nation', unpublished PhD thesis, Oxford 1982.

3. MANUSCRIPT SOURCES

Arthur Sanderson & Sons Ltd Co. Archives, Registry of Artists (1904–5), Jeffrey & Co. logbook (1861–85) and Charles Knowles & Co. pattern book (1884–1907).

Birmingham Reference Library, Elkington & Co. pattern books, Vols I–III.

British Museum, Department of Oriental Antiquities, MSS.2919–5/1/1913, Christopher Dresser's album of Japanese Drawings.

British Museum, MSS. Letterbook for 1875, no.5327, from Caspar Clarke, dated Teheran, 22 April 1875, to Christopher Dresser.

British Museum, MSS. Index to Minutes, Vols III–V (1825–60).

Brotherton Library, University of Leeds, MSS.1385 and 1386, letters from Dresser to George Augustus Sala, dated London, 4 July 1877 and 24 December 1877.

Christie's Archive, London, auction catalogues 1859–.

Chubb & Son Co. Archives, MSS. Chubb Collectana, Vols V–VIII (1873–84).

Courtaulds Co. Archive, London, J. W. & C. Ward logbooks (1884–1905).

Getty Center for the History of Art and the Humanities, Archives, Los Angeles, California, Papers of Sir Nikolaus Pevsner, *c.* 1920–83.

Greater London Record Office, Royal Society of Arts

MSS. Correspondence with Dresser, January 1857–30 March 1882.

Ipswich Museums and Galleries, MSS.R 1972–72, Christopher Dresser's sketchbook.

James Dixon & Sons Co. Archives, Sheffield, ledgers, sales books, pattern books and catalogues (1860s to 1890).

Jena Universitätsarchiv, Bestand Philosophische Fakultät, M.nr.364, Dresser's honorary D.Phil. 14 September 1859.

Kyoto Prefectural Library, MSS. Kyoto Governor's Records, 1877, no.5.

Linnean Society Archives, London, MSS.5 B, 215–220, Five botanical drawings by Christopher Dresser (1855–7) and MSS.5 B.230, Dresser's paper on 'Contribution to Organographic Botany' read for the Society, 1 April 1858.

Manchester Public Library, Royal Manchester Institution Letterbook, MSS.M6-1-49-7, letter to Christopher Dresser regarding lecture on 'Decorative Art', dated 31 January 1862.

Public Record Office, Chancery Lane, London, National Registry of Companies, no.299, 12 February 1873, Alexandra Palace Co. registered, no.188, 23 February 1887, Art Furnishers' Alliance, official and final liquidation proceedings.

Public Record Office, Kew, London :
Board of Trade Files, Register of Companies, BT.31, Board of Trade Patent Office Registered Designs, BT.43.
Education Department Papers, Department of Science and Art Minute Books, E.D.28.
Foreign Office Papers, Correspondence Japan Legation, F.O.262 & F.O.46.

Royal Doulton-Minton Co. Archives, Stoke-on-Trent, MSS.1-1905, pattern books, catalogues, ledgers, estimate books, art work and Christopher Dresser file.

Sheffield City Libraries, James Dixon & Sons records (uncatalogued).

Tiffany & Co. Archive, New York, Tiffany's Blue Book (1878), letter from Christopher Dresser to Louis Comfort Tiffany, dated London, 25 July 1878.

——, various newspaper cuttings related to Dresser's collection of Japanese art manufactures and his stay in America.

——, Messers Leavitt Auctioneers catalogue of 'The Dresser Collection of Japanese Curios Articles selected for Tiffany & Co.' (18 June 1877).

Tokyo National Archive, MSS.2a-9-394, Report on the Austrian Exhibition in 1873.
MSS.2a-10-2025 'Naimusho Nishi' (Reports of the Interior Department) (1877).
MSS.2a-9-303, 'Kobusho Nempo' (Reports of the Industrial Department) (1877).
MSS.2a-35-6-1831, Ishida Tametake's report of Dresser's journey in Japan.
MSS.2a-10-2501, Records of Government Officials: Ishida Tametake.
MSS.2a-10-3862, Records of Government Officials: Sakata Haruo.
MSS.2a-9-624, 'Kobusho Nempo' (Reports of Industrial Department), permission for Dresser to travel freely in Japan.
MSS.2a-9-391, 'Kobusho Nempo' (Reports of Industrial Department), report on the South Kensington donation to Tokyo National Museum (1877).

Tokyo National Museum Archive, Acquisition Catalogue, Vol. II, no.7, letter from Dr Christopher Dresser to Machida Nishinari, dated London, 13 March 1880, and no.28, letter from Machida Nishinari to Christopher Dresser, dated Tokyo, 13 October 1880.

United States Patents and Trademarks Office, Washington, Registry of Paperhangings, Div.15.nos.9975–9987 (15 May 1877), designs by Christopher Dresser for Wilson & Fennimore Co., Philadelphia.

Victoria & Albert Museum, Far Eastern Department, Christopher Dresser's albums of Japanese drawings: DJ.76-1905 and DJ.161-168-1905, Mori Niho albums, DJ.104-1905 Kion Album.
Christopher Dresser's album of Japanese 'Mon' (crest) patterns D.209-1905.
Christopher Dresser's drawings of Japanese porcelain in his collection D.397-541/1905.

Victoria & Albert Museum, National Art Library, MSS.86.EE.3, Christopher Dresser, 'Notes on four Japanese ceilings, of which copies were presented to Dr. Dresser by the Japanese Minister of Interior, with the Minister's letter and a description of the preparation of lacquer' (1878).
——, MSS.55.AA.47, Vols I–IV, Henry Cole Miscellanies.
——, MSS.86.FF.64, Gottfried Semper, 'Practical Art in the metal and hard materials, its technology, history and styles', (London 1852).
——, Elkington & Co. pattern books, Vols 1–12 (1851–90), recent acquisition.

Victoria & Albert Museum, Prints and Drawings Department, Box 230, nos.3925–3996. Christopher Dresser's botanical diagrams.
——, PD.179 nos.1058 & 979. Christopher Dresser's drawings of Indian turban and Indian dagger.
——, wallpaper frieze by Christopher Dresser, probably William Woollams (1877).
——, E.655, 660, 663-1953. Jeffrey & Co. wallpapers exhibited at Paris Exhibition in 1878, recently attributed to Dresser.
——, recent acquisition, Christopher Dresser's pattern books, Vols I–II.
——, 94J, 29,30,30A. Jeffrey & Co. Collectana, Vols I–III (1838–1915).
——, 93.H.56-57, William Woollams & Co. pattern books (1865–6).
——, WS.Box37, John Line & Co. pattern book dated 1880.
——, A.205.D.122-1905, Owen Jones's drawings of the Chinese and Japanese court in the South Kensington Museum (1865).
——, E.280-1963, Edward W. Godwin's sketchbook containing drawings from Dresser's diapers.
——, Christopher Dresser's pattern books, 2 vols, *c.*1867, from Charles E. Fewster's Collection, recent acquisition.
——, two wallpapers by Dresser, produced by Jean Züber, Rixheim, Alsace, 1903 and 1904, recent acquisition.

Wedgwood, Josiah & Sons Archives, Stoke-on-Trent, Pattern books 8 and 9 (1867–72) and Majolica pattern books, I and II (1869–88) and estimate-book (1869–78).

Wellcome Institute for the History of Medicine, London, Japanese books from Dresser's collection:
Chodo Zue (1804), furniture designs.
Shiniki Ipputsu (1801), drawings.
Horimono Ehon (*c.*1750), patterns for carving.
Gaho (1861), a picture book.

INDEX